THE WEAPONS LEGACY OF THE COLD WAR

cy of the Cold

Hill

ng

xon, OX14 4RN
17

rancis Group, an informa business

ndro Pascolini 1997

r LC control number: 97019614

ield Road, Louth, Lincolnshire LN11 7AJ,

Contents

Preface

The chapters in this volume were presented to the 18th summer course of the International School on Disarmament and Research on Conflicts (ISODARCO) held at the Certosa di Pontignano (Siena), Italy, between 29 July and 8 August 1996.

The organization of the school was made possible by the financial contributions of two organizations and the generous collaboration of several individuals without which these meetings would have not been possible and to whom goes our deepest gratitude: The John D. and Catherine T. MacArthur Foundation; Prof. Alessandro Pascolini and Prof. Dietrich Schroeer, directors of the course and editors of the book; the Physics Department of the University of Rome 'Tor Vergata'; Prof. Maria Vegni, of the Biology Department of the University of Siena; The Regional Council of the Toscana Region; Dr Isabella Colace of the ISODARCO office in Rome. For hospitality we are indebted to Mr Andrea Machetti and all the personnel of the Certosa di Pontignano.

All opinions expressed in the chapters of this book are of a purely personal nature and do not necessarily represent the official view of either the organizers of the school or of the organizations with which the writers may be affiliated.

Carlo Schaerf
(President of ISODARCO and Director of the School)

Notes on the Contributors

Georgi Arbatov (Russia) is the Director of the Institute for the USA and Canada, as well as a member of the Russian Academy of Science. He is the author of *The System: An Insider's Life in Soviet Politics.*

Eric Arnett (USA) is leader of the Project on Military Technology at the Stockholm International Peace Research Institute. He is the author of the annual chapter on 'Military Research and Development' in the *SIPRI Yearbook*, as well as editor of *Nuclear Weapons after the CTB* and *Military Capacity and the Risk of War.*

Oleg Bukharin (Russia) works on arms control issues at the Moscow Institute of Physics and Technology, and at Princeton University where he is currently a staff member of the Program on Nuclear Policy Alternatives.

Francesco Calogero (Italy) is Professor of Theoretical Physics, University of Rome I 'La Sapienza'. He is currently on leave while serving as Secretary General, Pugwash Conferences on Science and World Affairs. Together with M. de Andreis he has recently published a SIPRI Research Report, *The Soviet Nuclear Weapons Complex.*

Anatoli S. Diakov (Russia) is Professor of Physics at the Moscow Institute of Physics and Technology where, together with Frank von Hippel, he has established the Center for Arms Control, Energy and Environmental Studies. His current activities include work on plutonium disposition, transparency and nuclear arms reduction.

Ioury E. Federov (Russia) is Professor of Political Science in the Department of Political Science of the Moscow State Institute of International Relations of the Ministry of Foreign Affairs of the Russian Federation.

Gert G. Harigel (Switzerland) is an Emeritus Senior Physicist at CERN (Organisation Européene pour la Recherche Nucléaire). He is a founding and council member of the International Network of Engineers and Scientists for Global Responsibility and secretary/treasurer of the Geneva International Peace Research Institute.

Hilal Khashan (Lebanon) is Associate Professor of Political Science at the American University of Beirut. He is currently on study leave in the Department of Political Science at the Florida State University. He has written *Inside the Lebanese Confessional Mind* and *Partner or Pariah*.

Patricia Lewis (UK) is the Executive Director of the Verification Technology Information Centre in London. She was a consultant to the UK government during the CFE Treaty negotiations and has published widely on the verification of arms control and disarmament treaties.

Arto Nokkala (Finland) is a retired lieutenant-colonel (GSO) and former Senior Research Officer of the Department of Strategic Studies in the Finnish National Defence College. Currently he is a visiting researcher at the Tampere Peace Research Institute of the University of Tampere, Finland.

Alessandro Pascolini (Italy) (*co-editor*) is Professor of Physics at the University of Padua and Vice President of ISODARCO.

Dietrich Schroeer (USA) (*co-editor*) is Professor of Physics at the University of North Carolina at Chapel Hill. He developed a course on science, technology and military affairs and is author of *Science, Technology and the Nuclear Arms Race*.

Hartwig Spitzer (Germany) is Professor of Physics at the University of Hamburg and a member of its Center for Science and International Security. He has been co-organizer of several conferences on security issues and global development problems. He is currently chairman of the International Network of Engineers and Scientists for Global Responsibility.

Frank von Hippel (USA) is Professor of Public and International Affairs, Princeton University, and chairman of the Research Arm of the Federation of American Scientists.

Lamberto Zannier (Italy) is Head of Disarmament, Arms Control and Cooperative Security of the North Atlantic Treaty Organization.

Ciro E. Zoppo (USA) is Research Professor Emeritus of International Relations in the Political Science Department of the University of California at Los Angeles. His most recent publication is *The Future Role of the United States in European Security*.

Introduction

The theme for the 1996 summer school of ISODARCO and of these Proceedings is 'The Weapons Legacy of the Cold War: Problems and Opportunities'. One attractive feature of ISODARCO is that it has always built its discussions on a technological base. Hence the inclusion of the word 'weapon' in the title. At the same time there is much contact with policy implications, as indicated by the words 'Cold War' and 'legacy.' This school and these Proceedings are a review of the current situation in international security as created by the Cold War, and how the end of the Cold War is likely to change the situation. Since the end of the Cold War is creating changes in many aspects of international security, the range of topics covered is quite broad. But the weapons legacy of the Cold War, and the possible changes in it, tie the contributions together.

The chapters are arranged into four groups. The first three chapters discuss changes in technology policy after the Cold War. Dietrich Schroeer asks how important advanced military technology will be now that the superpower confrontation no longer dominates international security. Gert Harigel describes the military–industrial complex. Georgi Arbatov explores the problems experienced in converting military technologies to civilian uses.

Problems of nuclear weapons are examined in five chapters. Frank von Hippel and Oleg Bukharin evaluate the security of fissile materials. Ciro Zoppo considers the potential for accidental nuclear war, Anatoli Diakov writes about the Russian view of nuclear disarmament and Eric Arnett about the implications of the comprehensive nuclear test ban for weapon modernization and nuclear proliferation. Francesco Calogero asks whether a world free of nuclear weapons is desirable, possible and probable.

General arms control after the Cold War is considered from a NATO perspective by Lamberto Zannier and, in terms of contributions that verification could make to it, by Patricia Lewis and Hartwig Spitzer.

The final set of papers considers post-Cold War regional issues that have weaponry implications. Ioury Federov reports on Russia's current nuclear policy, Arto Nokkala considers the political implications for Northern Europe of the Cold War military legacy, while Hilal Khashan illustrates the connection between changes in the world order and the progress of militant Islam.

Dietrich Schroeer and Alessandro Pascolini

1   The Future of High Technology in Military Affairs

Dietrich Schroeer

Introduction

This chapter considers two related questions: 'How important is technology in military affairs?' and 'How has the importance of technology changed with the end of the Cold War?' The answers to these questions are vital in deciding how to structure military operations, for deterrence and for fighting possible future wars. How much money should be invested in research and development? What kind of equipment should be bought for military forces? What tactics and strategies should be developed for future operations of military forces?

Questions about the usefulness of technology in military affairs have been asked for a long time. Some argue that improvements in technology, such as the development of the modern battleship or the tank, have completely revolutionized warfare in weaponry, tactics and strategy. Others claim that through leadership and adaptability the human factor continues to be most important.

The controversy about the importance of technology was sharpened during World War II, particularly with the advent of nuclear weapons. The development of nuclear weapons swung the pendulum towards a faith in technology as the most important factor. Nuclear weapons required high-technology delivery and control systems. That led to the creation of the most advanced military technologies of jet aircraft, intercontinental ballistic missiles (ICBMs) with multiple warhead and precision guidance, nuclear-powered missile submarines and surveillance satellites. In contrast, the primary military strategy of the nuclear weapons was relatively simple, in the sense that mutual assured destruction implied an all-or-nothing outcome. The tension between the strategically simple view of full-scale nuclear annihilation as the ultimate deterrent, and the complex high-technology approach of the nuclear war fighters has been one version of this continuing controversy about the usefulness of technology in military affairs. This is particularly so since many strategists have seen nuclear weapons as a cheap replacement for expensive conventional armaments.

Now the Cold War has ended, and the second superpower – the Soviet Union – no longer exists. Have there been any concomitant changes in the importance of technology in military affairs? On the nuclear level, the situation has changed from the superpower competition, in which techno-logical imperatives appeared to drive the development of the very best technologies available, to one of stewardship. The focus in advanced mili-tary technologies has now switched to conventional warfare. We no longer ask how high technology can aid in deterrence between the superpowers, but whether high technology can prevent or win wars between and with developing and third-world countries. The new calibration point for technol-ogy is no longer a war in Europe between the North Atlantic Treaty Organi-zation (NATO) and the Warsaw Pact Organization. Instead, many see the model for the future in the Gulf War between Iraq and the Western coalition, or in the peace-keeping operation by NATO in Bosnia.

The answers to these two questions have many practical implications. For the United States they guide decisions about strategic modernization of nuclear weaponry; the effort to be devoted to research and development (R&D) on advanced technologies; the relative emphasis on offensive and defensive technologies, for example the kind of ballistic missile defence to be deployed and the level of emphasis on precision-guided weaponry; and the relative funding for manpower and for equipment for the different serv-ices. Globally, this question guides discussions about client–state relation-ships, the proliferation of advanced military technologies, the level of arms sales to other countries, the threat of independence movements and guerrilla warfare and about arms control.

We first consider the importance of technology in military affairs, summa-rizing contrasting arguments that either accept or reject technology as the most important factor in military affairs. In this review a distinction will be made between technology as devices and technology as an approach or a system. We then consider how the end of the Cold War has changed this technological situation. Here we analyse the implications for the technologi-cal future of the post-Cold War changes in the political, strategic and tech-nological situation. Finally, we examine several specific issues raised by these two questions.

The Importance of Technology in Military Affairs

Technology affects military affairs on two levels: on the first level, technology creates devices, such as tanks, guided missiles and surveillance satellites; on the second level, technology is a world view, an approach towards solving problems; it creates an enthusiasm for technical solutions, an emphasis on quantitative cost–benefit analyses and an interest in efficiency.

Arguments that Technology is Vital for Military Affairs

The enthusiasm for technological solutions can be expressed in the aphorism, 'Save lives, not ammunition.' This enthusiasm is particularly strong in the United States.[1] Colin S. Gray talks about a 'US strategic culture' that is particularly technology-oriented.[2] The preference for the technological approach often translates into a desire to use technological devices to replace manpower. This enthusiasm for technological devices is often based on analyses of historical technological arms races. Such analyses focus on developments in naval warfare, such as the steam-driven iron-clad battleship and the submarine; in land warfare, such as the machine gun and the tank; and in air warfare, such as air combat and strategic bomber forces. In most cases it is clear that these technologies have indeed changed warfare. However, it is not equally clear what conclusion can be drawn about the future of technology in warfare.

The most convincing success of technological warfare in recent years has been the Gulf War in 1991 between Iraq and a coalition of the United States plus its allies. This war was between a superpower and a second-tier military power that was willing to fight a technology-based war. Operation 'Desert Storm' appeared to have been so successful because of the overwhelming technological advantage of the coalition. Such technological devices as cruise missiles, stealth bombers and night-vision goggles, together with total air superiority and battlefield information from AWACS and JSTAR surveillance aircraft, seemed to carry the day. Secretary of Defense Richard Cheney said, 'This war demonstrated dramatically the new possibilities of what has been called the "military–technological revolution in warfare".'[3] Future Secretary of Defense William Perry said that 'a new class of military systems ... gave U.S. forces a revolutionary advance in military capability'.[4]

There are some analyses that have cast doubt on the ultimate usefulness of the most advanced military technologies in the Gulf War. The effectiveness of the *Patriot* anti-tactical-ballistic missile has been challenged.[5] Major technological flaws have been found in the flow of target information and battle damage assessments.[6] In spite of such criticisms, the Gulf War of

1991 is generally seen as the ultimate example of technological success in military affairs.

There is a long-standing tradition of glorifying the contribution made by technologies to the development of bigger and better devices. Analysts revel in creating lists of technologies with promising futures.[7] Similarly, the US Department of Defense regularly publishes a 'wish list' of critical technologies that it wants to develop. The most recent Cold War wish list of technologies to be promoted includes software engineering, machine intelligence and robotics, simulation and modelling, passive sensors, signal and image processing, hypervelocity projectiles and propulsion, and biotechnology.[8] This list calls for R&D in the most advanced cutting-edge technologies, all most useful on a high-technology, high-intensity battlefield. Should one not expect changes in such lists in response to the end of the Cold War?

The impact of technology goes far beyond the hardware that it creates. It also provides a style of operations through technological systems and through ways of structuring military forces. Ultimately, technology is the source of a way of looking at the world through faith in technological solutions, through the performance of quantitative cost–benefit analyses and through the substitution of technology for manpower.

A strong proponent of the usefulness of this technological outlook has been the historian Martin van Creveld, who claims that 'technology does not just represent an assemblage of hardware but a philosophical system. As such, technology affects not only the way war is conducted and victory is sought, but the very framework that we use for thinking about it.'[9] He believes that, whenever the technological devices of opponents are comparable, the deciding factor is the way in which these devices are utilized through technological training, doctrine and organization. Even if this argument of the usefulness of a technological world view is not always factually true, as long as it is accepted as a guide to military planning, it becomes *the Truth*.

Ultimately, van Creveld enters a *caveat*, when he accepts that this pro-technology approach can go too far: 'It would be erroneous to believe that, just because technology represents a very good starting point for thinking about war, it therefore represents the only or even the best starting point. Merely because technology plays a very important part in war, it does not follow that it alone can dictate the conduct of a war or lead to victory.'[10]

Arguments Against Technological Enthusiasm

Just as the Gulf War of 1991 is cited as the primary example of technological success in military affairs, the wars in Vietnam and Afghanistan are cited as primary evidence for the failure of technology in military affairs. In

Vietnam the technological superiority of the United States could not overcome the guerrilla tactics of the North Vietnamese forces, particularly since the conduct of the war was restricted by political considerations.[11] In Afghanistan the technological superiority of the Soviet military forces was equally unable to win that guerrilla war.[12] Both of these wars can be used to argue that technological devices are insufficient in the face of opposition by forces who refuse to fight at an advanced technological level.

Many people have argued that technological devices do not win wars. Wheeler and Booth have said that 'particular innovations in military technology have occasionally had a decisive effect on events ... But such breakthroughs are rare.'[13] Jonathan Alford has said that 'technology always delivers less, arrives later and costs more than forecast'.[14] And Timothy Garden has talked about a technology trap:

> In the West, the cornucopia of novel technologies has meant that we have increasingly sought a technical answer to every security concern. If we devote increasing resources to the expanding range of opportunities, we may find ourselves less and less able to afford to procure the weapons that we need for our security. This is the Technology Trap, and it has as its bait 'the neat solution'.[15]

And John Erickson has argued that 'The villain of the piece in more than one case has been made weapons technology along with *Homo technicus* ... The political determinants remain of prime importance.'[16]

Many believe that an emphasis on technology encourages arms races. The very concepts of arms races, such as 'technological imperative', 'action–reaction phenomena' and 'offence or defence dominance', are intrinsically grounded in a technological outlook on life.[17] The result of this technological mind-set is a worst-case approach, in which the emphasis is on the technological question of what is possible, rather than the political question of what is probable.[18]

Arms races can be both stabilizing and destabilizing, but they are more usually the latter. The instability comes as both sides want to avoid ever being dangerously inferior. But international security cannot be seen as a zero-sum game, in which a gain by one side must inevitably mean a loss by the other side. This is particularly true in the case of deterrence, which relies on the absence of a motive to attack.

Many believe that a technological world view overly encourages quantification and reliance on technical experts. The question is how best to allocate scarce resources, how to set priorities in technology development, how to compromise between a small quantity of the very best equipment and a larger quantity of not-so-advanced equipment and how to make the trade-off between equipment and personnel. The question should be, which technologies most improve security?

The problem is that questions of allocation are most easily addressed by quantitative cost–benefit analyses, by a quantitative technological approach. Stanley Hoffman has called this approach a quest 'for mathematical formulas that tend to give a reassuring sense of certainty even when they measure the immeasurable ... [an] oversimplification and overrating of purely technical but calculable elements over intangible ones'.[19] The resulting problem is known as the McNamara fallacy, named after Robert S. McNamara in his role as Secretary of Defense during the Vietnam War, when he applied quantitative cost–benefit analyses to all military affairs.[20] This cost–benefit approach leads to worst-case scenarios, which emphasize what can be done efficiently in terms of technical fixes, rather than what ought to be done effectively. We think about what we can accomplish with what we have, instead of thinking about what we need to accomplish, and then select the means with which to do it. The cost–benefit approach also overemphasizes quality of arms at the expense of larger numbers of lower-quality weapons.[21]

Many believe that an overemphasis on technology has led to a decrease in national security, because national security is at heart a political rather than a technological problem. As Wheeler and Booth put it, 'We are inundated by technological changes ... future international security is at root a political and not a technological problem' and 'technology rarely deserves the centrality which it is usually accorded. The latter has been encouraged by the pre-eminence of strategists in the contemporary debate about East–West affairs, and by the way they have made "strategy" and "security" almost synonymous.'[22]

The concern is that this fixation on technology leads to a neglect of the important political and social aspects of problems. Michael Howard said it very well:

> Let me repeat the analogy ... about the drunk who lost his watch in a dark alley but was found looking for it under a lamp post because there was more light there. The light provided by our knowledge of technological capabilities and our capacity for sophisticated strategic analysis is so dazzling as to be almost hypnotic; but it is in those shadowy regions of human understanding based on our knowledge of social development, cultural diversity and patterns of behavior that we have to look for the answer.[23]

Obviously there must be a middle ground in military affairs where technology, strategy and politics can meet. Albert Wohlstetter has said that 'The cardinal choices ... cannot be made solely on the estimates of the feasibility

of some piece of hardware. They are political and military strategic decisions. Technology is an important part, but far from the whole of strategy.'[24]

Military Technology after the Cold War

What issues related to technology have changed as a result of the end of the
Cold War? There are four obvious changes. First, nuclear weapons have lost
in importance. The end of the superpower confrontation has brought unprecedented levels of nuclear disarmament with START II and beyond. At
the same time, concerns about chemical and biological weapons have increased. Second, the collapse of the Soviet Union has ended the confrontation between two forces based on high-technology military weaponry. This
may lead to the end of high-tech arms races. Third, the end of the bilateral
world of the United States and the Soviet Union is bringing to an end a large
number of client-state relationships. No longer can Cuba protect itself against
the United States by calling on the Soviet Union for assistance. In the past
these client-state relationships gave great influence to the superpowers.
Consequently, client states of one superpower were limited in the extent to
which they could engage in conflicts with the clients of the other superpower. Neither Egypt nor Israel could be allowed to win the war of 1973, for
fear that the two superpowers might be dragged into the war, and end up
fighting each other, possibly with nuclear weapons. These positive aspects
of client relationships may be changing with the end of the Cold War. For
example, when Iraq was a client state of the Soviet Union, was it less likely
to use chemical weapons than it is now? Finally, the end of the two-power
nuclear umbrella may lead to an increase in lower-level conflicts, such as
civil wars and international terrorism. Let us examine a couple of areas in
which the relative importance of technology will change in the post-Cold
War period.

The End of Superpower Arms Races

With the collapse of the Soviet Union, the importance of nuclear weaponry
and its associated advanced technologies has diminished. Now that the
confrontation between NATO and the Warsaw Pact Organization is no longer
the major determinant of military technologies, there is not the overwhelming need for the Western nations to keep up with a high-technology Soviet
military. We might expect that the desire for cutting-edge technologies
would be somewhat decreased. In the future we may expect to see less
reliance on technical experts and on technical fixes. We may expect to see
the end of arms races driven by technological imperatives and the end of

action–reaction chains. Instead of engaging in arms races, we now worry about the survival of the former Soviet Union. This is a totally new post-Cold War question. John Mearsheimer claims that we will soon miss the Cold War. He believes that Europe will 'return to the multipolar system that, between 1648 and 1945, bred one destructive conflict after another'.[25]

What Wars should be Planned for?

The argument about the usefulness of technology in military affairs sometimes takes on an alternative form: do weapons developments drive doctrine, or vice versa? Technological enthusiasts believe that technology does drive tactics. But technological pessimists, such as Robert O'Connell, have long argued that technology should not be and is not the determinant of strategy. He says, 'It is true that, once a developmental sequence has begun, the technological imperative becomes nearly absolute. But at the beginning and end of every such sequence is a point when human choice can and does exert itself.'[26] Now that the superpower arms race is over, we are in a position to let security needs guide our technological developments. Perhaps we can now direct our concerns towards asking how to spend our limited military resources to meet challenges that we judge worthwhile, rather than looking for problems to solve with the technologies that have become available.

The end of the Cold War has reduced the threat of global nuclear conflict. There can now once again be wars between superpowers and second-tier countries, such as Iraq. The end of the Cold War has disrupted the client–state relationships of various countries, as many nations are no longer clearly defined as client states for one or the other of the superpowers. Hence these former client states may no longer feel themselves to be so restricted in what they can do, since their actions do not impinge so directly on superpower relations. We may also in the future see more wars involving a single superpower with a former client state.

Some analysts have proposed drastic changes in future military force structures in response to these changed probabilities. Wiesner *et al.* propose a 'mission-up' review of military forces for the United States. They argue that, by the year 2000, the foreseeable missions can be accomplished with an annual budget of $115 billion.[27] This is a reduction of over 50 per cent compared with current military budgets. The reasoning behind such drastic budget revisions is that 'U.S. forces were shaped for conflict with a superpower. The emerging multi-lateral world calls for a smaller, more flexible and far less expensive military.'[28] Instead of a superpower confrontation we may expect more guerrilla and terrorism wars. We can expect to see increases in ethnic conflicts. These issues *are* becoming more important with the end of the Cold War: consider the ethnic tensions and collapse in the former Soviet Union, and the collapse of Yugoslavia. In such lesser wars, technology is not so obviously the winning card.

Some people suggest that the military should exploit the present opportunity and use technology to change from offence to defence dominance.[29] However, Glaser suggests that, because of surviving Cold War attitudes, defence dominance for the United States might be seen as superiority by Russia, which could destabilize its deterrence relationship with the United States: 'The worlds of defense-dominance and U.S. superiority lack the important advantage of providing both countries with a high degree of confidence in their security.'[30] Perhaps some defences could be developed that would not threaten stability. This might be the case with a change in ballistic missiles defence from the strategic defences of 'Star Wars' to a post-Cold War short-range Theater Missile Defence (TMD). Indeed TMD systems, such as an advanced *Patriot* and a naval missile defence, are being developed. But an expandable Theater High Altitude Air Defence system (THAAD) is not in that post-Cold War spirit.

Some thought has been given to developing more relevant post-Cold War military technologies. In lesser wars the infantry might become much more important. Technologies are under development to provide better 'defensive kill' weapons for the infantry,[31] but the technologies for performance enhancement of the infantry soldier are still organized mostly in Cold War terms, such as sustainment, mobility, survivability, lethality and improvements in C^{3}I (command, control, communications and intelligence).[32]

There are efforts to develop new types of weapons for use in lower-level conflicts, where civilians might be at great risk because they are intermingled with military forces. Such 'non-lethal weapons' are an attempt to develop technologies for 'terrorist or contingency scenarios where injury to hostages or civilians is a significant concern. ... [May such] less-than-lethal technologies ... be useful in theatres such as the former Yugoslavia?'[33] Such weapons might include sticky foam, incapacitation by laser blinding, and so on, and these are seen by some as suitable for counter-terrorism, or even peace-keeping operations.[34] But on closer examination these technologies do not appear quite so non-lethal. The obvious problem with these 'soft-kill solutions'[35] is that the level of damage must be gauged carefully so as to be disabling, but non-lethal. On the whole, technological preparation for lower-level wars has been lacking so far.

US Military Funding after the Cold War

How has the US administration and military responded to the end of the Cold War? The perception of nuclear weapons is indeed changing. Thomas

Schelling is grateful that nuclear weapons are seen as non-conventional, that everyone has accepted them as being different.[36] Nina Tannenwald concludes that we are now reduced to a basic deterrence role for nuclear weapons.[37] So it has become possible for the NATO alliance to give up reliance on tactical nuclear weapons, without a conventional build-up to make up for any possible resulting military weakness. Of course, there is a concomitant danger. It used to be accepted that any superpower war would be mutual suicide because it would turn into a nuclear war. But if nuclear weapons are no longer so important, might an end to mutual assured destruction increase the frequency of non-nuclear wars?

By 1994, the Posture Review of the US Department of Defense (DoD) recommended large specific reductions in strategic forces to meet START-II levels, even while opposing additional cuts in other areas. The *Trident* submarine-launched ballistic missile (SLBM) fleet is to be reduced to 14, all carrying D-5 missiles with five warheads each. The ICBM deterrent is to consist of 450 to 500 *Minuteman*-3 missiles, each with single warhead, but these missiles are to undergo a $5.2 billion modernization.[38] The 50 *Peacekeeper* ICBMs are to be deactivated by the year 2003. The strategic bomber force is to consist of only 66 B-52s. Both the B-1 and B-2 bombers are to evolve into a conventional strike weapon that can hit heavily-defended targets such as military headquarters and enemy radar stations with laser-guided weapons.

A 'bottom-up' review in 1993 by the then Secretary of Defense Les Aspin attempted to go beyond this DoD posture statement and define the overall force structure based on the needs for national security. However, in the end the review was really 'top-down', in the sense that it was driven by budget limitations imposed from above.[39] This review saw a need for a fairly ambitious conventional posture that would allow the United States to fight and win two simultaneous 'Desert Storm equivalent' regional wars.

Ultimately, the review argued that, within a few decades, the threat to the United States may come, not from a small rogue regional power, but from what has come to be known as a 'peer competitor' – in essence, a new superpower, such as China, a resurgent Russia or perhaps even India. This argument translated into a request for more of the same Cold War arms races, except that now the Soviet Union was replaced by this hypothetical peer competitor. Some analysts are cynical about this planning: 'Future war, in fact, may let former nuclear war planners retread a few of the scenarios conceived for a face-off with the Soviets.'[40]

The overall strategic requirement to be able to fight almost simultaneously two 'major regional conflicts' has been transformed by the military into the desire for more high-tech weaponry. This desired equipment includes precision strike capability for the B-1 and B-2 bombers, new fighter aircraft, start of research and development for the next generation of aircraft by establishing a Joint Advanced Strike Technology Program, smart and brilliant anti-armour ammunitions, development and deployment of the V-22 helicopter, and preservation of the carrier and submarine industrial base. These requirements clearly focus on improved high-technology weapons and on power projection.[41]

Victor Utgoff argues that the US technological superiority in weaponry maximizes success in war, produces better weapons that reduce defence costs, reduces casualties, deters attacks, avoids technological surprise, aids possible future reconstitution of larger forces, maintains R&D capabilities, provides civilian technology spin-offs, takes advantage of a technologically skilled citizenry, allows better technological assistance to allies and improves manufacture that can reduce production costs.[42]

Other technological enthusiasts use worst-case arguments to conclude that the 'U.S. will need a wide technology base from which to draw'.[43] Martin Libicki has speculated that in the next war the United States will require even more technology to overcome a technologically sophisticated opponent: 'For example, the site of ports, docks and piers are well known and shipping is almost impossible to hide. ... Using unmanned aerial vehicles/GPS guidance/warheads costing perhaps $250,000 each, a well-financed foe could launch 1,000 such weapons with the expectation that many would get through.'[44] Such worst-case fears seem overstated. It seems unlikely that a second- or third-tier nation can employ cruise missile technology that requires a total system including satellites imagery for maps. Can such a nation acquire, deploy and launch a large number of cruise missiles that cost over $1 million each?

Arms Control

The old centrepiece of arms control is the Strategic Arms Reduction Talks (START) process which focuses on nuclear weaponry. The response of the technologists, at least in the United States, is to move from the designing of nuclear weapons to 'weapon stewardship'. Of course, these changed jobs involve very similar job descriptions to the old ones: for example, the development of computer codes to describe nuclear explosions. The US Department of Energy is launching a nuclear Stockpile Stewardship and Management Program to ensure a safe and functioning nuclear arsenal. Here a 'science-based' approach is supposed to replace actual nuclear testing.

The START-II Treaty indeed deals with advanced technologies, such as the high-accuracy multiple independently targeted reentry vehicle (MIRV) warheads on ICBMs. However, with the end of the Cold War, the START process is now getting to the level where Great Britain, France, China and perhaps even India may have to become involved if even lower levels of strategic nuclear arms are to be reached. If so, future START treaties may possibly be somewhat less technology-oriented. It will be much harder to control technologies that may be of use in lower-level conflicts. Thus it is not clear how much of a role technology will actually play in future arms-control efforts.

The Gulf War: The Future of Military Technology?

Finally, we examine in more detail one recent war that may shed some light on the importance of advanced technologies in military affairs, both in the recent past and in the future. In 1991, a coalition of military forces led by the United States liberated Kuwait from occupation by Iraqi forces. In this war an enormous quantity of high-technology weaponry was used and the coalition forces won the war with very few casualties of their own. Consequently, the 1991 Gulf War has been held up as a model proving the usefulness of advanced-technology weaponry in military affairs. Furthermore, it took place as the Cold War was ending; hence many analysts want to see it as a model of future technological wars. But various analyses of the Gulf War challenge the view that advanced technology won the war, and doubt that it can serve as a model for the future. A report by the US General Accounting Office (GAO) has cast doubt on the actual usefulness of technology in the Gulf War, while Cordesman and Wagner see the Gulf War as a set of lessons showing its limited relevance to future wars.

The GAO report suggests that the claims for the pinpoint precision of the advanced technologies in the Gulf War were 'overstated, misleading, inconsistent with the best available data, or unverifiable'.[45] The report challenges the effectiveness of the Stealth bomber, the *Tomahawk* cruise missile and much of the smart weaponry. The authors of the report are not convinced that such expensive high-tech equipment was cost-effective in many cases compared to lower-tech weaponry. In particular they were concerned about the relatively poor performance of sensors for identifying targets and assessing battle damage. They conclude that, 'The cost of guided munitions, and the limitations on their effectiveness demonstrated in Desert Storm need to be addressed by the Department of Defense.'

Some specific conclusions of the GAO report were the following:

(1) Sensor capabilities must be enhanced, in order to identify valid targets and produce timely battle damage assessments. (2) Many high-tech weapons could not be used in adverse weather and at the desired bombing altitudes. (3) Higher cost

aircraft were not necessarily more effective than lower-cost aircraft. (4) It could not be proven that guided munitions were cost-effective; hence the increasing reliance on guided munitions may not be appropriate. (5) A different theater of operations may limit the effectiveness of complex or advanced technologies. (6) Many of DoD and manufacturers' postwar claims about weapon system performance were 'overstated, misleading, inconsistent … or unverifiable'.

While Cordesman and Wagner[46] are somewhat more impressed by the technological successes of the Gulf War, they too have doubts. They are particularly concerned that analysts might draw overoptimistic conclusions about the usefulness of technology from the successes in the Gulf War. They divide the lessons from the Gulf War into four categories: the uniqueness of the Gulf War, tactical lessons, technical lessons and human factor lessons.[47]

They emphasize that the Gulf War was unique in many ways, and hence no guide to the future. The unique features include the fact that Iraq gave the Western coalition nearly half a year to bring all its high-tech weapons into play. There was sufficient time to generate TERCOM maps of Iraqi targets for US cruise missiles. This advantage is not a consequence of the Cold War and it is unlikely to hold in future wars. Further, in the Gulf War power projection was simplified by unique host country facilities and capabilities: the application of high-tech weaponry in military affairs requires an advanced supporting infrastructure, and this infrastructure was available in Saudi Arabia, not because of the end of the Cold War, but rather as a legacy of the Cold War, when Saudi Arabia was a Western client state. There is no reason to expect access to such support infrastructures in most future wars.

Because Iraq was a Soviet client state during the Cold War, it adopted Soviet tactics to go with its Soviet weapons. Because of the Cold War history in Europe, the coalition forces were well prepared to overcome these tactics. This legacy of the Cold War is unlikely to be repeated in other future wars. As the developer of high-tech weaponry during the Cold War, the coalition forces were well prepared to utilize their own technologies, while Iraq had used its acquired Soviet technology previously only in a war with technologically inferior Iran during the 1980s. This kind of advantage for the weapon-producing countries may hold in the future. In the Gulf War, the coalition fought a 'blind' enemy. During the Cold War the Coalition had developed the C³I and battle management required for a high-tech war. It had also developed tactics to attack and destroy the communications links of the opponent. These Cold War technologies were successfully applied here, except for problems with intelligence. It is quite possible that other future wars would also be fought against such a blind enemy.

The Gulf War provided unique territorial conditions for the exploitation of technology. The tactics and training developed during the Cold War by the coalition forces for a European conflict with the Soviet Union were well suited for the desert terrain in which the Gulf War was fought. A high-tech war is likely to be most successful in such terrain. However, most future wars are more likely to take place in mountains, as in Bosnia, and in areas where civilians and military forces are more intermingled.

Cordesman and Wagner draw several tactical lessons from the Gulf War, a number of them referring to the fact that the successful tactics for the Gulf War were those developed in preparation for a war against the Soviet Union. Iraq adopted Soviet tactics and therefore played into the strongest hand held by the coalition, namely its preparation to use high-tech weapons to defeat Soviet tactics. The successful coalition tactics were a Cold War legacy. In the future, as fewer nations are client states of a superpower, a weaker opponent is unlikely to fight in the predictable style of one specific superpower.

Cordesman and Wagner also draw various technical lessons from the Gulf War. The negative technical lessons are mostly about a failure of intelligence. This failure led to the overestimation of the destructiveness of coalition weaponry. This in turn was caused by inadequate reconnaissance, intelligence and targeting technology. The source of this problem was an overreliance on high-tech weapons combined with a superpower mentality left over from the Cold War. In general, the technical lessons suggest that the Cold War did not prepare the coalition for the kind of low-level conflict likely to be the war of the future. Luckily in this case, Iraq fought in a 'Cold War' style, not a low-level war.

Cordesman and Wagner also draw some lessons from the Gulf War about human factors. The human factors that were favourable to the coalition during the Gulf War were the result of the Cold War. High-quality leadership, training and readiness of NATO forces had been developed to make up for Soviet numerical superiority. With the end of the Cold War Soviet challenge, such advantageous human factor effects may decrease, and the West may be less ready for future wars.

The greatest failure in the Gulf War was in damage assessment. The damage inflicted on Iraq was consistently overestimated. This problem is probably not a direct legacy of the Cold War, but it is the result of overenthusiasm about technology and its successes, which is an attitude induced in US forces during the Cold War, with its emphasis on high technologies to overcome quantitative advantages. There is considerable controversy about the ultimate cost-effectiveness of the high-tech weaponry of the coalition. The contrast between 'the best technology at any price' and a strict cost–benefit approach will have to be sorted out in the future. The Cold War legacy is an emphasis on the very best. But there is the suggestion that the best did not do as well (per unit cost) as did some inferior technologies. Overall, because of all these lessons, Cordesman and Wagner are not convinced of the technological success of the Gulf War. And they doubt its usefulness as a model for the future.

In the end, John Keegan summarizes it well: 'it would be unsafe to conclude from the course and outcome of the Gulf War that high-technology operations guarantee unlimited success in all circumstances'.[48]

Conclusion

The ultimate question for this chapter is raised by Cordesman and Wagner when they ask to what extent we should worry that the Gulf War may create 'expectations that future conflicts will produce equally decisive outcomes with equally limited casualties'.[49]

The Cold War encouraged the development and deployment of the best possible military technologies. Those technologies are most likely to pay off in wars where the opponent accepts the technological challenge, as was the case in the Gulf War. The usefulness of Cold War technologies in lower-level conflicts is not established and clearly the Cold War led to an attitude of technological overoptimism among many in military affairs.

The post-Cold War world presents different military challenges than that of the superpower arms races. Among military planners and the developers of military technologies there has so far been little response to the new situation. Questions of quantity versus quality, of balance between preparing for large or small wars, or of the development of a true defence, have not been thoroughly addressed. We expect that the technological challenges of the post-Cold War era will be radically different. But we do not yet know how they will be different. And the Gulf War does not seem to be a good guide to that new technological future.

Notes

1   Brigadier W.F.K. Thompson said, 'The national style of the Americans springs from their being the leading technological country, and their natural reaction to any problem is to look for a technological answer'. (As quoted in Asa A. Clark IV and John F. Lilley (eds), *Defense Technology*, New York: Praeger, 1989, p.273).
2   Colin S. Gray, 'U.S. Strategic Culture: Implications for Defense Technology', in Clark and Lilley, *Defense Technology*, pp.29–48.
3   As quoted in Eliot A. Cohen, 'The Mystique of U.S. Airpower', in L. Benjamin Ederington and Michael J. Mazarr (eds), *Turning Point: The Gulf War*, Boulder, CO: Westview, 1994, p.53.
4   William Perry, 'Desert Storm and Deterrence', *Foreign Affairs*, **70**, (4), 1991, p.66.

5   For scepticism about the *Patriot's* success, see Theodore A. Postol, 'Lessons of the Gulf War Experience with Patriot', *International Security*, 16, (3), Winter 1991/2, pp.119–71 – with a rebuttal by Robert Stein, 'Letter to the Editor', *International Security*, 17, (1), Summer 1992, pp.199–225; Eric Schmitt, 'Israelis Question Effectiveness of Patriot Missiles', *International Herald Tribune*, 3 November 1991; Eliot Marshall, 'Patriot's Scud Busting Record is Challenged', *Science*, 252, 3 May 1991, pp.640–41; Constance Holden, 'GAO Shoots Down Army on Patriot', *Science*, 258, 9 October 1992, p.223; Matthew Bunn, 'GAO Reports Dispute Accuracy of Missile Defense Claims', *Arms Control Today*, October 1992, p.37; John Conyers, Jr., 'The Patriot Myth: Caveat Emptor', *Arms Control Today*, November 1992, pp.3–10; George Lardner, Jr., 'New Data Take Some of the Luster off Patriot Missile's Gulf War Claims', *International Herald Tribune*, 9 April 1992.

6   General Accounting Office, 'Operation Desert Storm – Evaluation of the Air War', Washington, D.C.: Government Printing Office, Report GAO/PEMD-96-10, July 1996; see also a summary in Tim Weiner, '"Smart" Weapons were Overrated, Study Concludes', *New York Times*, 8 July 1996, pp.A1, A7.

7   For example, Timothy Garden extols the potential of beams and lasers, computing, fission/fusion weapons, ASATs, chemical weapons, materials science, biotechnology and electronics including smart weapons: *The Technology Trap: Science and the Military*, London: Brassey's, 1989, Section 3.

8   'Pentagon Identifies 21 Key Technologies for Maintaining U.S. Military Lead', *Aviation Week & Space Technology*, 134, (21), 20 May 1991, p.57.

9   Martin van Creveld, *Technology and War: From 2000 B.C. to the Present*, New York: Free Press, revised and expanded edition, 1991, p.232.

10   van Creveld, *Technology and War*, p.5.

11   Mark Clodtfelter, *The Limits of Air Power: The American Bombing of North Vietnam*, New York: Free Press, 1989.

12   Scott R. McMichael, *Stumbling Bear: Soviet Military Performance in Afghanistan*, London: Brassey's, 1991; Anthony H. Cordesman and Abraham R. Wagner, *The Lessons of Modern War, Volume III: The Afghan and Falklands Conflicts*, Boulder, CO: Westview Press, 1990.

13   Nicholas J. Wheeler and Ken Booth, 'Beyond the security dilemma: technology, strategy and international security', in Carl G. Jacobsen (ed.), *The Uncertain Course: New Weapons, Strategies and Mind-sets*, Oxford: Oxford University Press, for SIPRI, 1987, p.324.

14   As quoted in Garden, *The Technology Trap*, p.xi.

15   Ibid., p.6.

16   As quoted in Clark and Lilley, *Defense Technology*, p.14.

17   Wheeler and Booth, *The Uncertain Course*, p.326.

18   Ken Booth, 'New challenges and old mind-sets: ten rules for empirical realists', ibid., pp.46, 51.

19   Wheeler and Booth, ibid., p.314.

20   'The first step is to measure whatever can be easily measured. This is okay as far as it goes. The second step is to disregard that which can't be measured or give it an arbitrary quantitative value. This is artificial and misleading. The third step is to presume that what can't be measured easily isn't very important. This is blindness. The fourth step is to say what can't be easily measured really doesn't exist. This is suicide'. (Daniel Yankelovich, quoted in *Science*, 184, 1974, p. 677).

21   M. Handel, 'Numbers Do Count: the Question of Quality versus Quantity', *The Journal of Strategic Studies*, 4, (3) September 1981, pp.225–60; see also Franklin C.

Spinney, in *Defense Facts of Life: The plans/reality mismatch*, Boulder, CO: Westview, 1985.

22   Wheeler and Booth, *The Uncertain Course*, pp.313, 323.
23   Michael Howard, 'The future of deterrence', *RUSI Journal*, **131**, (2) June 1986, p.10.
24   Quoted in Clark and Lilley, *Defense Technology*, p.273.
25   John J. Mearsheimer, 'Why we will soon miss the Cold War', *Atlantic Monthly*, August 1990, p.35.
26   Robert L. O'Connell, *Of Arms and Men: A History of War, Weapons and Aggression*, New York: Oxford University Press, 1989, p.5.
27   Jerome B. Wiesner, Philip Morrison, and Kosta Tsipis, 'Ending Overkill', *Bulletin of the Atomic Scientists*, **49**, (2), March 1993, pp.12–23.
28   Philip Morrison, Kosta Tsipis and Jerome Wiesner, 'The Future of American Defense', *Scientific American*, **270**, (2), February 1994, p.38.
29   Wheeler and Booth, *The Uncertain Course*, p.326.
30   Charles L. Glaser, 'Nuclear Policy Without an Adversary', *International Security*, **16**, (4), Spring 1992, p.41.
31   Andrew C. Tillman, 'Weapons for the 21st Century Soldier', *International Defence Review*, (1/1994), pp.34–8.
32   Mark Hewish and Rupert Pengelley, 'New Age Soldiering', *International Defence Review*, (1/1994), pp.26–33.
33   Barbara Starr, 'Non-lethal weapon puzzle for US Army', *International Defence Review*, (4/1993), p.319.
34   Gary Stix, 'Fighting Future Wars', *Scientific American*, **273**, (6), December 1995, pp.92–8.
35   'The "soft kill" solution', *Bulletin of the Atomic Scientists*, **50**, (2), March/April 1994, pp.4–6.
36   Thomas C. Schelling, 'The Role of Nuclear Weapons', in Ederington and Mazarr, *Turning Point*, pp.105–15.
37   Nina Tannenwald, 'The Changing Role of U.S. Nuclear Weapons', in Michele A. Flournoy (ed.), *Nuclear Weapons After the Cold War: Guidelines for U.S. Policy*, New York: Harper Collins, 1993, pp.36–71.
38   William B. Scott, 'Shrinking ICBM Fleet Gets Needed Upgrades', *Aviation Week & Space Technology*, **143**, (2), 10 July 1995, pp.58–60.
39   Anthony H. Cordesman, *US Defence Policy: Resources and Capabilities*, London: Royal United Services Institute for Defence Studies, 1994, p.22: 'not how to shape the proper strategy and force mix, but rather how to ... fit a lower budget ceiling. ... There was little real examination of major changes to roles and missions.'
40   Stix, 'Fighting Future Wars', p.94.
41   Cordesman, *US Defence Policy*, pp.44–5.
42   Victor A. Utgoff, 'Military Technology Options for the Future', in Barry M. Blechman, William J. Durch, David R. Graham, John H. Henshaw, Pamela L. Reed, Victor A. Utgoff, Steven A. Wolfe, *The American Military in the Twenty-first Century*, London: Macmillan Press, 1994, pp.143–95.
43   David A. Fulghum, 'Planners Mull Future Wars', *Aviation Week & Space Technology*, **141**, (10), 5 September 1994, p.105.
44   As quoted in Fulghum, 'Planners Mull Future Wars', p.106.
45   GAO, 'Operation Desert Storm', and Weiner, '"Smart" Weapons Overrated'.
46   Anthony H. Cordesman and Abraham R. Wagner, *The Lessons of Modern War: Volume IV: The Gulf War*, Boulder, CO: Westview Press, 1996.
47   Ibid., particularly Chapter 1, 'Analyzing the Lessons of the Conflict', pp.1–32.

48   John Keegan, 'The Ground War', in Ederington and Mazarr, *Turning Point*, p.77.
49   Cordesman and Wagner, *The Gulf War*, particularly Chapter 1, 'Analyzing the Lessons of the Conflict', pp.1–32.

2 The Impact of the Military–Industrial Complex on Society

Gert G. Harigel

Introduction

A major legacy of the Cold War is the military–industrial complexes in many countries. A major hope for the end of the Cold War is that these complexes may decrease in size and importance. To judge whether this hope is realized, it is important to have a baseline for comparison. This report aims to provide that baseline for the military–industrial complex.

There is no unique definition for the concept of a military–industrial complex. The lowest common denominator could be: 'It is a close technical collaboration between military and industry to their mutual benefit.' In democracies this complex has various appearances. It may have the structure of a lobby putting pressure on politicians, who in turn impose desired actions first upon their parliamentary committees and then on the government itself (as, for example, in the United States). A lobby may exercise influence on a group of countries which are linked together by a defence treaty. Beginnings of such a structure can be seen in the European Community. In dictatorships the complex is already incorporated into the governing system, when both partners are state-controlled under a planning system (as, for example, in the former Soviet Union).

The military–industrial complex lives primarily on public funds that are dispersed by politicians. In many countries defence is high on the political agenda. Many justifications are given for maintaining a large weapons industry and a strong army. They range from provision of national or international security, guarantee for peace and independence, to preservation of ethnic principles and religious values. The defence industry provides jobs, thereby

19

becoming an asset for the economic well-being of a country. The liabilities of weapons, such as their possible use for destruction or their eventual obsolescence after ever-shortening time intervals, are rarely discussed. When furthering this complex, moral considerations are often neglected, or destabilizing global aspects of armaments are not taken properly into account.

The development of military–industrial complexes can be traced back to Europe at the time of the industrial revolution, eventually discharging their weapon potential during World War I, causing disastrous destruction and enormous loss of human lives. During this war, weapons were still directed selectively towards military targets, so that casualties among the civilian population were only at the level of a few per cent. The victorious nations dismantled the enemies' military industries afterwards, but did not prevent their quick rebirth. World War II saw a repetition of this cycle, albeit with much higher civilian casualties. It was followed almost instantaneously by the tremendous arms build-up during the Cold War. It is this later period which we now examine in some detail.

The main players during the four and a half decades following World War II were the former Soviet Union and the United States. Both superpowers may have been aware of the effect of the enormous military spending upon their societies; perhaps they hoped to achieve an economic victory over the enemy without bloodshed, rather than to gain a military one. Criticism of the complex in Eastern Europe, particularly in the former Soviet Union, is surfacing only slowly, whereas public voices from the West began their warnings as early as the 1950s. Dwight D. Eisenhower became very conscious of the consequences of the peacetime weapon build-up in the United States while he was president. In his presidential farewell address of 1961 he gave a warning:

> In the councils of government we must guard against the acquisition of unwarranted influence, whether sought or unsought, by the military–industrial complex. The potential for the disastrous rise of misplaced power exists and will persist. ... In holding scientific research and discovery in respect, as we should, we must be alert to the equal and opposite danger that public policy could itself become the captive of a scientific–technological elite.
>
> This conjunction of an immense military establishment and large arms industry is new in the American experience.[1]

At an earlier time, in 1953, he had said:

> Every gun that is made, every warship launched, every rocket fired signifies – in the final sense – a theft from those who hunger and are not fed, those who are cold and are not clothed. This is not a way of life at all, in any true sense. Under the cloud of threatening war, it is humanity dangling from a cross of iron.[2]

Any analysis of the impact of the military–industrial complex upon society has to integrate many very different items; some of them can be quantified, others escape such an evaluation. It is possible to describe in numbers the usage of raw material, the environmental impact, the clean-up cost of weapon production sites of radioactive and toxic materials, and the cost of converting industries or economies. Human knowledge and labour invested in armament production, which might otherwise have been available for civilian production, improvements in living conditions or conservation of nature, is extremely difficult to value. Hence these latter aspects are beyond the scope of this chapter.

Our discussion is limited to some easily accessible and verifiable data. This paper is subdivided into sections on (1) military expenditure compared with other government spending, (2) the trade in major conventional weapons and its impact on developing countries, (3) weapons of mass destruction and their past and future repercussions on the environment, (4) environmental problems caused by the use and elimination of land mines, and (5) some remarks on the conversion of industries and workforces from military to civil production. The conclusions are drawn from these discussions, but indirectly reflect the author's personal feelings and experience of World War II and its consequences, which have resulted in a deep-seated scepticism about military solutions of conflicts.

Military Expenditures

There are many ways to assess the impact of government military spending upon society. It can be seen as a share of the overall government 'discretionary spending', as a part of the gross national product (GNP) or gross domestic product (GDP), or the way it influences the wallets of individual citizens and their quality of life. The absolute value of these expenditures for each country can be compared with its standard of living. At the same time, military spending can and should also be evaluated on a global scale. Should weapon transfers have priority over civilian development aid programmes? All this has to be seen against the backdrop of the desired military balance and readiness for defence of human values and national borders. Each of these evaluations may lead to different conclusions about the necessity and desirability of the military–industrial complex.

We begin by reviewing historical world military expenditures, so as to detect changes with the end of the Cold War and to evaluate the potential for the future. Most of the data, covering military expenditure up to the end of 1995, are taken from the comprehensive articles in various annual yearbooks on armaments, disarmament and international security from the

Stockholm International Peace Research Institute (SIPRI).[3] For readers who have access to the World Wide Web, SIPRI graphics of the military spending trends are available for all countries for 1984 to 1994. These can complement the selected tables presented in this report.[4]

The military budgets of various countries are shown in Table 2.1. The world average of the percentage of the GNP going into military budgets in 1993 was 3.3 per cent. Particularly notable in Table 2.1 are the high percentages for military spending in several countries. There are two countries which can at present least afford their high military expenditures because of severe internal economic problems, namely Russia and North Korea. Two rich oil-producing countries, Saudi Arabia and Iraq, were probably persuaded by the manufacturers to buy more weapons than they possibly needed.

Table 2.1   Military spending in 1995 for selected countries (current $ billions),[1] and percentages of GNP in 1993 [2]

Country	Military budget	% of GNP	Country	Military budget	% of GNP
United States	254	4.7	Spain	7	1.8
Russia	63	21.5	North Korea	6	26.6
Japan	54	1.0	Turkey	6	5.8
France	41	3.4	Norway	4	3.1
United Kingdom	35	3.6	Pakistan	4	6.4
Germany	34	1.6	Iraq*	3	74.9
China	29	2.7	Belgium	3	1.8
Italy	16	2.1	Denmark	3	2.0
South Korea	14	3.6	Greece	3	5.5
Saudi Arabia	13	11.2	Syria	3	8.3
Netherlands	9	2.4	Iran	2	3.5
Canada	8	2.0	Portugal	2	3.0
India	8	3.3	Libya	1	5.1
Australia	7	2.4	Vietnam**	1	5.7
Brazil	7	1.3	Cuba	0.3	2.7
Israel	7	9.4			

Notes:
1 Center for Defense Information, 'Last of the Big Time Spenders: Proposed 1997 U.S. Military Budget Dwarfs All Others', *The Defence Monitor*, **25**, (4), 1996, p.4.
2 Britannica Book, 'Britannica World Data, Nations of the World, United States', in *Britannica Book of the Year, 1996*, London: Encyclopaedia Britannica, 1996, pp.741–4.
* Data from 1991; ** data from 1994.

The fairly high military expenditures in Israel, Syria, Turkey and Greece may be understood to result from tensions in those regions.

We now examine in some detail the situation in the United States, for two reasons: first, it is the richest nation in the world; second, reliable data are available on its spending policy, both in the military and the civilian sector. As seen from Table 2.1, the military budget of the United States dwarfs those of all the other countries. In 1996, the United States spent more than twice as much on its military as the combined total of its potential adversaries, China, Russia, Iran, Iraq, Syria, North Korea, Cuba and Libya. The United States also leads in arms production and sales, as will be shown later. Data for the past and present will first be presented and then put into the perspective of the total budget and accumulated government debt.

The annual military spending of the United States since the 1950s oscillated between about $400 billion and $250 billion (in constant 1995 dollars),[5] peaking during the Korean War, the Vietnam War and the Reagan build-up in the 1980s. In response to the collapse of the Soviet Union, the spending went down and appears to have levelled off at about $270 billion. The military spending may be compared with the total US governmental expenditure in 1995 of $1539 billion (32.0 per cent social security and Medicare, 17.6 per cent defence, 15.2 per cent interest on the national debt, 14.5 per cent income security, 7.5 per cent health, 13.2 per cent other) and with a revenue of $1346 billion.[6] The debt accumulated during the last decade amounts to $2.3 trillion and the total national debt approaches $5 trillion.

In 1994, 63 per cent of governmental purchases of goods and services were by states and local authorities, and 37 per cent by federal agencies.[7] The proposed US 1997 federal 'discretionary' spending includes (in $ billion)[8] military: $255; education: $27; health: $24; justice: $23; resources and environment: $21; international affairs: $19; veterans' services: $19; science and space: $18; housing assistance: $17; social services: $15; transport: $14; general government: $13; other income security: $12; economic development: $9; energy: $5; agriculture: $4; commerce: $3; and other: $3. Thus slightly more than half of it goes into the military budget, only 5 per cent is spent on each of the categories of education and health. The other category of federal spending is 'mandatory' expenditures, money the federal government must spend automatically. It includes entitlements, which are money for benefits provided directly to individuals, such as social security, Medicare, Medicaid, food stamps and federal retirement. It also includes interest payments on the national debt. However, these figures do not reflect the large expenditures of the individual states and cities on health, education and roads.

Official figures for 'National Defence' understate the full extent of military spending by omitting several important costs. Such understatements are probably common to figures given by other countries. Table 2.2 estimates the full cost for the United States of preparing to maintain its military strength, and paying for past expenditures, while Table 2.3 shows the impact of military spending in the United States and selected major industrialized countries upon the wallet of the average citizen.

There is a noticeable downward trend in the data for the United States, Russia and China, an upward tendency for Japan and Germany, while the

Table 2.2   Estimated defence spending ($ billions) in the United States for fiscal year 1996

National defence spending		263
Military-related spending		
Foreign military aid	5	
International peacekeeping	0.4	
Space (military)	3	
Military retirement pay	17	
Veterans' benefits	39	
Military share of interest on the national debt	167	
Military-related subtotal		231
Total military and military-related spending		494

Source: See Table 2.1, note 1.

Table 2.3   Military budget per citizen (dollars) in various countries, 1997[1] and 1993 [2]

	1997	1993	1993 % of GNP
United States	963	1 153	4.7
France	707	740	3.4
United Kingdom	600	587	3.6
Japan	432	335	1.0
Russia	429	504	21.5
Germany	416	375	1.6
China	24	47	2.7

Notes:
1   Center for Defense Information, 'The 1997 Military Budget: A Ticking Time Bomb', *The Defence Monitor* **25**, (4), 1996, p.6.
2   See Table 2.1, note 2.

data for the United Kingdom and France are essentially constant. These percentages for major industrialized countries may not seem particularly large, except for Russia, since all taxpayers pay according to their income. However, spending even a part of this money for alternative purposes, such as aid for developing countries, could have important beneficial effects. Extrapolations into the future contain necessarily large uncertainties and depend upon many factors, such as changes of governments or political situations and economic conditions. Equally important for future expenditures is the question whether wasteful military spending can be controlled. A few examples are given here to illustrate the extent of this problem and its implications for the future.

The trend in the costs of some weapons reveals two important aspects: prices per unit tend to go up substantially, and weapons projects are hard to stop. Examples are (1) the B-2 *Stealth* bomber: originally 132 planes were planned at $0.56 billion each; now 20 cost $2.2 billion each; (2) the *Seawolf* submarine: originally 30 were planned at $1.5 billion each, now three cost $3 billion each; and (3) the C-17 transport aircraft: originally 210 aircraft were planned for a total of $39 billion, after two years, 120 aircraft are to cost a total of $43 billion.[9] The Eurofighter, to be built by a European consortium, showed a similar cost explosion.

An example of the tendency of projects to continue even as the costs rise is the strategic missile defence effort of the United States. More than $70 billion has been spent on the nation's ballistic missile defence (BMD) programmes since their beginnings in the 1950s. President Clinton's 1997 budget request includes $2.8 billion of research and development (R&D) money for BMD. Building and deploying a single-site national missile defence system could cost $29.2 billion. Studies by the technical community showing the exaggerated claims for BMD, such as the study of the American Physical Society 'Science and Technology of Directed Energy Weapons',[10] have caused only a temporary slowdown of the programme.

The military spending in the United States is and will be determined by the so-called 'bottom-up review' of September 1993.[11] It requires the ability to fight two nearly simultaneous major regional conflicts: $1.2 billion is requested for 1995 to 1999 to implement this plan. It was never stipulated who these two enemies might be, and what are their military potentials.

The military–industrial complex affects the R&D efforts of the United States and thereby, the future. Of the projected R&D expenditures for 1997 of $73 billion, 53 per cent is committed to R&D on military and nuclear weapons, while only 17.6 per cent, 11 per cent and 4.5 per cent go to health, civilian space and energy respectively.[12]

Often military research is praised as the motor for advance in science and technology. It cannot be denied that there have been substantial spin-offs from military research, such as radar, infrared photography of the environ-ment and so on. However, most experts agree that, had the R&D money been spent directly on the civilian research, more useful results would have been obtained. The planned joint Russian–US venture to build a space station is in the view of many scientists an example of wasteful spending, since most of the planned research can be done under almost equivalent conditions much more cheaply on earth. The station, including its operation over a decade, may cost in the region of $100 billion.[13] The purpose seems to be to keep engineers and companies in the weapons complex busy. It can be argued that this may have a positive effect as far as it provides peaceful work for a number of scientists and engineers from the former Soviet weapons factories, who could otherwise be tempted to work for 'rogue' states. For more than two decades following World War II, the field of elementary particle physics profited from the wish 'to have a large number of physicists ready and well-paid, in good health, in case of another war. But around 1970 things began to change for several reasons.'[14]

A worldwide study of decision making on weapon systems at Oxford University found that

> much of the power and momentum of the arms race lies in the early stages of decision making, when a weapon is on the drawing board in the lab, and at the testing and developing stages. Frequently, by the time these stages are complete, so much money has been spent that the programme must continue – the 'no turning back' point is passed. But very often at this point even senior politicians, let alone parliamentarians, are still unaware of the project. ... Do members of parliament have ultimate financial control over defence decisions? ... Only one NATO parliament, the US Congress, has a defence budget that is itemized in such a way that Representatives can see how much money is being spent on a particular weapons system. ... The national parliaments, except Congress, lack adequate powers properly to control defence expenditure.[15]

It appears that even in democracies the spending by the military–industrial complex is almost out of control and beyond supervision by the citizenry.

Production and Trade of Conventional Weapons

To evaluate the effect of arms production and trade on society as a whole, both from an economic and a security point of view, one has to consider it as part of the entire world trade. The total world trade in 1993 was about $24.3 trillion, the share of the United States was $6.4 trillion. The total world exports (external trade) were $4.2 trillion. The US weapons exports were $9.9 billion out of the world total weapons exports of $22.8 billion.

Arms production in most parts of the world has a downward trend, but there are at the same time important efforts to raise the technological quality of the arms produced. Financially, one effect may balance the other. In 1992, the 100 major arms-producing companies had combined arms sales of about $166 billion, followed by a decline of about 6 per cent in the following year, and 2 per cent in 1994.[16] The statistics for these companies show a shift during 1993 in the regional distribution of arms sales. There was a drop of sales by Western European companies and an increase for the United States and Japan. The 12 leading companies are two French, one British and nine US firms. This confirms that the centre of the military–industrial complex is in the United States.

Worldwide export deliveries of major conventional weapons in 1994 are estimated to have been $21.7 billion in constant 1990 US dollars; in 1993, they had been $24.5 billion. This global volume of delivery of major conventional weapons appears to have been stable during the period 1991–3, after a period of rapid decline between 1987 and 1991.[17] The share in the arms sales provided by the top 100 arms-producing companies shows no significant regional or national variations in 1992, 1993 and 1994.

The largest reductions in trade with conventional weapons can be found in the share supplied to developing countries, going down from 66 per cent in 1985 to 58 per cent in 1994, and the Middle East, going from 31 per cent in 1985 to 24 per cent in 1994. The relative share of world sales supplied by developing countries has remained almost constant over the last few years.

Leading supplier countries and the value of trade in major conventional weapons are shown in Table 2.4. Data in this table do not include trade in

Table 2.4 Leading suppliers by country of major conventional weapons for 1990–95 (values in constant 1990$ millions)

Suppliers	1990	1991	1992	1993	1994	1995	1990–95
USA	10 648	12 568	13 794	12 802	12 821	9 804	72 437
USSR/Russia	10 459	4 657	2 841	3 631	962	3 905	26 455
Germany, FRG	1 656	2 520	1 503	1 686	2 483	1 964	11 812
UK	1 509	1 143	1 099	1 213	1 493	1 663	8 120
France	2 220	1 071	1 108	1 368	1 021	815	7 603

Source: Ian Anthony and Herbert Wulf, 'The trade in major conventional weapons', in *SIPRI Yearbook 1990*, pp.219–316; Pieter D. Wezeman and Siemon T. Wezeman, 'The trade in major conventional weapons', in *SIPRI Yearbook 1995*, pp.491–582; and Ian Anthony, Pieter D. Wezeman and Siemon T. Wezeman, 'The trade in major conventional weapons', in *SIPRI Yearbook 1996*, pp.463–533.

smaller weapons such as rifles, hand grenades and land mines. Russian arms sales remained stable (within 10 per cent) from 1980 till 1989, they dropped substantially in 1991 and further in 1994, to recover recently to 25 per cent of its pre-collapse value, regaining second place after the United States and making it the largest arms seller to the developing world.[18] The reliability of these numbers is reduced by fluctuations in the exchange rate for the Russian ruble. For the immediate future, Russia's main export articles remain raw materials such as oil, gas and timber – and arms. The arms sales by the United States have remained fairly steady. In 1994, Germany took second place for a short time; faced by the demand for weapon reduction by the Treaty on Conventional Forces in Europe, the choice was either to destroy or to sell the surplus accumulated by the German unification.

Major recipients of these conventional arms are listed in Table 2.5. Saudi Arabia showed large fluctuations in its weapon imports, probably due to the Gulf War and the large commitments to it. Japan had a large drop in imports, which was compensated by an increase in its own weapon manufacturing. Turkey increased its imports considerably, which might reflect the trouble with its Kurdish population on the border with Iran and Iraq. India had a drop in imports, probably due to its economic crisis in 1991.

Table 2.5   Leading recipients of major conventional arms for 1990–94 (values in constant 1990$ millions)

Recipients	1990	1991	1992	1993	1994	1995	1990–95
Saudi Arabia	2 459	1 208	1 080	2 534	1 309	961	9 551
Japan	2 272	2 386	1 608	1 260	829	799	9 154
Turkey	804	954	1 640	2 288	2 089	1 125	8 900
Egypt	755	1 234	1 274	1 191	1 884	1 555	7 893
Greece	1 221	559	2 632	891	1 185	489	6 977
India	1 599	1 799	1 419	724	445	770	6 756

Source: Pieter D. Wezeman and Siemon T. Wezeman, 'The trade in major conventional weapons', in *SIPRI Yearbook 1995*, pp.491–582; Ian Anthony, Pieter D. Wezeman and Siemon T. Wezeman, 'The trade in major conventional weapons', in *SIPRI Yearbook 1996*, pp.463–533.

Table 2.6 shows that, apart from the substantial decline from the height of the Cold War in 1986 to its end in 1990, there has been a significant reduction since 1990 in exports of major conventional weapons by countries belonging to the industrialized world. This development may be attributed

Table 2.6   Exports of major conventional weapons for 1986–95 (values in constant 1990$ millions)

	1986	1990	1991	1992	1993	1994	1995	1990–95
World total	44 854	31 296	25 819	24 533	24 744	22 841	22 797	152 030
Developing world	2 775	1 627	1 705	1 725	2 197	1 158	1 410	9 822
Industrialized world	42 079	29 669	24 114	22 808	22 547	21 683	21 387	142 208

Source: As for Table 2.5.

primarily to the reduction of exports from the former Soviet Union. Exports by developing countries remained essentially constant and insignificant.

Imports by developing countries of conventional weapons accounted for more than half of their world trade. As seen from Table 2.7, there has been a substantial drop during 1990–95. Imports by least developed countries (LDCs), which are a subset of the developing world, dropped by an order of magnitude, largely due to the end of the Afghanistan war. Arms delivery into regions of conflict is an unfortunate but common phenomenon. Sometimes it goes on in spite of internationally declared embargoes. Table 2.8 lists as an example the US arms exports to such areas of conflict for two time periods. Some reductions in exports can be seen. Total US deliveries dropped from about $3.5 billion per year in the period 1987–91 to about $2.7 billion per year in the period 1991–3, perhaps partially as a result of

Table 2.7   Imports of major conventional weapons (values in constant 1990$ millions)

	1986	1990	1991	1992	1993	1994	1995	1990–95
World total	44 854	31 296	25 819	24 532	24 743	22 842	22 797	152 029
Developing world	29 583	18 095	13 995	12 072	13 293	13 252	16 073	86 781
LDCs	1 731	3 103	1 703	313	414	128	456	34 017
Industrialized world	15 271	13 201	11 824	12 460	11 450	9 590	6 724	65 249

Source: As for Table 2.5.

Table 2.8   US arms exports to various areas of conflict (values in constant 1995$ millions)

Recipient	1987–91	1991–93
Southern Europe		
Spain	2 900	500
Turkey	3 700	2 300
Middle East/North Africa		
Israel	5 000	2 000
Morocco	210	80
Egypt	2 600	2 400
Sub-Saharan Africa		
Chad	60	5
Somalia	40	5
Liberia	10	0
Kenya	50	20
Zaire	20	0
Asia		
Pakistan	825	30
Philippines	310	180
Indonesia	360	70
Latin America		
Guatemala	30	0
Haiti	0	0
Colombia	130	60
Brazil	270	120
Mexico	410	90

Source: William D. Hartung, 'U.S. Conventional Arms Transfers: Promoting Stability or Fueling Conflict?', *Arms Control Today*, **25**, (9), November 1995, pp.9–13.

diminishing competition between the two superpowers for regional superiority after the end of the Cold War. In particular, there was a drastic reduction in sales to Sub-Saharan Africa. However, as the recent conflicts in the Central African nations of Burundi, Rwanda, Zaire, Sudan and Nigeria show, these wars would probably not have escalated so much without previous weapons deliveries.

Noteworthy is the drop in deliveries of arms to Pakistan, probably in connection with the end of the Afghanistan war, which allowed the United States to resume its efforts to curtail Pakistan's nuclear weapon ambitions.

US military aid to Somalia from 1981 to 1989 amounted to a staggering $296 million; the weapons involved had to be recaptured by the UN forces during their intervention.

US weapons sales during the four decades 1950 to 1990 to the Middle East amounted to $85 billion, most of them going to Saudi Arabia ($41.5 billion), Israel ($17.3 billion) and Iran ($11.3 billion). The Soviet Union in turn provided Iraq with ample weapons. This kept the Iran–Iraq war going for over eight years.

As arms become less readily available, wars may perhaps become of shorter duration and be less destructive. This is to be hoped for, since the material losses and the death toll from past conventional wars have been mind-blowing. Michael Renner reports[19] that the Iran–Iraq war of 1980–88 cost $416 billion up to 1985, surpassing the combined earnings of $364 billion from all oil sales to that point. He also reports that, 'According to the Arab Monetary Fund, the Iraqi occupation of Kuwait and the war to reverse it cost the region some $676 billion.'

A US official pointed to the importance of the Wassenaar Arrangement on Export Controls for Conventional Arms and Dual-Use Goods and Technologies, saying that 'Nonproliferation controls are great [for nuclear weapons], but the bulk of the wars are conventional. We're gonna say we have a regime for stuff that nobody uses but we don't have a regime for stuff that everybody uses?'[20]

Arms trade and proliferation to LDCs is one of the saddest aspects of our time. These countries still suffer from their colonial period, the wars leading to their independence and innumerable civil wars afterwards, wars that probably could have been avoided if they had not been able to purchase weapons. Many of these countries are still shamelessly exploited by the industrial countries and suffer heavily from debts. Table 2.9 compares military expenditure and external public debt service with government revenue for selected developing countries and LDCs. For half of the countries shown in Table 2.9, the debt service plus military expenditure consumes more than 50 per cent of the total government revenue, condemning those countries to perpetual poverty. The International Monetary Fund predicts that the total external debt of LDCs will rise by 8 per cent in 1994, to $1.675 trillion.[21] The total debt as a fraction of exports and services continued to decline, however, and was expected to drop to 121 per cent in 1994.

The following are the words of Oscar Arias Sánchez, winner of the 1987 Nobel Peace Prize, and former president of Costa Rica, a land which abolished its army in 1948 and has come to enjoy one of the highest standards of living in Latin America:

Table 2.9 Military expenditure and external public debt service as percentage of current government revenue, 1987

Country	External debt service	Military expenditure	Debt service plus military expenditure
Argentina	23.6	15.8	39.4
Colombia	50.7	14.5	65.2
Chile	25.6	22.0	47.6
Egypt	11.8	19.6	31.4
Indonesia	35.5	13.9	49.4
Israel	13.1	30.9	44.0
Jordan	36.2	48.9	85.1
Morocco	30.9	19.5	50.4
Pakistan	20.4	40.1	60.5
Philippines	48.1	15.5	63.6
Sri Lanka	24.2	30.7	54.9
Zimbabwe	23.5	22.5	46.0

Source: Somnath Sen, 'Debt, financial flows and international security', *SIPRI Yearbook 1990*, pp.203–17.

> There is no greater immorality than to sell weapons to sub-Saharan Africa. Selling them weapons is the best way to condemn those countries to perpetual poverty. ... Official military spending is $700 billion a year, 14 times as much as is dedicated to development work. Developing nations spend $200 billion on their armies and weapons purchases. Just reducing military spending can help solve many of the problems of poverty.
>
> Developing countries spend more on debt servicing than on these basic needs [adequate food, safe water, primary health care, family planning and basic education], and little more than 6 per cent of the $40 billion international bilateral aid actually goes to the social sector.[22]

A Code of Conduct for Arms Transfers initiative is being organized by Oscar Sánchez. This Code would restrict arms from going to dictators, or to governments that commit serious human rights abuses, or governments that use arms against their own people. Sánchez pointed out that nearly all arms transfers today are made by the five members of the Security Council, and nearly all of them are going to governments that would not qualify under such a Code of Conduct.

Monitoring of the arms trade is important. Since 1992, some governments have been reporting some of their arms imports and exports on a voluntary basis to the United Nations Register of Conventional Arms. Some valuable information on the military–industrial complex can be deduced from these communications, even if they are not complete. The Wassenaar Arrangement on Export Controls may provide more transparency on weapons trade.

Total Cost of Weapons of Mass Destruction

Weapons of mass destruction are discussed separately here, because there is some hope that we may be able to curtail their production and to eliminate them eventually. The signing of the START treaties and the conclusion of the Chemical Weapons Convention and of the Biological Weapons Convention are all indications that humanity abhors weapons of mass destruction and sees them more as a burden than an asset in any war. The Nonproliferation Treaty, the Advisory Opinion of the World Court, the Report of the Canberra Commission and the Abolition 2000 movement (which unites more than 660 non-governmental organizations) all stress the importance of an urgent elimination of nuclear arms. However, even if these initiatives were all to be successful, the legacies of nuclear and chemical weapons would still be with us for a long time and would adversely affect society.

Table 2.10 shows that the nuclear weapons programme of the United States has cost it about $4 trillion in 1995 dollars from its inception in 1940 to the present. This is three times more than was spent on procurement for all of World War II, and is roughly equal to the US gross national product. The total includes most, but not all, of the direct, indirect and overhead costs required to develop, produce, deploy, operate, support and control US nuclear forces over the past 50 years.[23] An additional $500 billion to $1 trillion

Table 2.10   The cost of US nuclear weapons from 1940 to 1995 (constant 1995$ billions)

Building nuclear weapons	387
Delivery systems for nuclear weapons	2 000
Command, control, and defence against nuclear weapons	1 100
Retiring and dismantling nuclear weapons	15
Legacies of nuclear weapons programmes	385
Managing nuclear weapons	25
Total	3 900

Source: Stephen I. Schwartz, 'Four Trillion Dollars and Counting', *Bulletin of Atomic Scientists*, **51**, (6), November/December 1995, pp.32–5.

may be added to this total once all known costs are documented and ana-lysed, especially those costs that are related to operating and maintaining the arsenal. In the end the figure will likely be approximately equal to the $5 trillion US national debt. In short, one-quarter to one-third of all US military spending since World War II has been devoted to nuclear weapons and their infrastructure.

The spending on nuclear arms in the former Soviet Union is not known, but was certainly enormous.[24] To quote the Russian nuclear physicist, Andrei Sakharov:

> Every day I saw the huge material, intellectual and nervous resources of thou-sands of people being poured into the creation of a means of total destruction, something capable of annihilating all human civilization. I noticed that the control levers were in the hands of people who, though talented in their own ways, were cynical. Until the summer of 1953 the chief of the project was Beria, who ruled over millions of slave-prisoners. Almost all the construction was done with their labour. Beginning in the late fifties, one got an increasingly clearer picture of the collective might of the military–industrial complex and of its vigorous, unprincipled leaders, blind to everything except their 'job'.[25]

Has this enormous spending on nuclear arms benefited mankind? Politicians and the mass media try to make us believe that their existence has prevented a war between the two superpowers, without being able to give any proof for this statement. Not only have there been 140 wars since 1945, but the five declared nuclear powers have been involved in an average of five wars each since 1945, compared to an average of 0.65 wars each for all other countries. This is clearly not compatible with the assertion that nuclear weapons have helped prevent wars.

Some of the as yet unknown costs of nuclear war preparations are those of nuclear waste management, environmental remediation and storing nu-clear weapons. These are estimated to cost the United States at least $230 billion over the next half century, perhaps more than half a trillion dollars.[26] The latter figure is well in excess of the $375 billion it cost, in current dollars, to develop and build the tens of thousands of weapons that were assembled in the United States. Expectations are that well over $50 billion will be needed to clean up the plutonium complex at Hanford in the state of Washington. One contractor has estimated that the handling of 177 high-level waste tanks alone may cost up to $50 billion. Each of these tanks is the size of the Capitol dome in Washington, DC, with a volume of 210 000 cubic metres; they were designed to last only 25 years. They contain the enormous amount of radioactivity of 450 million curies; 11 tons of pluto-nium are in storage and 1.5 tons are dispersed in waste. Vitrification is considered by some experts as the way to store plutonium safely and permanently, but others disagree.

The legacy of nuclear tests in the atmosphere is still with the global population, since only a fraction of the radioactive fallout has decayed. The large amounts of radioactivity created by over 1500 underground nuclear explosions is largely confined to caverns, but some of it may leak into water aquifers. Thus the impact of the nuclear weapons on society is threefold: (1) the high cost of their production, maintenance and destruction, (2) radioactivity dispersed during nuclear explosion tests and manufacturing, causing significant health risks, and (3) the requirement of safe disposal of waste for durations that equal the lifetimes of many generations. Our budgets, health and ecology will be affected for a long time by the existence of the nuclear weapons complex.

The Chemical Weapons Convention (CWC) prohibits the development, production, acquisition, stockpiling, transfer and use of chemical weapons. This Convention was signed in 1993, and entered into force in November 1996 after the ratification by the required 65 countries. The main possessors of chemical weapons, the United States and Russia, have not yet ratified. It is estimated that the elimination of US chemical weapons will cost at least ten times as much as their fabrication. The cost was estimated as more than $8 billion in 1992,[27] perhaps as much as $20 billion, according to other sources. The CWC requires that the destruction of stockpiles should be completed in less than 10 years after its entry into force. There are 31 000 tons of chemicals in 3.6 million weapons.[28] A major problem is to find a place for the incineration plants. Many sites on mainland United States are under consideration, as well as the Johnston Atoll in the Pacific Ocean, south-west of the Hawaiian islands. For obvious reasons, nobody wants to have such a plant in his or her backyard. In the former Soviet Union there are claimed to be about 40 000 tons of chemical weapons agents in weapons, plus 30 000 tons dumped in the Baltic Sea. However, some experts estimate that 300 000 to 400 000 tons is a more realistic figure for the stored weapons. The health risks posed by the destruction of chemical weapons cannot be ignored. The possible leakage from dumped weapons into the Baltic Sea will threaten bordering countries for a long time.

The verification of disarmament treaties down to the very last detail is not possible and must rely to a certain extent upon trust. The necessary verification budgets for the technologies and the personnel for operation and bookkeeping will be proportional to the required degree of certainty. Costs for the verification of the CWC are not yet known.

The Impact of Land Mines

The human, ecological and economic effects of land mines provide one example of the social impact of the military–industrial complex. Negotiations on banning fabrication, trade and use of land mines are progressing slowly, but, if a ban were ever to take place, the social costs of land mines would continue to be very high.

Since World War II about 250 million land mines have been produced. Of these, 190 million are antipersonnel, with 110 million still in place. Two to five million land mines are still laid every year, while only 100 000 are removed each year. The density of land mines per square mile (2.6 square km) for the most affected countries is as follows:[29] Bosnia–Herzegovina 152; Cambodia 142; Croatia 92; Iraq 60; Egypt 59; Afghanistan 40; Angola 31; Eritrea 28; and Iran 25. These land mines claim 25 000 victims each year: 80 per cent of them civilians and 29 per cent children under the age of 14. Considering the low production price of antipersonnel land mines, ranging from a couple of dollars to about $100 apiece, it is difficult to understand why they attract manufacturers in 38 countries. Probably it is because they are made in small factories and do not require special technical skills.

The cost of clearing the land mines already in place has been estimated to be at least $33 billion, while the estimated cost of rehabilitation and prostheses for the world's 250 000 land mine-related amputees (increasing by 800 each month) is $750 million. As with the chemical weapons discussed above, the costs of eliminating deployed land mines are higher (by about two orders of magnitude) than their manufacture.

The loss of agricultural land, which may last for decades or even centuries, may reach one-third of the total in some countries, for example in Afghanistan and Cambodia. The partial ban on the use of antipersonnel mines that has recently been agreed upon in the framework of the Certain Conventional Weapons Convention has left most people unsatisfied.

Workforces and Conversion

The military–industrial complex has costs in technological competitiveness. Table 2.11 shows the percentage of total R&D funds and the number of engineers and scientists working directly or indirectly for the armament industry in four declared nuclear weapon states, and for the two countries that lost World War II. Some restructuring of the arms industry can be observed worldwide, but the conversion of military industries into competitive civilian operations is a difficult process for all countries, and appears to be painfully slow in the former Soviet Union.

Table 2.11   Funds, engineers and scientists going to military research, 1987

Country	Percentage of total R&D funds	Numbers of engineers & scientists
France	20	21 000
West Germany	5	8 000
Japan	0.8	3 000
United Kingdom	25	25 000
United States*	33	265 000
USSR	large	many

Note: * The percentage of total R&D funds increased further for 1997.

Source: Frank von Hippel, 'Contributions of Independent Analysts and Activists to Disarmament and the Conversion of Military Resources', Rillin et al. (eds), *Proceedings of Challenges*, pp.26–32.

The military sector represents a part of the economy that is largely protected from public scrutiny and economic competition. Does military spending create jobs? The Centre of Defence Information estimates that every billion dollars spent on military procurement produce 25 000 jobs.[30] If spent in the civilian sector, the same billion would create 30 000 jobs in mass transport, 36 000 in housing, 41 000 in education or 47 000 in health care. For example, the US Department of Defense has an arms sale staff of 6395 full-time employees who promote and service foreign arms sales by US companies at a cost of more than $450 million to taxpayers. Could these people not instead develop trade in civilian goods?

Conclusions

The preceding sections have presented data on the magnitude of the weapon build-up by the military–industrial complex. In the end this 'investment' does more harm than good for our societies on the human and financial level, leaving behind destruction of the environment, toxic and radioactive waste and obsolete weapons requiring disposal. Citizens should be better informed about the environmental damage resulting from the construction of nuclear weapons. Such weapons of mass destruction can now be abolished, since even leading military experts and commanders are now convinced that such weapons are of no use. Huge military spending should only be justified if there exist enemies who threaten the country from outside, or if such enemies are expected to emerge in the near future. For internal enemies, for instance where there are ethnic conflicts, there is no reason to have highly sophisticated weapons of mass destruction to neutralize them. A well organized police force should be sufficient to control internal upheaval.

We should therefore do everything possible to reduce the military–industrial complex, and to transfer engineers and scientists from military industry to civilian tasks. It is true that money saved by reducing the military is not automatically available for civilian projects. To be successful and give humanity a chance of survival, the minds and attitudes of people have to be changed, as argued by the *Russell–Einstein Manifesto*, away from the simplistic argument that security can be guaranteed by a weapons build-up. We have to convince everybody that war is a costly and ultimately primitive and immoral way to solve political problems. In particular, intellectuals and politicians have to tackle much more important aspects related to the well-being of humanity, such as facing up to the risk of climate change, forging a sustainable water strategy, sustaining freshwater ecosystems, preserving agricultural resources, understanding the threat of bio-invasions, confronting infectious diseases, shifting to sustainable industries and looking for renewable energy sources and environmentally sustainable public transport. Many of the scientists and engineers now working in the military–industrial complex could find these to be rewarding challenges.

Countless examples of arguments for choosing butter rather than guns could be given. Carol Bellamy, the Executive Director of UNICEF, said: 'In 1993, UNICEF estimated that $25 billion a year in extra resources would be enough to meet the basic needs of every man, woman and child for adequate food, safe water, primary health care, family planning and basic education.'[31] These $25 billion are only a small percentage of the yearly world expenditure on armaments!

Does the world need superpowers with huge military–industrial complexes, with ever more sophisticated and expensive weapons? Would the world not be better off with humanitarian superpowers, a functioning International Court of Justice and a well funded and respected United Nations to promote equitable living conditions for everybody who lives on our planet?

Notes

1   Alan L. Mackay, *A Dictionary of Scientific Quotations*, New York: Adam Hilger, 1991, p.83.
2   *The Defence Monitor*, **22**, (8), 1993.

3   Stockholm International Peace Research Institute, *SIPRI Yearbook: Armaments, Disarmament and International Security*, Oxford: Oxford University Press, 1989, 1993, 1995, 1996.
4   SIPRI: http://www.sipri.se/sipri/whatsnew.html.
5   Mike Moore, 'More security for less money', *The Bulletin of the Atomic Scientists*, **51**, (5), September/October, 1995, pp.34–7.
6   Britannica Book, 'Britannica World Data, Nations of the World, United States', in *Britannica Book of the Year, 1996*, London: Encyclopaedia Britannica, 1996.
7   Ibid.
8   Center for Defense Information, 'Discretionary Spending', *The Defence Monitor*, **25**, (4), 1996, p.5.
9   Danielle Gordon, 'Underfunding? Or Overprogramming?', *Bulletin of the Atomic Scientists*, **51**, (5), September/October 1995, p.38.
10 George E. Pake, Michael A. May, W.K.H. Panofsky, Arthur L. Schawlow, Charles H. Townes and Herbert F. York, 'Report to the American Physical Society of the Study Group on Science and Technology of Directed Energy Weapons', *Review of Modern Physics*, **57**, 1987, p.S1–S200.
11 Paul George, Robert Bedeski, Bengt-Göran Bergstand, Julian Cooper and Evamaria Loose-Weintraub, 'World military expenditures', in *SIPRI Yearbook 1995*, p.394.
12 Irwin Goodwin, 'Washington Reports: Clinton's 1997 Budget Proposes Small R&D Gains and Promises to Start More Battles on Capitol Hill', *Physics Today*, **49**, (5), May 1996, p.55.
13 Tim Beardsley, 'Science in the Sky', *Scientific American*, **274**, (6), June 1996, p.36.
14 Victor F. Weisskopf, 'Final Remarks', *Nuclear Physics*, **B36**, 1994, p.450.
15 Scilla Elworthy, 'Were We More Democratic 300 Years Ago?', in Rainer Rilling, Hartwig Spitzer, Owen Green, Ferdinand Hucho and Gyula Pati (eds), *Proceedings of the International Congress on 'Challenges, Science and Peace in a Rapidly Changing Environment'; Vol. I*, Berlin: Schriftenreihe Wissenschaft und Frieden, 1991, pp.52–62.
16 Elisabeth Sköns and Ksenia Gonchar, 'Arms production', in *SIPRI Yearbook 1996*, pp.411–62.
17 Ibid.; also Elisabeth Sköns and Ksenia Gonchar, 'Arms production', in *SIPRI Yearbook 1995*, pp.455–90.
18 Philip Shenon, 'Russia Now World's Main Arms Seller', *International Herald Tribune*, 21 August 1996.
19 Michael Renner, 'Budgeting for Disarmament', in Lester R. Brown (ed.), *State of the World 1995: A Worldwatch Institute Report on Progress Toward a Sustainable Society*, New York: W.W. Norton, 1995, pp.150–69.
20 Natalie J. Goldring, 'Wassenaar Arrangement in Limbo', *Basic Reports, Newsletter on International Security Policy*, (52) May 1996, p.3.
21 Carol Bellamy, 'Children Are Better Off, but the World's Effort Must Continue', *International Herald Tribune*, 23 October 1996.
22 Ibid.
23 Ibid.
24 Don J. Bradley, Clyde W. Frank and Yevgeny Mikerin, 'Nuclear Contamination from Weapons Complexes in the Former Soviet Union and the United States', *Physics Today*, **49**, (4) April 1996, p.40.
25 'Sakharov Speaks 1974', *Dictionary of Scientific Quotations*, p.216.
26 Glenn Zorpette, 'Hanford's Nuclear Wasteland', *Scientific American*, **274**, (5), May 1996, pp.72–81.

27   Paul Doty, 'The Challenge of Destroying Chemical Weapons', *Arms Control Today*, **22**, (8), October 1992, pp.24–5.
28   'U.S. Disclosure is Welcomed', *International Herald Tribune*, 24 January 1996; Heather Podlich, 'Factfile: U.S. Unitary and Binary Chemical Stockpiles', *Arms Control Today*, **26**, (1), February 1996, p.34.
29   Gino Strada, 'The Horror of Land Mines', *Scientific American*, **274**, (5), May 1996, pp.26–31; United Nations, Department of Humanitarian Affairs, 'The United Nations and Mine Clearance (Overview – June 1995), and Background Paper Summary, Expert Panels A-I', Loose Leaflet from International Meeting on Mine Clearance, 5–7 July 1995.
30   Private communication from Timothy Bruening.
31   Carol Bellamy, 'Children Are Better Off'.

3   Problems of Reconversion from the Military to the Civilian Sector

Georgi Arbatov

Introduction

To get rid of the redundant weapons left by the Cold War – and to do it in a way that does not endanger either peace and international security or the environment – is the natural first step in our efforts to overcome the dangerous legacy left by this period of intensive arms races and hostile and tense international relations. The second monster we have to tame is the defence industry, which grew beyond all reasonable proportions during the Cold War. It is especially visible in the former Soviet Union, which, while having a much smaller gross national product, tried to have military equality – or if possible even more than that – with the United States and its allies. This policy completely deformed the Soviet economy; by some assessments more than half of Soviet industry worked for defence.

The Defence Industry

In the minds of people, defence-related branches of industry appear to be closely linked with such important, almost sacred, issues as national security and patriotism, and are surrounded by solemn and strict secrecy, especially in the former Soviet Union. Hence for decades the defence industry was not only privileged but also became a kind of sovereign state within a state. This meant much less control by the public and an obvious development of this sector of the economy as an end in itself in accordance with the rules of the so-called 'Parkinsonian laws', even though ways to rationalize such a state of affairs were found rather skilfully. All of this became obvious from time to time, often revealed in scandals that erupted in this sphere in the West and lately also in the former Soviet Union.

The defence industry has for a rather long time enjoyed unusual political influence. My generation started to speak about it mostly only after the famous speech of President Eisenhower in 1961, in which he warned about the danger embodied in what he called the 'military–industrial complex'. In reality it was already a serious problem before World War II and even World War I.

In the 1930s, two books were published in the West that examined the dangers of the political influence of arms-producing firms (especially private ones) and the threat to peace they constituted. These were *Merchants of Death* and *The Private Manufacture of Arms*.[1] They had a strong, but alas not very lasting or effective, impact on public opinion. The warnings and appeals contained in the books were based mainly on the history of the period preceding World War I. Similar conclusions and warnings, as has already been mentioned, were made in the early 1960s by President Dwight Eisenhower on the basis of updated experience, which included not only the period before World War II but also the Cold War.

The danger was so obvious already at the end of World War I that even the 1919 League of Nations Covenant stated: 'The members of the League agree that the manufacture by private enterprise of munitions and implements of war is open to grave objections.' In the early 1920s, the League of Nations set up a Temporary Mixed Commission to investigate the problem ('mixed' because it included members from different fields, including military industry). The Commission cited six 'objections to ... untrammelled arms manufacture'. They were that, in the years leading to World War I, armaments enterprises (1) fomented war scares in their countries and abroad; (2) bribed government officials at home and abroad; (3) circulated false inflammatory reports on various nations' military strength to stimulate arms spending; (4) influenced public opinion by controlling certain newspapers and magazines; (5) played countries off against one another; and (6) organized international arms trusts that pushed up the price of arms.

Norman Cousins – the American author, publisher and public figure who died recently – wrote in one of his last books about all of this as an 'unremembered history'.[2] But maybe it is rarely remembered precisely because it has not yet become history even today, after the Cold War has ended, according to conventional wisdom.

While quite a few things have changed, many have not. First of all, the defence industry, whether private or state-owned, has a strong influence on the whole policy of governments, as we have clearly seen both during and, regrettably, after the Cold War. President Eisenhower said this so clearly because, being in the White House, he felt this pressure more than anybody else. In addition, governments have become the principal salesmen of armaments; whether this is for better or for worse is difficult to say. The government of course is supposedly more responsible. But at the same time, if arms sales become a government's policy, this means vastly increased quantities of the deadly merchandise, and also that commerce acquires grave political meaning, affecting much more strongly the whole system and substance of international relations. So if we are considering military arms, it would be foolhardy to make a judgement on what is more dangerous – private arms manufacture and trade or governmental control of these. The 20th century gives us more than enough proof that both can be bad.

But the core of the problem is of course the overinflation during the Cold War of the defence industry. An over-large defence industry is dangerous for several reasons. For one, its sheer existence undermines trust and sows suspicions about the country's intentions. For another, it is always tempting to sell armaments to other countries; as has already been mentioned, this destabilizes the situation. For a third, whether we want it or not, it encourages proliferation of weapons. This is so because, besides arms, technologies can also be sold; or the specialists who can create such technologies and arms can migrate to other countries. And last, but not least, such industry is a heavy burden for one's own economy.

Economics of Defence Reconversion

All these problems with an overinflated arms industry make the reconversion of the redundant parts of the defence industry so important. We already have some experience in this field and know how difficult this task is. The reasons for the difficulties are manifold – economic, political and technical. Some difficulties are created by the very complicated character of the problem itself, others by inertia from the past and by inherited suspicions, prejudices and misperceptions. Only some of these difficulties will be touched upon here, in view of the many dimensions and extremely complicated nature of the problem of reconversion. And there is also the obvious fact that much of this ground has been covered by specialists in the various fields. This permits me to limit my contribution to a few comments on problems which for different reasons are of some special interest to me.

It is logical to start with the obvious. And the obvious is the economy. Here we confront a none-too-rare contradiction between the economic interest of the nation as a whole (it obviously is served by reducing the defence industry to a reasonable size) and the interests of this particular sector of economy and its owners. Nations usually face the necessity of reconversion after big wars. A major source of experience on reconversion is how nations have dealt with this necessity in the past. This experience shows first of all that after big wars the major powers have coped with this problem, even though they sometimes encountered problems of unemployment and certain dislocations in sectors of the economy closely connected to the defence industry. The United States, for instance, managed not too well after World War I, but handled reconversion much better after World War II. As a rule, centrally planned economies could cope with both wartime conversion and postwar reconversion more effectively than could the market economies (which, by the way, became more and more centrally planned in wartime). This is natural and does not need special explanations. The Soviet Union, for instance, after World War II, accomplished reconversion without difficulties.

But in the former Soviet Union, with all its republics in transition and with a very clumsily and painfully done change to a market economy, the need for reconversion after the Cold War coincided with profound political changes. This has made the economy (and not only the economy) much less governable, which naturally aggravated the difficulties of the post-Cold War reconversion in Russia.

The major economic obstacle to reconversion has become the lack of investments needed to switch to the production of civilian goods, such as changes in equipment, retraining of personnel and so on. The ill-designed reform had as one of its results sky-high inflation, with prices increasing in five years several thousandfold. Despite endless talks about stabilization, this inflation continued, which made it practically impossible to obtain bank credits. Long-term credits were available only in absolutely exceptional cases, as a special favour from the government. As for commercial banks, they were ready to provide only very short-term credits – for days, weeks, or in the best case for months – and then with forbiddingly high interest rates. As for the government, it was not ready to face this problem, neither had it the resources to handle such a situation of severe economic crises.

Inflation had another adverse by-product. The enterprises that worked for defence were mostly high tech-oriented. So after reconversion they were supposed to produce high-quality and expensive civilian goods. But because of inflation, neither private consumers nor industrial enterprises had the money to create a really large-capacity market for their goods, even if they could find money for investments.

Another very serious problem that is particularly relevant to high-tech products is foreign competition. Since Russia opened up its markets to foreign companies, such high-tech products put out by newly reconverted enterprises simply could not compete on the market with the production of world-famous companies such as IBM, Sony, Hewlett-Packard and Motorola.

There have been many complaints about this from directors of reconverted enterprises. This problem is particularly acute since the usual way to beat the competition – to sell at lower prices – is closed to them. Because of very high taxes, the cost of home production is very high and enterprises have to set high prices. This is actually a problem not only for high-tech products, but for the whole industry and for agriculture. Therefore industry demands either that taxes be radically cut, or that high tariffs be imposed on imports; this would be a highly protectionist policy.

These problems will be resolved if Russia opts for a more reasonable economic policy. But they are not the only ones. Production for defence involves a guaranteed market and guaranteed prices and consumers, no competition, no need to worry about keeping costs low, and so on. To put it in a nutshell, defence involves an absolutely bureaucratic economy. To switch from this to an open market, with all the troubles and concerns it brings to the producer, is a really difficult exercise.

The Institute for the USA and Canada has been involved in efforts to help reconversion from the beginning of the 1990s. In particular, it has worked to organize some cooperation with the Americans (and maybe tempt them into some investments). We worked at first with the American investment company Battery March, and then, under the auspices of both governments, with Pepperdine University. In the course of this work people from the Institute made some trips to the USA, together with groups of leading directors of some of our defence enterprises. We could witness the evolution of their views as they progressed from complete rejection of the realities of the conditions of a market economy (and one had to adjust to these conditions in producing civilian goods after reconversion), through doubts and suspicions, to recognition of the changes as imminent. Some even started to like the changes. However, some of the directors remained absolutely immovable; we have to accept as a fact of life that not everybody will be able to change.

This piece of personal experience confirms once more that the task of reconversion is very complicated, but we have to do it for both economic and political reasons. Of course the West, America in particular, could help, and this help is welcome, but we are not speaking here about investments: this is a broader question which is very important for the future of Russia, but which depends on political stability in Russia and on its ability to create an attractive climate for private foreign investments.

But in this case another question may be even more important than investments: how to open the world high-tech markets to Russia as a seller. This would encourage the Russian defence industry to convert sooner and give it an opportunity to earn some money for its own conversion. Some openings are already in existence: the Americans have agreed to use our missiles to launch some of their satellites; they have also agreed to buy an engine for their heavy space-launch vehicle. But some other bigger and more important projects were rejected. These include the plan to build across Russia a transcontinental glass fibre communication cable as part of a global system, as well as the Russian proposal to participate in the creation of a worldwide satellite communication network. There are presumably more such examples, those mentioned are ones the author has heard about by sheer chance. But such examples remain rare, and do not as yet play a serious role in determining the fate of Russian industry.

At the same time, one thing is absolutely clear: the main difficulties for reconversion come from the present situation inside the country, not from the outside. The most important of them is the dismal state of the Russian economy, although there is a certain interdependence; not only does the unconverted part of the redundant defence industry lie idle, bringing not a ruble to the ailing economy, but it hangs around the economy's neck like a giant burden, like an albatross, which makes any attempts at economic revival even more difficult.

This makes even more important the military reform about which Russia has already been talking for more than five years, but towards which nothing really has been achieved so far. And this reform should be based on a new military doctrine; but the last attempt by Russia to produce a new doctrine led to an obvious 'miscarriage'. Only under the conditions of a carefully established doctrine will it be clear what kinds of defence enterprises, and how many of them, should be retained and maybe even modernized to safeguard national security. Only then can Russia decide what really is no longer needed and should be reconverted or closed – although already many defence enterprises which should undergo reconversion are easily identified.

The Politics of Defence Reconversion

This brings us to the second series of difficulties which interfere with the attempts to change – the political ones. First of all, there are people in Russia (as well as in other republics of the former Soviet Union) who just do not agree with the end of the Cold War, with all the changes which have taken place in recent years. Some of them are obsessed with imperial ambitions or messianic zeal. Others simply do not trust the West, particularly the Americans, think that they will fool the Russians and believe that the 'end of the Cold War', as well as the 'shock therapy' of the economic reform in general, are sly gimmicks the West has put into action to destroy Russia as a great power. While such people and ideas are to be deplored, it must be said that Russia does not have a monopoly on this kind of dangerous trash: similar people, and similar ideas about Russia, may also be encountered in the West. Such a state of mind, whether it is sincere or prompted by vested interests, naturally rejects any disarmament and reconversion.

Other people, on both sides, are simply not sure whether the new kind of international relations is permanent, and worry that this may be a very short-lived episode in history. These people argue that we should therefore be prudent, and not dismantle our military might, including our defence industry, until the future is more certain. In the West such people find support for their scepticism in the instability of the former Soviet Union, in some dubious policies such as the war in Chechnya, and in the 'patriotic' diatribes of some politicians from the extreme left or extreme right. In Russia, such people find support for their scepticism in some real or imagined manifestations of 'imperial' behaviour of the United States, as the one and only superpower, in such acts as the planned expansion of the North Atlantic Treaty Organization towards the East, in its vast military budget and so on. Such views can very easily become self-fulfilling prophecies.

These are usually the high-sounding pretexts under which, very often, other, very down-to-earth considerations are discernible. These include practical fears about one's own job if the director or leading personnel of a redundant enterprise are involved. Or there can be fear about the future of the enterprise itself and (particularly in Russia) about the whole town or a part of a city with all of its social infrastructure that depends on that enterprise.

Combined with economic difficulties and military uncertainties, these fears can put very strong brakes on the process of reconversion. One should not forget that, even if one does not count the military itself, the defence industry, with its workforce and other people depending on it, represents a very large and important part of the voting constituency of politicians. The dismal state of the formerly privileged defence industry has pushed a large number of these people into the embrace of the communists or the nationalists on the extreme right. The presidential campaign witnessed a very hard fight for their votes. This led among other things to some concessions in foreign policy and to a slowdown of the disarmament and reconversion processes, which shows that at present the military industrial lobby still has strong leverage on policy makers.

The number of concessions given to this lobby is of course rather strongly limited by the extremely difficult economic situation in Russia, as well as by the lack of professional experience and the often outright feebleness of the government and of most new governmental or semi- or quasi-private organizations which today manage the Russian economy. The government's weaknesses make it possible not to panic in spite of some rather bellicose speeches. But at the same time we have to understand that, without serious new efforts inside and outside Russia, the elimination of the legacy of the Cold War, including disarmament and reconversion of the redundant part of the defence industry, will not move forward. To put it even more strongly, without such efforts Russia will remain exposed to the danger of moving in the direction of a new Cold War.

Reconversion of Military Forces

Finally, we digress slightly from the main topic. Apart from redundant weapons and an inflated defence industry, we have one heritage from the Cold War which may be even more dangerous than technologies: the people in uniforms who were programmed to spend their life learning how to kill and destroy and in case of war to do it. Suddenly this skill, this profession of soldiering, is no longer needed. There is cause for concern, not only about the possible support by some of these people of the political opposition or, in extreme cases, their participation in possibly violent activities, but also about the fact that some of them might possibly become 'guns for hire', helping to spread something which can be even more precious than weapons for a militarily weak but aggressive country, or even a political action group – their martial art and science, strategic and tactical abilities, as well as their ability to use modern arms effectively. Such people are to be found among some of the military personnel who spent their best years in Afghanistan and Chechnya, as well as among Iranians and others.

A special case in this respect are the peoples of those countries which had to fight long-term wars, especially those who have grown up in conditions of war, never went to school, did not master any peaceful profession and know nothing apart from war. The most vivid case of this is Afghanistan, where the war did not end after the withdrawal of Soviet troops. The country is full of young people ready to fight for certain ideals, which may not be very clear to them but are ascribed by them to the Koran, ideals which they cannot even read, the simple reason being that they had no chance to become literate enough to study the holy book.

The danger is that there are available many experienced soldiers and officers who will be ready to participate in any conflict as volunteers or mercenaries. This is also a new post-Cold War phenomenon which demands the attention of the world community and, if necessary, international measures.

Notes

1   H.C. Engelbrecht and F.C. Hanighan, *Merchants of Death*, New York: Dodd & Mead, 1934; P. Noel-Baker, *The Private Manufacture of Arms*, New York: Oxford University Press, 1937.
2   N. Cousins, *The Pathology of Power*, New York: W.W. Norton, 1987.

4 US–Russian Cooperation on Fissile Material Security and Disposition

Frank von Hippel and Oleg Bukharin

Introduction

Reductions in the nuclear weapons arsenals of the United States and the former Soviet Union (FSU) have created the challenge of securely storing and disposing of about a million kilograms of weapons plutonium and highly-enriched uranium (HEU). Reprocessing in Western Europe, Russia, Japan and India has added to this total a stockpile of almost 200 000 kilograms of separated 'civilian' but weapons-usable plutonium.

There is particular concern about the short-term security of fissile materials in Russia because of the enormous economic and political dislocations in that country. Cooperative international efforts, to assist Russia in strengthening the security of its fissile materials and in arranging for their disposal, are described below and their adequacy is assessed. However, international cooperative efforts to increase the security of weapons-usable fissile materials and eliminate surplus stocks must focus on the long-term global problem as well as the special short-term problem in Russia.

Fissile Materials

According to current usage in the arms control community, 'fissile' isotopes are fissionable isotopes which can sustain an explosive chain reaction if assembled in a 'critical mass'.

51

Uranium-235

Uranium-235 is the only relatively abundant naturally occurring fissile isotope. It is diluted in natural uranium with 140 times as much U-238, which cannot by itself sustain an explosive chain reaction. Uranium has to be isotopically 'enriched' to at least 20 per cent U-235 before it becomes 'highly enriched' uranium (HEU) and weapons-usable according to IAEA (International Atomic Energy Agency) convention. 'Weapons-grade' uranium, used in fission nuclear explosives, is enriched to more than 90 per cent in U-235. The advantage of higher enrichment is that the critical mass is smaller. The IAEA uses 25 kilograms of U-235 in highly-enriched weapon-grade uranium as its standard for a 'significant quantity' required to make a first-generation implosion fission explosive.

Many processes have been developed to enrich uranium. Gaseous diffusion has been the primary enrichment process in the past. The state-of-the-art method today uses gas centrifuges. Using such enrichment processes, the former Soviet Union and the United States each produced several hundred thousand kilograms (several hundred tonnes) of weapon-grade uranium. The United Kingdom, France and China each produced in the order of 10 000kg, and South Africa produced and Pakistan may have produced several hundred kilograms. Israel and India are both believed to have enrichment programmes but are not known to have produced significant quantities of weapon-grade uranium. The United States, Russia, France, United Kingdom, Germany, Netherlands and Japan have also enriched uranium to low-enrichment levels (2–5 per cent U-235) to fuel light water reactors and, in some cases (notably the United States and Russia) have enriched uranium to weapon-grade to fuel their naval power, research and weapons materials production reactors.

Plutonium-239

A number of fissile isotopes have been created in nuclear reactors by neutron capture on heavy non-fissile isotopes. The artificial fissile isotope that has been created in largest abundance is plutonium-239 (half-life of 24 400 years). It is created by neutron capture on U-238 making U-239, which converts by two subsequent radioactive decays to Np-239 and then to Pu-239.

The United States produced about 90 000kg of weapon-grade plutonium[1] and the former Soviet Union somewhat more. The IAEA uses 8kg as its estimate for the amount of plutonium required to make a first-generation implosion weapon, including production losses. The Trinity and Nagasaki bombs each contained 6.1kg. For the plutonium coming out of excess US nuclear warheads, a 'planning figure' is 4kg.

The rate at which a nuclear reactor fissions uranium determines the rate at which fission heat is produced. A useful number to remember is that the fission of one kilogram of U-235 per day releases heat at the rate of about one gigawatt (10^9 watts). Power reactors convert about one-third of the released thermal energy into electrical energy. Therefore a typical one-gigawatt (electric, GWe) power plant will have a thermal rating of about three gigawatts (thermal, GWt).

A 3-GWt light water power reactor, operating at a typical average of 75 per cent capacity, would fission about (3GWt)×(0.75 years)×(365 days/year)×(1000 grams/GWt-year) = 800 000 grams = 0.8 tonnes of U-235 and produce almost 0.6 tonnes of Pu-239 per year. However, almost two-thirds of the produced Pu-239 is fissioned while the fuel stays in the reactor core, reducing the amount of plutonium in approximately 20 tonnes of discharged spent fuel to about 0.2 tonnes. The combined capacity of the world's nuclear reactors is about 350GWe, about 90 per cent of it in light-water reactors. The approximately 7000 tonnes of spent fuel discharged annually from these reactors contains about 65 tonnes of plutonium (65 000kg).

When a neutron in a nuclear reactor is absorbed by a Pu-239 nucleus, the probability of fission is about two-thirds. The other third of the time a Pu-240 nucleus is produced. Pu-240 can also absorb a slow neutron to become Pu-241, which in turn can absorb a slow neutron to fission or become Pu-242. All these plutonium isotopes are weapons-usable. However, weapons designers prefer relatively pure Pu-239, and 'weapon-grade' plutonium is defined in the United States as containing less than 6 per cent Pu-240. The production of weapon-grade plutonium requires that the uranium fuel in which plutonium is produced not be exposed too long to neutrons. Otherwise, an increasing fraction of the Pu-239 will capture neutrons and fission or be converted to Pu-240. The production of weapon-grade plutonium therefore requires much more frequent refuelling than is economically optimal.

The fresh fuel used in light-water reactors today typically contains 4 to 5 per cent U-235. When the 'spent' fuel is discharged, it contains about the same percentage of fission products, about 1 per cent unfissioned U-235, and about 1 per cent plutonium formed as a result of neutron capture in the U-238 in the fresh fuel. Currently, about 2300 tonnes of spent light-water fuel is being reprocessed and over 20 000kg of plutonium is being recovered annually in Britain and France. Russia has a smaller-scale commercial reprocessing plant, where it reprocesses some East European (Bulgarian and Hungarian) and FSU spent fuel. India and Japan also have small reprocessing plants for spent power reactor fuel.

However, virtually all nuclear utilities in Europe and Japan have found reprocessing a convenient interim measure to deal with spent fuel in the absence of politically acceptable solutions involving interim surface or permanent underground storage. Reprocessing contracts require that foreign customers take back their separated plutonium and 'high-level waste' (concentrated fission and transmutation products immobilized in glass). Thus the owning country still faces the problem of storing or disposing of its radioactive waste and must have its separated plutonium fabricated into fuel for other nuclear reactors, such as 'mixed-oxide' (MOX, uranium–plutonium fuel). Plutonium recycling is both controversial and expensive. In order to keep their reprocessing customers, France and Britain have been forced to store 'temporarily' increasing stockpiles of both high-level waste and plutonium. Russia is similarly storing the radioactive waste and plutonium of its customers. At this point, France and Britain have each accumulated at their reprocessing plants over 50 tonnes of stored separated power reactor plutonium (mostly foreign in France, mostly domestic in Britain) and Russia has accumulated about 30 tonnes.

Disposal of Excess Weapons Materials

Russia's serious internal economic and political instabilities have created great concern in the West about the possibility that Russian plutonium or highly-enriched uranium might appear on the black market. This has led to various initiatives to help Russia dispose of its excess stocks of fissile materials.

From Weapons Components to Fissile Materials

In the United States, the dismantling of nuclear weapons takes place at the Pantex plant near Amarillo, Texas. Plutonium 'pits' from the primary fission triggers of the dismantled weapons are stored in bunkers at Pantex. HEU-containing secondary bomb components are disassembled at the Y-12 site in Oak Ridge, Tennessee. After removal from the secondary, the HEU is melted into ingots. The United States has put about 10 tonnes of weapon-grade uranium under IAEA safeguards in a storage vault at the Y-12 facility.

In Russia, weapons components containing nuclear materials ('physics packages') are dismantled at Arzamas-16 and Yekaterinburg-45. Plutonium pits and uranium secondaries are placed in containers. Some are then sent for long-term storage to Chelyabinsk-65 and Tomsk-7. Much of the weapon-grade uranium is sent to Tomsk-7 to be oxidized for transport to a uranium-enrichment facility, where it is blended down to low-enriched uranium.[2] Neither the United States nor Russia has yet undertaken large-scale conversion of plutonium 'pits' of primaries to metal ingots or plutonium-oxide powder.

U-235 Disposal

Under the February 1993 agreement, the United States has agreed, in principle, to buy from Russia over a period of 20 years approximately 500 tonnes of excess 90 per cent enriched weapon-grade uranium. The rate of purchase would be at least 10 tonnes per year during the first five years and 30 tonnes per year for 15 years thereafter. Russia has agreed to clean the HEU of chemical contaminants and dilute it with 1.5 per cent enriched uranium to an enrichment level of about 4.4 per cent. At the prices prevailing at the time of the deal, the low-enrichment uranium (LEU) would be worth about $12 billion. Deliveries of HEU-derived LEU to the United States began in 1995.

In order for the United States to verify that the LEU is derived from weapon-grade uranium, the United States is allowed to sample the material coming into the blending point, to witness shredded HEU metal from Russian warheads being converted into an oxide powder in furnaces, and to seal containers of oxide before they are shipped to the blending facilities. In return, Russia is permitted to monitor the further blending of the LEU to enrichments specified by fuel fabricators and then its shipment to the fuel-fabrication facilities.

If deliveries of Russian LEU reach the equivalent of 30 tonnes of weapon-grade uranium per year, they could satisfy approximately one-half of the LEU requirements of US power reactors. US and Canadian uranium miners and the US uranium-enrichment complex have therefore raised various objections to this deal. As a result, the US Department of Commerce has required that an equivalent amount of natural uranium, bought from non-Russian sources, will have to be given back to Russia. Russia will therefore be paid only for the difference between the value of this natural uranium and the LEU, that is for the enrichment work. As a compromise with the uranium miners, recently passed US legislation has finally created a gradually increasing quota for the sale on the US market of the stockpile of 'Russian' natural uranium that will be created in connection with the importation of the Russian low-enrichment uranium.[3]

There have also been difficulties in getting political acceptance of the reduction of US uranium-enrichment activity that will result from the imports of Russian LEU. In July 1993, a government-owned corporation was created to manage the US enrichment complex as a first step towards privatization. To compensate this emerging US Enrichment Corporation (USEC) for the loss of business that will result from the purchase of the Russian LEU, USEC has been made the sole agent for the contract. However, the management of USEC has complained about the price negotiated by the US government for the embedded separative work in the LEU. It has attempted to establish Separative Work Unit prices (SWU)[4] that would result in profits comparable to those which it would receive if the SWUs were produced in its own US enrichment plants.[5]

However, Russia's Ministry of Atomic Energy (MinAtom) rebuffed USEC's proposals to drop its price, so the Clinton administration has provided a short-term subsidy by giving USEC some surplus government-owned enriched and natural uranium. For the longer term, the administration expects that the USEC can be motivated to negotiate mutually acceptable prices by the threat that the government will otherwise allow other organizations to compete to be the agents for sale of the Russian LEU.[6]

It might be hoped that Euratom and Japan would also purchase blended down weapons uranium from Russia. The British fuel-cycle company, British Nuclear Fuel Services, and MinAtom have been exploring the possible purchase over 20 years of LEU produced by blending down, in Russia, 100 metric tonnes of weapon-grade uranium.[7] Trade between Russia and Japan is complicated because of their political dispute over the Kurile Islands; Japanese fuel fabricators have thus far refused to purchase LEU derived from weapons uranium.

The United States also plans to dispose of some of its excess weapons uranium. In March 1995, President Clinton announced that he was declaring as surplus an additional 200 tonnes of excess weapons-usable fissile material, of which 38 tonnes were plutonium.[8] The part of this excess HEU which is suitable for use as nuclear fuel will be blended down to LEU.[9] An initial decision has been made to transfer 50 tonnes for blending.[10] Some of the over 90 per cent enriched HEU which was already in the form of UF_6 is being blended down at the Portsmouth enrichment facility.[11] The International Atomic Energy Agency has been invited to subject this down-blending process to international safeguards.[12] The quantity of U-235 that the US is transferring to civilian use or disposal is smaller than that being bought from Russia because the United States originally produced less HEU and because the United States has decided to retain a very large stockpile of weapon-grade uranium for future use as naval reactor fuel.

Plutonium Disposal

One problem which has slowed progress in planning for plutonium disposition is that, in contrast to the situation for surplus HEU, it would cost more to make reactor fuel with plutonium than it would cost to buy low-enriched uranium fuel – even if the plutonium is free. Nevertheless, a large-scale industry is being established in Western Europe to fabricate separated power reactor plutonium into 'mixed-oxide' (MOX) fuel, in which several per cent of plutonium is mixed with natural or depleted uranium. France and Belgium have in operation – and Britain soon will have – industrial-scale facilities, each capable of fabricating annually several tonnes of plutonium into MOX fuel.[13] These facilities, however, do not currently have the capacity to keep up even with the rate of plutonium separation in West Europe. Nor, it appears, do either Western Europe or Japan have any extra power reactor capacity to absorb MOX fuel fabricated elsewhere.

To the countries that are involved in MOX production and their major customers (Germany and Japan) the obvious answer to this problem is to build a MOX plant in Russia.[14] Indeed, MinAtom would like to use its plutonium-disposition problem as a justification for building a new generation of 0.8GWe 'BN-800' fast-neutron reactors, originally proposed as plutonium breeder reactors.[15] However, Russia does not have the funds to build the new reactors. Another MOX proposal would have Russian and/or US weapons plutonium fabricated into fuel for use in Canadian heavy-water reactors. However, MinAtom opposes the idea of shipping weapons plutonium out of the country. Furthermore, it would presumably want to be paid for the MOX fuel if another country benefited from its fuel value.

The United States, which opposes reprocessing, fears that any increased production of MOX could undermine its anti-reprocessing position. The US government is therefore investigating alternatives to MOX for plutonium disposition which would meet what a National Academy of Sciences study dubbed the 'spent-fuel standard'.[16] This standard requires that the plutonium be made as inaccessible as in spent fuel, where the plutonium is protected by a mixture of fission products which create a lethal gamma-ray field around the spent fuel. The leading alternative to MOX being considered in the United States is to embed small cans of plutonium-containing glass in large canisters of fission product-containing glass as the fission products, from which the plutonium was originally separated, are solidified in a waste form suitable for underground disposal.

In Russia, 'vitrification' of the fission product waste from reprocessing has been carried out since 1986 at the Chelyabinsk-65 commercial reprocessing plant. This infrastructure could also be used to implement a 'can-in-canister' plutonium-disposition approach. However, MinAtom rejects the idea of disposing of plutonium as waste.[17]

At the G-7 'nuclear summit' with Russia, which was held in Moscow in April 1996, it was agreed to convene an international meeting of experts in France by the end of 1996 'to identify possible development of international cooperation' in the disposition of weapons plutonium.[18] Whatever is ultimately done, it is important that it does not make the risk of diversion worse. This is a real danger because it is more difficult to safeguard nuclear weapons materials in process than in storage.

Securing Existing Stockpiles

Even if the disposition of excess weapons uranium and plutonium were to proceed at the maximum planned pace, much of this material will have to be stored for 20 years, and significant quantities of weapons-usable material will remain in military and civilian use indefinitely thereafter. It is therefore critical that the security of all weapons-usable fissile material be upgraded as rapidly as possible. This is of particular concern for Russian stockpiles because of the instability associated with the current very difficult political and economic transition in that country.

Amounts of weapons-usable fissile materials ranging from significant to huge are stored, processed or used at approximately 100 sites in Russia. The security of these materials reportedly varies from relatively stringent at warhead-production facilities to inadequate at large fuel cycle facilities and civil research institutes. Published accounts of the small diversions of fissile materials that have occurred thus far from naval fuel storage facilities, research institutes and fuel cycle facilities indicate that the principal threat of diversion of nuclear materials is posed by insiders.

The collapse of the Soviet Union has weakened many of the arrangements for monitoring and controlling the movements of personnel, greatly increased the permeability of Russia's national borders and made nuclear workers much more accessible to criminals interested in corrupting or intimidating them. In order to maintain nuclear material security, Russia must introduce a Western-style integrated material protection, control and accounting system designed to closely monitor fissile materials. Lack of Russian funds for such a system has led to a number of Western initiatives. The US 'Soviet Threat Reduction Act' of October 1991 (now better known as the 'Nunn–Lugar Program') has authorized the US Department of Defense (DoD) to spend approximately $400 million a year in cooperative programmes to assist the former Soviet Union in 'the transportation, storage, safeguarding and destruction of nuclear and other weapons [and] the prevention of weapons proliferation'.

The Government-to-Government Programme

In September 1993, the US Department of Defense and MinAtom signed an 'Agreement on Cooperation' in the area of materials protection, control and accounting, with the initial project being the development of a model safeguards system at a low-enriched uranium (LEU) fuel fabrication plant in Electrostal, 50km east of Moscow.

MinAtom's reluctance to offer its more 'sensitive' facilities for cooperative efforts apparently stemmed from concerns about the audit and inspection rights upon which the US Department of Defense insisted. The DoD programme was also made less attractive to Russia's economically stressed nuclear facilities by the fact that it used US goods and services almost exclusively.

In 1994–5, the United States offered reciprocal access to US facilities, starting with an invitation to visit a US plutonium storage facility at Hanford, Washington in July 1994. This led to an invitation to visit the plutonium storage facility at the reprocessing plant in Chelyabinsk-65 in October 1994 and then to an agreement to start upgrading security at this and a number of other major civilian research and fuel cycle facilities with large inventories of weapons-usable fissile materials.

The 'Lab-to-Lab' Programme

The government-to-government programme did not really develop momentum, however, until after direct collaborations organized between US and Russian technical experts from their national nuclear laboratories focused on rapid upgrades of nuclear material security. In contrast to the government-to-government programme, about half of the lab-to-lab programme funds are spent in Russia on salaries and equipment.

The lab-to-lab programme began in 1994 with two pilot projects. At the Kurchatov Institute of Atomic Energy in Moscow (the former Soviet Union's first nuclear reactor development laboratory), US and Russian experts designed and built a comprehensive physical security system at a critical assembly building containing about 70kg of weapon-grade uranium for a zero power mock-up of a space reactor. At the Institute of Experimental Physics in Arzamas-16 (the former Soviet Union's first nuclear weapons design laboratory), the lab-to-lab programme helped to fund a project to develop a modular computerized detection and tracking system for HEU and plutonium items. These initial successes established the bona fides of the lab-to-lab programme and encouraged Russian and US advocates of international cooperation on nuclear security issues.

Participation in the lab-to-lab programme has increased and, as of June 1996, included six US national laboratories (Los Alamos, Brookhaven, Livermore, Sandia, Oak Ridge and Argonne) and eight institutions in Russia (Arzamas-16, Chelyabinsk-70, Institute of Automation, Institute of Inorganic Materials, Institute of Physics and Power Engineering, Kurchatov Institute, Production Association 'Eleron' and Tomsk-7). The funding level has climbed to about $100 million a year.

At this point the government-to-government programme covers virtually all MinAtom facilities where large inventories of weapons-usable materials are used for non-military purposes. The lab-to-lab programme overlaps with the government-to-government programme and, in addition, covers MinAtom's weapons design institutes. A DoE–MinAtom cooperative effort has also been launched on upgrading safeguards and security at Russia's warhead production and disassembly facilities, as well as improving the security of fissile materials in transit.

In May 1996, a team of US experts visited a nuclear navy base near Murmansk as a first step in a US DoE initiative to improve the security of the storage facilities for fresh fuel for Russia's nuclear submarines. And the US Department of Energy and Gosatomnadzor (Russia's civilian nuclear regulatory agency) are working to improve nuclear safeguards at research reactors and facilities not affiliated with either MinAtom or Russia's Ministry of Defence. Thus far, however, there has been no systematic effort to enhance the capabilities of the guard forces at Russian nuclear facilities. In this case, an organizational obstacle stems from the fact that the guard forces are provided, not by MinAtom, but by the Ministry of Internal Affairs.

Secure Storage

As Russia is drawing down its nuclear forces, large amounts of HEU and all plutonium are going into storage in the form of warhead components.[19] Initially, the material is stored at the warhead dismantling sites and the existing storage facilities of the plutonium complexes of Chelyabinsk-65 and Tomsk-7.[20] However, it is planned later to put the plutonium – and perhaps some HEU – into long-term secure storage.[21] The first of these high-security storage facilities is being built near the town of Chelyabinsk-65 with assistance from the US Nunn–Lugar programme. However, almost five years after this project was first proposed, only a concrete floor for a first unit has been laid. This facility, initially with capacity for 25 000 containers, is currently scheduled for operation in 1999.

Progress in building this storage facility was delayed first by the decision to change the location of the first storage facility from Tomsk-7 to Chelyabinsk-65 and then by proposed changes in the design of the facility. Another significant delay was due to an impasse over MinAtom's request for US assistance in the funding of the actual construction of the facility, to pay for Russian salaries and materials. The Department of Defense insisted on limiting assistance to US goods and services for the design ($15 million) and construction ($75 million) phases. However, in the summer of 1995, the United States finally did commit itself to contributing to the cost of purchasing Russian construction materials. The Clinton administration has therefore requested and received permission from Congress to use an additional $29 million for this purpose and may ultimately provide an additional $46 million to bring its total support for the construction phase up to a total of $150 million – half of MinAtom's estimate of the total cost of the facility. In addition, $50 million in Nunn–Lugar funds have been budgeted for the manufacture in the United States of containers for the fissile material components.

In exchange for this assistance, MinAtom has agreed in principle to make the storage arrangements 'transparent', so that the United States will be able to verify that the safeguards at the facility are adequate and that the materials are not removed for reuse in weapons. However, in negotiations over the implementation of these security arrangements, Russia has made it clear that it expects them to be made in the context of broader reciprocal transparency arrangements which would cover excess US fissile material as well.

Thus far, only the storage of weapons plutonium has been discussed. However, in Chelyabinsk-65, Russia also has about 30 000kg of plutonium separated from East European, Finnish and FSU spent fuel, contained in over 10 000 containers stored in a 50-year-old warehouse. Although the monitoring of the interior of this facility and its access controls are being upgraded under the government-to-government programme, the inadequacy of its design is being ignored while a modern, high-security storage facility is being built nearby for weapons plutonium. Thus far, the Nunn–Lugar programme has apparently not seriously concerned itself with the upgrading of the storage of such weapons-usable fissile materials in Russia that are not actually derived from dismantled weapons. Weapon-grade plutonium is also accumulating in storage facilities at Tomsk-7 and Krasnoyarsk-26, at a combined rate of about 1.5 tonnes a year. This plutonium too should be securely stored.

Stopping Further Production of Fissile Material

Given the huge surplus of HEU and separated plutonium, it would make sense to have a moratorium on further production. In fact, the final four of the US Pu-production reactors were shut down in 1987 and 1988.[22] Production of HEU for weapons in the Soviet Union ceased in 1988 and a gradual phase-out of the production of plutonium for weapons began in 1987.[23] By 1993, 10 out of Russia's 13 plutonium-production reactors had been shut down.

Russia, however, continues to operate three plutonium-production reactors (two in Tomsk-7 and one in Krasnoyarsk-26) because they produce by-product heat and electricity for the populations of the neighbouring cities. The aluminum-clad uranium-metal fuel used in these reactors cannot be stored long-term in water. It is therefore reprocessed, producing approximately 1.5 tonnes of Pu per year. The Russian government has reported that, starting in October 1994, new plutonium from these reactors is being converted to stable oxide and placed in storage.

In June 1994, Russia reconfirmed that it would shut down these three reactors by the year 2000; the United States agreed to work with Russia to replace them as regional sources of heat and electricity; and Russia and the United States agreed to develop a system of bilateral monitoring of the plutonium produced in the interim. Subsequently, the United States sponsored feasibility studies of energy replacement options for the Tomsk and Krasnoyarsk reactors. These studies found that replacement power plants would cost billions of dollars and, in the case of replacement nuclear reactors, would take up to 10 years to complete.[24]

Thus it has been agreed that the most feasible approach in the short term is conversion of the cores of the existing reactors to a fuel cycle that does not generate weapon-grade plutonium and improves the safety of the reactors. According to the estimates in the joint study, core conversion for the three reactors could be implemented in 32 months at a cost of $80 million to the United States and a similar cost to Russia.[25] In the meantime, the arrangements for bilateral monitoring of the plutonium being produced by the reactors are being delayed until Russia is satisfied with the level of US assistance.

Transparency and Irreversibility

Since 1995, efforts are being made to take advantage of Russia's new openness to on-site inspections to negotiate a comprehensive set of agreements between the United States and Russia to exchange information on stocks of nuclear warheads and fissile materials, and to arrange for the verification of their reduction. The US and Russian governments have repeatedly expressed their interests in transparency. Indeed, one of the statements issued at the May 1995 summit was titled 'Joint Statement on the Transparency and Irreversibility of the Process of Reducing Nuclear Weapons'.

This statement asked for reciprocal exchanges of detailed information on aggregate stockpiles of nuclear warheads, on stocks of fissile materials and on their safety and security. It has also asked for a cooperative arrangement for reciprocal monitoring at storage facilities of fissile materials removed from nuclear warheads. There has been considerable US–Russian discussion at the technical level, and diplomatic activity to work out the implementation of these agreements. However, all of these initiatives have become bogged down before achieving concrete results.

Transparency Arrangements for Dismantled Nuclear Warheads

In March 1994, US Secretary of Energy O'Leary and Russian Minister of Atomic Energy Mikhailov agreed to 'reciprocal inspections by the end of 1994 of facilities containing plutonium removed from nuclear weapons [as a step towards concluding] an agreement on the means of confirming the plutonium and highly enriched uranium inventories from nuclear disarmament'. Defining the procedures for such inspections has been difficult. Progress has been impeded by the fact that some marginally classified weapons design information would be revealed in the process. It was therefore decided that the inspections could not go forward until an 'Agreement for Cooperation' had been negotiated.

The US Department of Defense has proposed to the Russian Ministry of Defence specifics on the proposed bilateral stockpile declarations, including declarations of the historical stockpiles of warheads up to the present. The United States has also proposed declarations of stored surplus warheads together with verification measures such as 'unique identifiers' (such as seals, tags and/or radiation 'fingerprints'). In the same context, the United States has proposed declarations of total stocks of HEU and plutonium, by enrichment or isotopic composition, by form and by location, as well as historical production by site, back to 1970.

None of the proposals so far officially proposed or discussed includes verification of active stocks of warheads beyond those warheads on strategic missiles subject to being counted under START agreements. Nor, apparently, has declaration of the quantities of fissile material in individual warhead types so far been proposed, although they could be used to verify declarations of fissile material stocks in warheads.

Placing Civilian and Surplus Military Fissile Material under IAEA Safeguards

In September 1996, Russia joined the United States in discussions about placing civilian and surplus military fissile material under IAEA safeguards. A major obstacle to such a placement appears to be financial: both the costs of preparing Russian and US facilities for the application of international safeguards and the costs to the International Atomic Energy Agency of extending inspections to so many facilities.

An additional obstacle is concern about the possible leakage of weapon design information through the IAEA to potential proliferant states. The most important concern expressed within the US nuclear weapons establishment has been about revealing to the IAEA the amount of plutonium in modern warhead 'pits'. Either the governments will have to decide that knowing the amount of plutonium in a modern pit would not be that useful to a proliferant, or they should move ahead with the process of turning the pits into non-weapons form.

Defence Conversion

MinAtom's 10 closed nuclear cities, with a combined population of about 700 000, are today in a critical situation. The cities receive only minimal governmental funding, they are isolated from Russia's developing markets by guarded double fences and their underemployed workers cannot relocate because of Russia's underdeveloped housing market. These cities cannot be left to economic and social collapse: such a collapse could result in a haemorrhage of nuclear materials into the black market. Russia's nuclear arsenal is shrinking and its nuclear power capacity is likely to remain at its current level well into the next century. The collapse of the closed cities can be avoided only if useful commercial work is created for workers to replace weapons work that is no longer needed.

This problem has long been recognized by Moscow, and planning for the conversion of the nuclear complex began in 1989. However, the Russian conversion programme has largely failed because of a lack of market skills, secrecy, centralized control and, above all, insufficient investment. Some of the West's nuclear security initiatives discussed above are helping by creating jobs and helping the nuclear cities to develop new long-term missions. There is a need, however, for a dedicated defence conversion programme which would focus on helping proliferation-sensitive nuclear facilities to establish commercially viable, non-nuclear enterprises.

The Defense Enterprise Fund established by the Nunn–Lugar programme spent a total of $152.7 million in 1994–5 to build housing for retired missile officers and to start non-military production at four non-nuclear defence facilities. The International Science and Technology Center (ISTC) was established in 1992 in Moscow with funding from the United States, the European Union and Japan in order to give key weapons scientists an alternative to emigration. The Industrial Partnering Program (IPP), established in 1994 in the US Department of Energy, has also focused most of its attention on research and development institutes.

The IPP appears to have the most potential for the nuclear cities as well, since it starts with direct technical contacts between US and Russian experts, and has the direct involvement of US industry. Ultimately, however, the success of this and other conversion efforts will depend upon the willingness of Western companies to invest significant funds in projects in the closed cities.

Conclusion

The Cold War nuclear arms race is over. However, the thousands of nuclear weapons and hundreds of tonnes of weapons-grade fissile material will not disappear overnight. Prevention of their diffusion to rogue states and terrorist groups is of paramount importance for international peace and security. In particular, there remains a serious problem of security of the huge stock of HEU and plutonium in Russia. The Russian government and the international community are working to upgrade the security of fissile materials.

Much, however, remains to be done. Dismantling of nuclear warheads, safe and secure management and disposition of fissile materials, and environmental restoration must become the principal tasks of the US and Russian nuclear complexes. Fissile material operations must emphasize international cooperation and transparency. The complexes themselves must be reduced in size and reconfigured to fulfil these post-Cold War tasks. Workers and facilities must be redirected to commercial non-nuclear activities.

Notes

1   *Plutonium: The First 50 Years: United States plutonium production, acquisition and utilization from 1944 through 1994*, US Department of Energy DOE/DP-0137, 1996.
2   The cities are a part of MinAtom's network of ten 'closed' cities. They now have names but they are still most widely known by these box numbers.
3   This legislation is described in *Nuclear Fuel*, 25 September 1995, p.3.
4   Short for kilogram Separative Work Units, a measure of the amount of enrichment work provided by the separation facility. For example, 6.7 SWUs are required to produce one kilogram of 4.4 per cent LEU, with 0.3 per cent U-235 remaining in the depleted uranium 'tails'.
5   In fact, there is considerable uncertainty about the size of USEC's loss or profit – and even about its very existence. See 'Outlook on USEC', *Nuclear Fuel*, 11 October 1993.
6   'USEC Privatization Preparations Mesh Opinions of Several Agencies', *Nuclear Fuel*, 20 May 1996, p.3.
7   Private communication with a BNFL representative, June 1995.
8   *Plutonium: The First 50 Years*, Table 15.
9   Of the excess HEU, 65 per cent has commercial value, 15 per cent does not, and the status of 20 per cent remains to be established. See 'DOE Issues Draft EIS on HEU Disposition', *Nuclear Fuel*, 6 November 1995, p.19.
10 William J. Broad, 'Quietly, U.S. Converts Uranium into Fuel for Civilian Reactors', *New York Times*, 19 June 1995.
11 'USEC Says It Has Begun Blending US HEU', *Nuclear Fuel*, 19 June 1995, p.19.
12 'IAEA Considers Applying Safeguards to HEU Down-blending at Portsmouth GDP', *Nuclear Fuel*, 20 May 1996, p.5.
13 The MELOX plant at the Marcoule site in France has a designed capacity of 120 tonnes MOX per year and could be expanded to 160 tonnes per year in the future. The

PO plant in Dessel in Belgium has a capacity of 35 tonnes per year. The Sellafield MOX plant in the United Kingdom has a designed capacity of 120 tonnes MOX per year and is expected to come on line in 1997/8. See 'COGEMA Preparing Addition of MOX Capacity at Melox, La Hague', *Nuclear Fuel*, 25 September 1995, pp.10–12; 'BNFL Wants to Be a Leading Player in Disposal of Weapons Plutonium', *Nuclear Fuel*, 8 April 1996, pp.12–13.

14   'Germans, French Propose Competing Technology for Russian MOX Project', *Nuclear Fuel*, 3 June 1996, pp.11–13.

15   V. Mikhailov, V. Bogdan, V. Murogov, V. Kagramanian, N. Rabotnov, V. Rudneva and M. Troyanov, 'Utilization of Plutonium in Russia's Nuclear Power Industry', *Post-Soviet Nuclear Complex Monitor*, 18 March 1994, pp.9–17.

16   Committee on International Security and Arms Control, National Academy of Sciences, *Management and Disposition of Excess Weapons Plutonium*, Washington, DC: National Academy Press, 1994; *Management and Disposition of Excess Weapons Plutonium: Reactor-Related Options*, Washington, DC: National Academy Press, 1995.

17   'Russia's Nuclear Fuel Cycle', in *Moscow Summit on Nuclear Safety*, Moscow: Russian Information Agency Novosti, 19–20 April 1996, p.8.

18   Declaration of the G-7 nations plus Russian leaders, 'Moscow Nuclear Safety and Security Summit Declaration', 20 April 1996.

19   Assuming that Russia dismantles 1500–2000 warheads a year and an average warhead contains 15–30kg of HEU, then 20–60 tonnes of HEU a year is recovered from dismantled weapons.

20   V. Menshikov, 'On the Situation with the Storage of Plutonium and Enriched Uranium in Tomsk-7', *Yaderny Control*, February 1995, pp.3–4 (in Russian).

21   At least originally, the storage facility was intended for storing equal numbers of HEU and plutonium containers for a period of 80–100 years. See V. Golozubov, 'Main Design Principles for Russia's Weapons Fissile Materials Storage Facility', presentation at the International Workshop 'Reprocessing of Spent Fuel, Storage and Use of Reactor and Weapons Plutonium', Moscow, 14–16 December 1992.

22   *Plutonium: The First 50 Years*, pp.25,30.

23   V. Petrovsky, statement at the 44th UN General Assembly, 25 October 1989.

24   US–Russian Commission on Economic and Technological Cooperation, 'Report on the Nuclear Energy Committee', Washington, DC: 20–30 January 1996, p.5.

25   'Stopping Weapons-Grade Plutonium Production in Russia', Washington, DC: US Department of Energy, March 1996.

5 Unintentional Nuclear Fire after the Cold War and Arms Control

Ciro E. Zoppo

The Problem of Accidental Nuclear War

The focal point of this inquiry may be succinctly stated, notwithstanding its empirical complexity: after the demise of the Soviet Union and the collapse of the bipolar East–West adversarial system, is accidental nuclear war still possible?

Before framing a hypothetical answer, accidental nuclear war must be redefined to fit the changed and changing strategic circumstances of the last five years or so. Simply put, accidental nuclear war is defined, for our purposes, as the firing of some strategic nuclear weapons. Such launch of a limited number of nuclear warheads would occur because of actions not properly authorized by a legitimate command authority, a technological mishap or a partial systemic failure of the warning and command system.

Unless some radical changes have taken place in the organizational and operational set-up of the American and Russian command structures, limited firings would not necessarily be restricted to a single silo, a single ballistic missile from a strategic submarine or one launch control centre. As will be detailed later, an appreciable number of intercontinental ballistic missiles (ICBMs) or submarine-launched ballistic missiles (SLBMs) could be involved.

The possibility, and hence the risk, of accidental nuclear war or unintentional nuclear fire has been ever-present from the outset of the nuclear age. Incalculable as it may be to predict accidental or unauthorized launches of nuclear weapons, intuitively it may be said that such a possibility increased when technology made it operationally possible to launch missiles on warning and enhanced the readiness of strategic nuclear forces in the United States and the former Soviet Union. Operational-alert modifications in both nuclear powers may have mitigated this problem but it has not disappeared. In fact, the territorial fragmentation of the former Soviet Union has removed ground-based warning stations that used to be on the peripheral reaches of the Soviet state. Ground-based warning stations are now at the borders of Russia, reducing the reaction time available to Russian military and civilian nuclear decision makers.

This situation is as much a product of the imperatives of the technology of strategic forces as it is of political intentions and military doctrines.[1] Consequently, the end of the Cold War has not eliminated the possibility of accidental and inadvertent nuclear launches. Major modifications in the structure of national nuclear forces and their operational procedures could reduce the risk. As will be suggested, American and Russian strategic nuclear forces would have to be radically altered to abort such a possible outcome. Russian strategic forces have continued to be on hair-trigger alert procedures.[2]

Focus on Russia and the United States

The initial focus of this analysis will be on the United States and Russia in particular. West European nuclear nations and the case of China will be noted only when obviously relevant to the examination of the problem. Because tactical nuclear weapons are hardly deployed, if at all, in the non-strategic forces of the United States and Russia, the scope of the analysis is strategic systems. Tactical nuclear weapons are discussed only when relevant to the possibility of unintentional nuclear fire.

In regard to the major nuclear powers – the United States, Russia, Britain, France and China – this examination of unintentional nuclear fire does exclude calculated strategic pre-emptions, totally automated launch-on-warning sequences and escalation to strategic alerts as coercive measures in situations of international crises. No intentions to go to nuclear war by the leaderships of the major powers exist or should be induced by a generated acute crisis. Nuclear coercion may be an aspect of analysis, but only if it is imbedded in a Russian internal political crisis resulting from severe political instability. The attack on dedicated international targets would not be an explicit intention of those involved in the domestic political upheaval.

Even before the end of the Cold War, the major nuclear powers had developed nuclear policies that made the deterrence of nuclear war itself the primary security objective. Without such an objective, it would have been practically impossible to promote and achieve any nuclear arms control.

Since the end of the Cold War, the scope and approach of nuclear arms control has been broadened. An example is the redeployment and partial destruction of tactical nuclear weapons. Implicitly, it may be said that by now the protagonist nuclear powers have redefined the central mission of their strategic nuclear forces as existential deterrence. Consequently, except as an *ultima ratio*, these nations have no intention to use nuclear war, however limited, as an instrument of foreign policy.

Unpredictability

If there are no intentions to use nuclear weapons as an instrument of national security to pursue the national interest, are nuclear accidents or unintentional launches nevertheless likely? With the intellectual tools currently available for analysis it is impossible to answer the question with any kind of probable predictability. Nevertheless, the consequences of malfunctions or operational confusion in the command and control systems leading to unintentional nuclear fire could be so grievous that a focus on that possibility continues to be warranted. Such an event, even if limited to a single nuclear warhead, would be different in kind from other accidents, like those involving nuclear reactors, or other calamities.

For example, the probability of nuclear accidents cannot be assessed with the rigour available to assessments of air travel safety. Moreover, the consequences of an unintentional nuclear launch are magnitudes above the loss of an aircraft and its passengers. But noting the beliefs and attitudes of those in charge, and of the experts prior to nuclear accidents that have occurred, will illustrate and validate the question. Before the 1979 Three Mile Island nuclear reactor accident, there was a widespread view among specialists that the risk of a reactor catastrophe was extremely low and that nuclear power had been rendered safe. Before the 1985 accident of the space shuttle *Challenger*, NASA's confidence about space launch safety was so high that teachers and politicians were permitted to join shuttle crews. There were hardly any expectations of disaster in regard to Bophal and Chernobyl before they happened.[3]

Scott Sagan, in his seminal work on nuclear safety, has examined theories on the relationship between organizations and accidents. He found two competing schools of thought that synthesize the literature. The first, which he labelled the 'high reliability theory', contends that extremely safe operations are possible with hazardous technologies, if appropriate organizational design and management techniques are followed. The second, labelled the 'normal accidents theory', argues that serious accidents with complex high-technology systems are inevitable.[4]

In regard to unintentional nuclear fire in an era no longer organized by Cold War assumptions of ideological rivalry, and most important given the transitional character of both Russian politics and the international environment, the normal accidents theory seems to offer a more useful guide to analysis. The main reason for this assumption lies in the facts of transitional politics that characterize the current situation. Although not inevitable, the possibility of a serious accident seems more plausible if cast in the mould of the normal accidents theory. The inevitability of results that is found in both the optimist and pessimist schools of thought has a certain determinism that is the subject of debate and remains unresolved in science. Moreover, neither school of thought addresses a primarily transitional system or situation.

Problem Awareness in the United States

In the United States, among civilian experts analysing the policy requirements of nuclear deterrence and the military forces charged with the control of strategic weapons, there was awareness of the problem of effective control of nuclear weapons. The symbiotic relationship between men and technology in strategic forces was a subject of study at the RAND Corporation in the 1950s and beyond. Since the early 1980s, it has been known that the military in charge of US strategic nuclear weapons have been aware of the problems connected with the personnel and the technological aspects of command and control. A special programme was set up for individuals whose duties gave them access to nuclear weapons. The Personnel Reliability Program was to screen those who would be involved in sensitive nuclear operations. More than 100 000 people had been screened by 1982. The individuals who passed the screening successfully had to show evidence of emotional stability and good social adjustment, and have no problems with alcohol or drug abuse.[5]

In 1975 alone, 5128 US military personnel were removed from access to nuclear weapons because of violations of the Personnel Reliability Program. In 1976 and 1977, these numbers were 4966 and 4973, or more than 4 per cent per year. In 1977, 1289 personnel were removed because of significant physical or psychological traits or aberrant behaviour, substantiated by competent medical authority. In addition to medical reasons, 828 were disqualified for negligence, 350 for court-martial offences and 885 for evidence of contemptuous attitudes towards regulations and the law. These traits might prejudice the reliable performance of duties connected with the operation of the strategic forces. From a military standpoint, the primary concern was command control so that the weapons would be launched according to plan. However, accidental or unauthorized weapons launches could also result.

More recent figures are not readily available, but it is doubtful that the nature of the problem or the range of figures has changed radically. It would be extraordinary if Soviet/Russian strategic forces had no such problems. During the last three to four years, some information on this kind of personnel problem has begun to filter into the public domain in Russia.[6]

Another aspect is primarily technological, although obviously the ultimate decisions are human. Computers have been intimately involved with the operations of strategic nuclear forces. During an 18-month period in the late 1970s, for example, the North American Air Defense Command had 151 false alarms. Four resulted in increasing the alert status of US strategic bombers and ICBMs. A major false alert, lasting six minutes, occurred when a technician mistakenly mounted a training tape of a Soviet nuclear attack on a US strategic forces computer. When the US general in charge was asked how it became possible to know that it was an error and not a real attack, he explained that his command had an instantaneous communication set-up with all the technological sensor sites or tracking stations. The officers in charge ascertained that, in fact, none was tracking any missiles. They then knew that it had to be a computer error.[7] The current Russian command and control system is based on a communication network basically resembling the approach used by the United States in those days; however, the US system uses more up-to-date technology. Incompetence, not evil design, may suffice to cause unintentional nuclear fire.

Having much smaller nuclear forces, Britain, France and China may not face the magnitude of the problem confronting the United States or Russia, but they must confront essentially the same kind of problem in command and control. Because Britain and France are relying almost exclusively on SLBMs, the organizational aspects of their strategic forces do not have to be concerned with ICBMs and require a somewhat different command-and-control configuration. However, command and control of strategic nuclear submarines is more difficult than it is for land-based ICBMs. Logically, the risk of accidents and unauthorized behaviour increases with the size of the nuclear arsenal and the number of personnel to service it.

The history of the Unites States' experience with nuclear weapons is being re-evaluated and has revealed accidents, near accidents, false warning incidents and other organizational dysfunctions that raise some questions about the safety of nuclear strategic operations. Notwithstanding improvements made during recent years in this sector, potentially serious safety and security problems remain in the existing nuclear forces of the nuclear states.[8]

Moreover, there are psychological and political consequences to consider in connection with an unintentional nuclear launch. Although in peacetime an accidental launch need not trigger a launch-on-warning or launch-under-attack response, the possibility exists. This kind of situation was illustrated by the January 1995 incident concerning the launch of a single Norwegian non-military rocket. The Russians apparently entered the early phases of launch-on-warning procedures when the launch of a Norwegian scientific rocket triggered a false warning that activated President Yeltsin's nuclear command suitcase and initiated an emergency conference with his nuclear advisers. It could be surmised that a cause of the misperception may have been a reduced effectiveness of the warning system due to the general deterioration of the military infrastructure. This deterioration is a general phenomenon for all services.[9] The probability that even a single nuclear explosion would lead to an exceedingly tense international crisis which might lead to war cannot be ignored.

Context Assumptions

A number of assumptions govern the present analysis, as follows. Only the next decade is considered and although chemical and biological warheads could be mated with existing strategic delivery mechanisms, only nuclear weapons are considered.

START agreements will remain limited to Russia, the United States and the nuclear successor states of the former Soviet Union. British, French and Chinese forces will not be included, although some modernizing and modest changes in deployment will be taking place in these forces. Of the former Soviet Union, only Russia will remain a strategic nuclear power. In the Lisbon Protocols to the START-I Treaty, the Ukraine, Kazakhstan and Belarus agreed to give up or eliminate all nuclear weapons from their national territories and accede to the Nonproliferation Treaty. Kazakhstan and Belarus have done so already. The Ukraine has recently concluded the process of transferring the last remaining strategic nuclear weapons to Russia.[10]

During this period there will be no nuclear disarmament by the nuclear powers, only reductions in nuclear weapons by the United States and Russia. The US government maintains that strategic nuclear forces are the linchpin for national security. So emphatically, does the Russian government. French strategic thinkers are already at work reshaping the rationales that legitimize the continuation of nuclear deterrent forces, although they recognize the loss of a designated or definable enemy.[11] Nuclear deterrence, however implausible in the rationales of US, European, Chinese and Russian foreign policies, will remain the doctrinal, operational core of the strategic forces of the nuclear powers.

However, in logic, the core assumptions of nuclear deterrence as they developed in the postwar period have been made politically obsolete, for the time being, by the radical changes in East–West relations. The repudiation of Communist ideology as the matrix for state action and organization, and the attendant disintegration of the Soviet Union and the Warsaw Pact, have destroyed the ideological justifications for US and West European containment policy. The changes have also undermined the cardinal assumptions of deterrence theory in a bipolar world and some of the operational rationales of strategic nuclear forces. The central axiom of nuclear deterrence was predicated on the existence of an immutable and implacable enemy. This articulated a set of assumptions that premised deterrence, such as the concept that the enemy's potentially aggressive intentions can be held in check only by rational cost–risk calculations of adversary deterrent policies, as derived from the actual or contingent deployment of strategic nuclear forces. Notwithstanding counterforce operational rationales, particularly in US military doctrine, populations are the ultimate targets under any conceivable nuclear deterrent doctrines. For the French and the British, they are in fact the primary targets.

As tactical nuclear weapons are eliminated from the inventories of American and Russian forces – either through destruction or mothballing – the possibilities of unauthorized use of battlefield, tactical nuclear weapons are accordingly largely eliminated. The US Army and the surface US Navy are practically denuclearized now. The United States has withdrawn all its nuclear artillery shells from deployed units and nuclear warheads from short-range ballistic missiles. So has Russia. Nuclear warheads from cruise missiles and attack submarines are also being withdrawn by the United States, although it is not clear whether Russia is following suit. Nuclear land mines and nuclear air-defence warheads have been destroyed. Total denuclearization is in the offing for the tactical nuclear forces.[12]

By mutual agreement, Russia has also withdrawn tactical nuclear weapons from its military forces. If current trends hold, and all former Soviet tactical nuclear weapons are returned to Russia to be either destroyed or stockpiled, the Russian armed forces will no longer deploy tactical nuclear weapons and the forces of the Ukraine, Kazakhstan and Belarus will be totally denuclearized. However, it should be pointed out that, while this outcome reduces or eliminates the dangers of unauthorized and accidental use of tactical nuclear weapons, it also removes available options in potentially escalatory sequences in crisis management and intra-war deterrence. Consequently, in a situation of crisis, escalation might go from the conventional to the centrally strategic, with no intermediate steps. An example of the linkage between tactical and strategic is to be found in France's nuclear deterrent. In French doctrine, before the end of the Cold War, tactical nuclear weapons were designated as shots across the bow or as a way to show resolve before escalating to the central strategic level.[13]

Another assumption underwriting the analysis is that in the decade ahead no European nation is expected to go militarily nuclear. Italy and post-Franco Spain did not develop policies for a nuclear option. Sweden, after a national debate, renounced a military nuclear option,[14] as did Switzerland. Nuclear renunciation remains anchored in Germany's defence policy, and there has been no change in Japan's policy regarding nuclear weapons. In any case, whatever the internal political evolution within Russia, it is generally expected that in the decade ahead there will not be a return to an adversarial, confrontational posture in Russian foreign relations *vis-à-vis* the United States and its European or Asian neighbours.

For the time period under consideration, it is assumed that there will not be deployment by the United States of a comprehensive Strategic Defense Initiative (SDI)-level system of defence against ballistic missiles. But research and development in components amenable to renegotiation under the ABM Treaty will continue. A smaller version, named Global Protection Against Limited Strikes (GPALS), was funded by the US Congress. Under the 1992 Missile Defense Act, Congress requires the Secretary of Defense to develop and to deploy a single-site ABM system consistent with the 1972 ABM Treaty.

It is also assumed that there will be no technological breakthroughs in anti-submarine warfare to invalidate the relative invulnerability of the strategic submarine. Consequently, when land-based strategic nuclear forces are greatly reduced and some systems eliminated or phased out, deterrence will increasingly depend on the less vulnerable strategic sea-based systems. These are the systems without permissive action links, and are the most difficult to command and control without making the strategic submarines vulnerable to pre-emptive attack. It is moot how much arms control can be effected to undercut the danger of unintentional nuclear fire before they are shorn of their utility as a deterrent. This is the kind of problématique in which arms control must operate.

Finally, the difficulty, nay the impossibility, of acquiring data which are relevant, up-to-date and sufficient to address the problem of unintentional nuclear fire forces analysis to be often inferential or conjectural.

Command and Control in a Politically Transitional Russia

When addressing the problem of unintentional nuclear fire, Russia is pivotal to the discussion. Command and control of Russian strategic nuclear forces and related organizational and technological systems are central to understanding the actual situation. The problem relates to two fundamental aspects: the military organizational and the technological; and, eminently, the political, in internal politics and foreign affairs. It is useful to review the changes that have occurred in American and Russian nuclear policies, and the record of nuclear incidents of the past and more recent events that are germane to the problem of unintentional nuclear fire.

Yeltsin and Bush officially ordered the removal of population targets from the Russian and American target assignments. The United States also announced the stand-down from alert status of the strategic weapons which are the subject of START-I reductions. The Clinton administration has continued this policy. Russia has also announced a stand-down from alert status of some of its missile forces, while some remain on combat alert. According to former Defence Minister Grachev, the missiles will have no specific designated targets.[15] Does this mean that an accidental launch could hit anywhere, at random? If so, it may not be possible to forewarn the recipient of such fire about the location of impact. While the benign intentions of the Russian and American presidents are unquestionable, verification of their unilateral directives changing the US and Russian strategic target plans is well nigh impossible without active operational verification that would invalidate the highest levels of national secrecy.

Intelligence and Accidents

This situation will perpetuate the need for intelligence on deployed Russian weapon systems for the United States, and on US and other Western nuclear weapon systems for the Russians. The November 1992 collision of a US and a Russian submarine practically in Russian territorial waters, and of an American hunter–killer submarine, the *Grayling*, and a Russian strategic submarine in the Barents Sea in March 1993 show how active US operational intelligence and operational strategic deterrence continue to be. From previously known information in the public domain,[16] it may be surmised that, of the US submarines mentioned, the first was engaged in intercepting Russian intermilitary communications on the Kola peninsula and the second was tracking a Russian nuclear strategic submarine, whose targets are in the United States, so that it could destroy the latter, should it become necessary, before it launched its missiles.

According to Russian navy officials, the USS *Grayling* hit the Russian submarine just 20 yards away from the conning tower. Had it hit the conning tower, the Russian High Command claims, it would have been impossible to cut off the submarine's two nuclear reactors and 'a thermonuclear explosion would have been inevitable'. According to Russian official sources, the collision also endangered the Russian submarine's 16 multi-warhead SS-N-18 ballistic missiles,[17] which have a range of 5000 nautical miles. Although there are scientific reasons to doubt a nuclear explosion, the US submarine would have been engulfed by radioactivity from leaks even without an explosion. Communications with the US strategic command would have been unlikely, and the exact situation surrounding the explosion difficult to apprehend in a time-urgent manner. The United States has denied the possibility of such catastrophic consequences, but it was reported that the collision was brought up at the Clinton–Yeltsin Vancouver summit of April 1993.

During the Cold War, Soviet and US nuclear submarines engaged in 'close encounters' routinely, but their dangerous manoeuvres near the ocean floor were supposed to have been abandoned. However, as long as the United States operates according to a counterforce strategy, the requirements of operational deterrence will keep the United States in a forward maritime posture. Situations of this kind will continue to occur at times. In February 1992, in a message to the UN Conference on Disarmament in Geneva, the Russian government suggested the end to nuclear alerts by putting all strategic weapons on 'zero alert'. But the United States responded that there would be no way to verify that either side had shifted the status of their respective missiles so that they would no longer be aimed at the former enemy.[18] During the Cold War, the USSR hardly ever went on high strategic alerts. The United States used them much more in order to signal determination.

The paradox of 'no political enemy' but the need to deter existing nuclear weapons with nuclear weapons will remain. With the continued existence of American and Russian strategic nuclear forces, militarily poised in adversary deployments, the issue of a potential test of the credibility of the US strategic guarantee to Western Europe will continue to exist in unforeseen and unforeseeable nuclear confrontations. The possible threat of 'accidental' or inadvertent nuclear conflict, from which Europe could not protect itself, will also be perpetuated.

The possibility, hence the risk, of accidental or inadvertent nuclear exchanges has been ever-present from the time the United States, the Soviet Union and other nuclear weapons states set up their strategic forces. Incalculable as it may be to predict accidental launches of nuclear weapons, the possibility will continue to exist, as long as launch readiness prevails. However, it should be noted that in the past false strategic alerts have been managed. The imperatives of technology and of military doctrines combine to create this possibility. Seemingly, the elimination of the adversarial US–Russian political posture has mitigated the risk of acute confrontation, but not eliminated all the risks inherent in the nuclear age.[19]

Technology also prompts another consideration. It is well known that over the years accidents have been frequent in the Soviet/Russian submarine force. Between 1986 and 1996 alone, there were 19 known accidents involving Russian nuclear submarines. Before then, 60 accidents had been catalogued. Although collisions have been the most prevalent accidents, 13 with Western submarines, the data also reveal recurring problems with missiles and missile tubes. Six accidents reported involved fires or explosions in missile tubes. One led to the ejection of a nuclear warhead in 1980, another caused the sinking of a *Yankee* class submarine in 1986. The earliest, recently reported accidental nuclear-related explosion on land was the explosion of an R-16 ICBM on its test launch pad in 1960. The blast killed unit officers and men and the commander-in-chief of the rocket forces. Another mishap only recently divulged was the crash of a military aircraft carrying nuclear weapons, causing several deaths from radiation in 1970.[20]

Transitions in Command and Control

In addition, during the continuing transition from the demise of the Soviet Union to the establishment of a parliamentary system in Russia and the transfer to Russia of nuclear weapons from other nuclear-capable former Soviet republics, command and control of nuclear forces may have weakened or become less certain. The disintegration of the central authority that legitimized and controlled the nuclear forces of the former Soviet Union, illustrated by the radical reorganization of the KGB, suggests the magnitude of the potential problem. The KGB was the main organizational instrument for command and control of the Soviet strategic forces.

The Russians have been too taken up with the fast-paced political and economic demands within the country and on its periphery to have addressed the issue beyond the attempt to consolidate civilian control over the military. Reportedly, as Yeltsin accepted the need for bypass surgery he at first considered delegating responsibility for security to Premier Chernomyrdin, but retaining the nuclear button. However, Russian state-run television noted that nuclear keys were also in the hands of the Defence Minister Igor Rodionov and Army Chief of Staff Mikhail Kolosnikov, and that without their cooperation the nuclear button would be useless. In fact, the Russian military, like the American, holds all of the authorization and unblock codes needed to launch a strategic attack. Ultimately, during his recent bypass surgery, Yeltsin did briefly delegate the nuclear button to Premier Chernomyrdin. Moreover, General Lebed ignored Prime Minister Chernomyrdin's call for unity during Yeltsin's hospital stay, telling a news conference in Moscow that Russia is near chaos and repeating the claim that the army is on the brink of mutiny. This contributed to his firing by Yeltsin. Seemingly, the final disposition of strategic command and control at the highest political level is not yet definitely resolved. A *sub rosa* struggle between the highest military and President Yeltsin and his political entourage continues. The Lebed feud with Grachev is indicative of the situation.[21]

During the abortive coup in 1991, the general staff stripped Gorbachev of nuclear authority, taking away his nuclear suitcase. Two of the conspirators, the defence minister and the chief of general staff, retained their suitcases and their authority. However, the nuclear commanders of the strategic missile forces, the navy and the air force agreed, in secret, not to obey commands from their immediate superiors. This weakened nuclear control authority for several months – among other things because the triad in Russian strategic nuclear forces is under three separate commands independent of each other.[22]

Russian nuclear strategy continues to be predicated basically on launch-on-warning. This means that strategic missiles would be launched presumably after an attack had been detected but before incoming enemy missiles hit targets on the territory of Russia. Strategic retaliatory doctrine is geared fundamentally towards this kind of option. The strategic general staff can exercise the option in one of two ways. One approach is the way the United States would implement launch-on-warning: send authorization to fire and unlock codes down to the individual commanders who perform the launch procedures. In the other approach, which is said to be unique to Russia, the general staff directly push the launch button from their war room near Moscow. This is a remote launch signal that bypasses the chain of command below the general staff. It goes directly to unmanned missile silos. Both these approaches to launch-on-warning allow three to four minutes for the detection of an attack, and another three to four minutes only for presidential decision making.[23]

The US launch-on-warning system also allows very little time for decision making. Once a US early-warning satellite gives the signal of a missile launch, it takes two and a half minutes to evaluate the signal. If the signal is seen as correct, a Missile Display Conference is called after 30 seconds. The technical information is assessed further and, if the situation is deemed serious, a Threat Assessment Conference is convened. Senior military officers evaluate the threat. Within eight and a half minutes of the original satellite signal, if the impending attack is deemed real, a Missile Attack Conference is called which includes all senior personnel and the president (if available). The time from issuing the order to fire to firing missiles in retaliation can be six minutes. In the period 1977–83 there occurred at least 255 Missile Display Conferences.[24]

The Russians have undertaken some actions to reassure the United States and its European allies about command and control and the alert status of their strategic forces. The organization of command and control for the Russian missiles has become much better known through a Russian policy of openness to American civilian and military experts, and openness to the Russian media as well. But the US government continues to have concerns regarding nuclear control at the highest levels.

The crisis in governance that has pitted President Yeltsin against the Russian Congress has underscored the fragility of the emerging system. Although the *Los Angeles Times* of 25 March 1993 reported that the CIA, in closed-door sessions before the crisis erupted, expressed confidence that the power struggle between Yeltsin and the Parliament did not pose a threat to the existing system for control of Russia's nuclear weapons, some Russian officials seemed less sanguine. In the same day's reportage, Mikhail Fedotov, Yeltsin's information minister, was quoted as saying that, if the Russian Congress voted to oust the president, but Yeltsin rejected the move, both the country and the armed forces would split into two armed camps. If that happened, 'each side will have a few thousand atomic bombs [and] ... you can imagine what the results would be'.[25]

Fedotov's fears may have been exaggerated. As Christopher Donnelly, Special Adviser to NATO's Secretary General, has explained, there never developed in the Soviet Union any civilian competence on security or significant civilian expertise in defence matters. One notable exception is Andrei Kokoshin, the Russian Federation's first deputy defence minister. His public statements reveal an in-depth expertise in nuclear doctrine and the technical aspects of deployments. Also noteworthy are the analyses of the emerging Russian strategic policy by Ioury Federov, of Moscow's State Institute of International Relations of the Ministry of Foreign Affairs. Federov's observation of the potential he claims in regard to nuclear weapons on Russian soil may be purely conjectural. Nevertheless, even with Yeltsin in power, the situation in the command and control of nuclear weapons is seen, by members of the US Senate Armed Services Committee, as possibly posing a security threat to the United States and Europe.[26]

As matters stand, the START agreements and other arms control measures to be implemented during the remainder of the decade do not intrinsically remove the possibility of accidental or unauthorized nuclear launches of US or Russian weapons. The magnitude of the potential problem is easily illustrated by the following facts. Should a breakdown in the chain of command or a malfunction in the warning system of either country occur, an operational response by US or Russian strategic forces might lead, not simply to the launch of a single missile, nor merely to the explosion of a single warhead on target. Unless the organization of American and Russian strategic forces has been radically changed in regard to organizational mandates and procedures, an unauthorized or accidental launch from Russia could involve six to 10 missiles, if a battalion, or 18 to 30 missiles, if a regiment. Until START II is implemented, each missile could carry up to 10 warheads. Comparably, a US launch could consist of either 10 multiple-warhead missiles or a squadron of 50, that is 500 warheads. MIRVs represent an additional element to be considered. A single Russian *Typhoon* submarine carries a potential 200 nuclear warheads. A US *Trident* submarine is more than equally endowed. Most Russian strategic submarines may be docked because of malfunctions and the cost of keeping them at sea, but their missiles are ready to fire. The warheads for American *Trident* submarines continue to lack insensitive high explosives.[27]

General Igor Sergeyev, commander-in-chief of the strategic missile forces, in an interview with *Krasnaya Zvezda* agreed that a missile can launch because of a malfunction. But he added that a new computerized automated system of combat command and control – as sophisticated as the US system – has the capability to override the malfunction. Those who have studied the issue of nuclear safety have pointed out that, as in the case of nuclear power plants and commercial airlines, the United States has a better record than the former Soviet Union. Therefore one could anticipate safer systems of control of nuclear weapons in the United States. The statement by General Sergeyev about the US system agrees, by implication, with this assessment. The rigid nature of a command and control system that may lead to nuclear inadvertence, on the one hand, and failure to retaliate to a real attack, on the other hand, continues to be of concern to the Russian military. Starting in 1992, one of the chief priorities of Russian strategic forces has been the development of a modernized battle management and communication system. Reportedly, it is only a matter of seconds from the moment the system has been activated to the moment the missile is launched.[28] The emergent Russian system may be more efficient than the previous one, but continues to be basically hair-trigger, as the 1995 incident of the Norwegian scientific rocket illustrated.

As noted, no prediction is possible about unintentional nuclear fire. As for the past, there have not been any – except for the nuclear explosion of a warhead on the test launch pad in Russia in 1960, noted above. Nor has there been an accidental nuclear war. However, some discussion of the organizational aspects of nuclear command and control specifically addressed to the Russian situation, and generically applicable to the United States and other nuclear states, can be useful in assessing the dynamic of command and control in this transitional period in Russia's political system.

At the technical operational level below the general staff, the safeguards on ICBM silos are said to be quite efficient. For example, if a crew in the silo tried to pick the lock on their blocking device (the Permissive Action Link or PAL), Russian duty officers can take steps to isolate the deviant launch crew electronically. Even if the crew manages to insert the unlock code, the general staff can send a special signal that will override and restore the blocking function. Technical safeguards become weaker in other strategic systems, particularly submarines and cruise missiles. On balance, Russia's technical safeguards for land-based ICBMs compare favourably with those of the United States.[29]

It would seem that on the technical side the command and control of Russian forces has been modernized to a high level of sophistication. From a military viewpoint, technological automaticity has its combat merits. From the viewpoint of political intentions and safety of operation, however, the human element in the equation for technology control must be considered ultimately the most critical. For the command and control of strategic nuclear forces, that element is the military organization responsible for the strategic forces and its relationship to civilian authority.

The benchmark of the Russian situation regarding unintentional nuclear fire is its transitional character regarding the reorganization of the technological and human aspects of the strategic nuclear forces. Developments regarding strategic technology after the Cold War, and their impacts on decision making in the United States, Russia and other nuclear powers, are highly complex and hard to predict.[30] Most crucial is the stability and integrity of the civil–military relationship at the apex of the command and control structure.

The re-election of Yeltsin may bring greater stability and better accountability in the political system and in civil–military relations. On the other hand, his health may perpetuate the instability inherent in the present situation. The absence of a stable political system, with established and tested institutional checks and balances, can undermine effective nuclear control. Ambiguous authority and the potential for sudden shifts of allegiance could cause a breakdown in the command and control system. If the political system becomes chaotic, and economic pressures lead to social pressures among the personnel in the strategic nuclear forces, there may be a loss of legitimate and competent control at the top of the chain of command. Under such circumstances, the new Russian strategic reorganization, with its heavy emphasis on the *Topol* mobile ICBMs, could create the possibility of insubordinate units in the field. Much would depend on who controls the Permissive Action Links. The possibility of insubordinate units already exists in regard to strategic submarines on patrol. For the foreseeable future, the context in which the possibility of unintentional nuclear fire is imbedded in Russia remains dynamic.

Arms Control of Unintentional Nuclear Launches

Arms control is defined as any measure taken unilaterally (whether reciprocated or not) and/or by tacit mutual agreement, or negotiated on a bilateral or multilateral basis, or by proclamation. Such measures may be verified by unilateral national technological means, with or without on-site inspection, by national or international verification, and so on, that singly or in the aggregate diminish or abort accidental or unintentional nuclear firings. The following discussion will focus primarily on the US–Russian strategic relationship. France and Britain will be included when directly related, but China the very least and only in general policy terms, given the paucity of pertinent available information.

Arms control pertinent to the problem of nuclear launch accidents deals with issues that fall into two groups of activities. The first includes strategic warning, command and control of strategic forces, and crisis management and communication. The second includes the technological characteristics of weapon systems, their target plans, the alert status and deployments of strategic forces, and the unilateral and joint measures taken primarily by the United States and Russia to manage strategic stability in this transitional period.

Arms control measures have been and can be proposed in all sectors which would help reduce the possibility of accidental and unintentional firings of nuclear weapons, or mitigate their impact. Crucial issues are the effects some of these measures would have on strategic stability and existing deterrence. Without going into explicit analysis, it may be posited that, on balance, they would generally strengthen stability in the current strategic situation. On the other hand, they may inhibit deterrence in pre-crisis and in crisis situations. However, if properly orchestrated these arms control measures would not inherently prevent the re-establishment of military redeployments that are more immediately ready to deter in a developing crisis and post-crisis situation.

Measures Dealing with Crisis Decisions

Politically Driven Measures

The following measures would fit into this first category.

- A Russian and American officially declared commitment not to go to strategic alerts during crisis. This avoids their use for crisis escalation and decreases the chances of unauthorized or accidental launches.
- No future deployment of anti-satellite weapons. Such a measure would ensure the survival of command-and-control mechanisms, safeguard the intelligence and surveillance needed during crises and preserve adversary communication – all tools necessary for crisis management. In his 1992 Statement on Disarmament, President Yeltsin announced that Russia was ready to negotiate the elimination of existing anti-satellite systems on the basis of reciprocity with the United States.[31]

- Reorganize and expand the arms control mandate of the joint American–Russian committee established under SALT I for clarifying and modifying any suspect behaviour by the other signatory, to include measures specifically agreed upon for preventing unintentional nuclear firings.
- Include in each of the American and Russian Crisis Management Centres high-level technically proficient personnel from the other country, on a reciprocal basis. These personnel must have their own communication channels to their national decision makers in crisis contingencies.
- Take all strategic bombers, with their personnel, off day-to-day ready alert. This has been done officially by the United States, with Russia presumably following suit. The United States has also stood down from the alert status of ICBMs scheduled for deactivation under START I, and called on Russia to do so as well. This procedure should be extended to all ICBMs on both sides.
- Redeploy strategic submarine forces to home ports, eliminating forward deployments, except for a limited number of boats mutually agreed upon. Verification could be relatively straightforward. The eventual goal would be to eliminate all forward deployments. This measure would be strongly resisted by both the Russian and American navies.
- Reprogramme strategic systems to eliminate salvo launches of ICBMs. Of concern in this context is the currently evolving Russian strategic doctrine which leans towards a structure of pre-emption.[32]

Technologically Driven Measures

The following measures would fit into this second category.

- There are three basic elements to an ICBM – the propulsion or rocket, the nuclear explosive warhead and the computer instructions or telemetry.[33] If the warhead is separated from the rocket and stockpiled in a different location, and if the guidance computer instructions are temporarily removed as well, it becomes impossible to send the warhead on target by mistake or intentionally. These changes in the operational status could be monitored adequately by the same remote control now being used to verify the dismantled stockpiling of warheads under present agreements. But should a severe crisis demand it, the components could be reassembled sufficiently quickly to return the missile to an operational status. Some questions arise about the impact on stability and deterrence at this point in the procedure. They can neither be defined properly nor answered without detailed analysis. Even then, it would be difficult, if at all possible, to generate the kind of data required for sufficient analysis.

- De-MIRV all strategic missiles: that is, return to single-warhead missiles. Admittedly, it would be difficult to achieve transparency in this operation without on-site inspection, which might reveal warhead design, thus increasing the vulnerability of the weapon to countermeasures.
- Eliminate land-based mobile strategic missile forces. These are inherently more difficult to command and control, and may not have sufficient transparency for purposes of verification. This decision has already been taken by the United States, which has invited Russia to eliminate those it possesses. However, the modernization of the Russian strategic forces is making the mobile strategic missile the backbone of the force. It is highly unlikely that the programme would be reversed.[34]
- Equip all strategic weapon systems, including SLBMs, with PALs. From the record it is expected that the measure would be strongly opposed by the US Navy in the first place, and by the strategic navies of the other nuclear powers. Signals give away a submarine's location, making it vulnerable in time of crisis. Moreover, even in non-crisis situations, if it is to be adequately verified it would lead to the same kinds of problems connected with de-MIRVing noted above.
- Equip strategic missiles with remotely controlled self-destruct mechanisms, independently developed on a national basis. Their design would be guarded with the highest secrecy by each nuclear power. Their codes would be periodically scrambled. This precaution would be required to invalidate any attempt by an adversary to abort a launch of missiles in self-defence. It is the kind of measure likely to be opposed by the military, whose principal duty is to maintain absolutely assured nuclear deterrence.
- Pledge no counter-city targets under any circumstances. The governments of Russia and the United States have officially declared that cities have been taken off their respective target plans. Again no effective verification is possible which does not take away the deterrent function of the strategic forces, particularly the British and the French, which are articulated by SLBMs, and are rationalized by military doctrines informed by finite deterrence based on countervalue targets. The complete failure of the 1958 Surprise Attack Conference is instructive. These forces would be undermined also by the deployment of effective strategic area defence, another potential way to cope with unintentional nuclear fire.

- Remove nuclear-armed cruise missiles from strategic air forces and stockpile them away from launch platforms. This is more feasible now, given the more extended time available for strategic warning.
- Promote research and development on ground area defence against a limited number of incoming missiles. If MIRVing is eliminated from the strategic forces of major nuclear powers, along with the capability to launch salvos of nuclear missiles, a much more modest missile defence against unintentional nuclear firings could be viable. Unlike the SDI (Strategic Defense Initiative) programme, it would not only cost less and be technologically less demanding, but would also not subvert the ABM Treaty. It could also be useful in deterring the belligerent use of nuclear weapons by emerging nuclear states in the developing world.

Conclusions

In order to be seriously considered by governments, the arms control measures indicated would have to be effectively verifiable by independent national means based on appropriate technology. The difficulty of verification varies with each measure. Each deserves its own in-depth analysis and, most important, must be defined so that it can be related to the other measures in regard to the effects on strategic stability and deterrence. Singly and in the aggregate these measures must be viable in the international political environment of this decade and beyond. Crucial to the enterprise will be the political developments within Russia and the Russian approach in foreign and security policies.

It is clear that the governments of the nuclear nations expect to maintain strategic nuclear forces as a hedge against an uncertain security future. It follows that arms control for diminishing or eliminating the consequences of accidental and unintentional nuclear fire is unlikely to be accepted if it does not contain the capability of preserving or reconstituting a robust nuclear deterrent within a manageable time. *Quod erat demonstrandum.*

Only deployed and reciprocal strategic defence systems with airtight area defence for urban populations could guard against the immediate effects of an accidental launch. For the United States, the deployment of such a system is years into the future, provided the funding for research and development on ballistic missile defence (BMD) does not fall victim to the Congressional budget axe. A more limited and cheaper system than originally planned, designed to defend the United States against accidental or unauthorized missile strikes, was authorized by Congress in November 1991.

In fact, there have been increases in BMD research in the Clinton defence budgets, but the priority has been shifted to battlefield theatre missile defence, rather than the defence of the American population. No similar programme is known to be under way in Russia. Although Yeltsin made reference to a joint global defence in the June 1992 Washington summit, the Russian government rejects any attempt to change the ABM Treaty. It argues that it is imperative to maintain the existing connection between strategic offensive and defensive weapons. The possibility for cooperation seen by the Russians is in the area of missile attack early warning systems.[35]

Total and verifiable nuclear disarmament would avoid the problem altogether, but is nowhere in sight. The basic structure of the strategic nuclear forces that emerged in the post-World War II period will continue to be a concrete reality, inherently dangerous in their potential for technological and organizational malfunctions. A mitigating result of the incessant march of technology has been the development of satellite intelligence and communications, including those with the adversary. These are useful means of avoiding escalation to inadvertent nuclear fire, especially in crises.

After START reductions of land-based ICBMs and the elimination of most deployed nuclear tactical systems, in times of escalating crises only the Arctic Ocean and adjacent northern waters would remain as forward strategic spaces in Europe for the United States. In the years ahead, strategic nuclear forces remaining in the air and at sea in Western Europe will be primarily French and British. Their composition will be shaped by the incipient national budgetary shortfalls and by the question whether they will become the subject of future arms control agreements. To date, French and British nuclear forces have not been included in the American–Russian arms control negotiations and agreements that have taken place or are projected.

Negotiated and projected US–Russian nuclear arms control is diminishing the quantitative arms race in strategic systems, and the threats that it produced to European security. A similar conclusion may be drawn about the qualitative arms race. In terms of the immediate future, the agenda and the funds for research on nuclear weapons and their delivery systems have practically disappeared in Russia. Russian government policy caused by fundamental political changes and dire economic conditions, as well as US and other Western subsidies to pay for the destruction of tactical nuclear weapons and the salaries of Russian scientists to divert them from military to civilian research, have seemingly eliminated the funding for research and development as a crucial Russian contribution to a technological arms race. Nevertheless, residual research continues in this area. For the first time since the advent of the nuclear age, the United States will have no nuclear warheads being manufactured or on order. The further assembly of the W-88 hydrogen bomb warhead, the last nuclear bomb still in production, was stopped in January 1992.

As extended deterrence becomes more a residual-threat deterrence because of the political and technological changes that have occurred, and as strategic arms control agreements between the United States and Russia successively dismantle each of the operational 'couplings' that linked the deterrent structure of the United States to Western Europe, the deterrent role of the United States in European security becomes less pivotal. Conversely, the role, the significance and the very *raison d'être* of West European nuclear forces become more important as potential nuclear deterrents – notwithstanding the fact that the US–Russian deterrent relationship will remain primary for the West.

Nevertheless, the actual and potential radical changes required in the nuclear relationship between the United States and its nuclear allies in Europe have not yet been substantively addressed in the ongoing redefinition of US and Alliance strategy. The future role of the United States in nuclear deterrence for the Alliance remains moot. It is difficult to imagine an acute crisis in Europe in the years ahead that would evoke the threatened or actual use of nuclear weapons by Russia or the United States.

Except in the area of those nuclear arms control agreements that have already been negotiated by the United States and the former Soviet Union and its nuclear successor states, European policy makers have hardly addressed any potential strategic military threats that might result as a consequence of the transition from the bipolar system of East–West relations in Europe. The central and almost exclusive role of the United States in the negotiation of nuclear arms control, and the perpetuation of East–West deterrence, are assumed. Policy preoccupation has been focused on the environmental threats posed by the conditions of nuclear technology in the civilian sector of the former Soviet Union and Eastern Europe.

Nevertheless, nuclear deterrence among the protagonist nuclear powers, the United States, Russia, Britain, France – and perhaps China – seems to be becoming nuclear reassurance. If this is actually true, it should be possible to come to grips cooperatively with the problem of unintentional nuclear fire.

Notes

1   Kurt Gottfried and Bruce Blair (eds), *Crisis Stability and Nuclear War*, New York: Oxford University Press, 1988, chs. 10 and 12.
2   US Government, 'Modernization of Nuclear Forces', *Foreign Broadcast Intelligence Service [FBIS] SOV*, 92-221, 16 November 1992, p.3; US Senate, Committee on Foreign Relations, Subcommittee on European Affairs, 'Nuclear Smuggling, and the Fissile-Material Problem in Russia and the CIS', Washington, DC: GPO, 104th Congress, Hearings on Loose Nukes, 22 August 1995, p.35.

3   Scott D. Sagan and Kenneth N. Waltz, *The Spread of Nuclear Weapons: A Debate*, New York: W.W. Norton, 1995, p.118.
4   Scott Sagan, *The Limits of Safety: Organization, Accidents and Nuclear Weapons*, Princeton, NJ: Princeton University Press, 1993, pp.13 ff. For organizational politics and change in the Soviet Union/Russia, see Stuart J. Kaufman, 'Organizational Politics and Change in Soviet Military Policy', *World Politics*, **46**, (3), April 1994, pp.355–82.
5   J. Muller and General James Hartinger, 'On Accidental Nuclear War', in Herbert M. Levine and David Carlton eds, *The Nuclear Arms Race Debated*, New York: McGraw-Hill, 1986, pp.40–42.
6   Ibid., and *FBIS-SOV*, 17 April 1995, p.47.
7   Muller and Hartinger, 'On Accidental Nuclear War', pp.42–3.
8   Sagan and Waltz, *The Spread of Nuclear Weapons*, p.119; Paul Bracken, *Command and Control of Nuclear Forces*, New Haven, CT: Yale University Press, 1983.
9   'Yeltsin Cited on First Use of Attaché Case', *Izvestiya*, 27 January 1995, *FBIS-SOV-95-018*, p.18. For the state of the Russian Air Force, see Benjamin S. Lambeth, 'Hard Times for the Russian Air Force', *Air Force Magazine*, July 1995.
10   'What's News – World-Wide', *Wall Street Journal*, 3 June 1996, p.1.
11   General Lucien Poirier, 'La crise des fondaments', *La Stratégie Française, Revue Stratégique*, No. 53 1/1992, pp.43–54; *Livre Blanc Sur La Défense*, Paris: 1994, pp.101–102, 117–20.
12   'President Bush's Initiatives on Nuclear Arms: Documentation', *NATO Review*, **39**, (5), October 1991.
13   See David S. Yost, *France's Deterrent Posture and Security in Europe*, London: International Institute for Strategic Studies, Adelphi Paper No. 194, Winter 1984/1985.
14   An analysis of the Swedish national debate on the decision not to go nuclear is in Jerome Garris, '*Sweden's Decision on a Nuclear Option*', Political Science PhD Dissertation, University of California at Los Angeles, 1974.
15   Interview with Russian Federation Defence Minister General Grachev, in *Rossiyskaya Gazeta*, Moscow, 21 October 1992, *FBIS-SOV-92-204*, p.2.
16   Art Pine, 'U.S. and Russian Subs Collide Under the Ice in Barents Sea', *Los Angeles Times*, 23 March 1993, p.A9.
17   Carey Goldberg, 'Russians Call Sub Crash a Near-disaster', *Los Angeles Times*, 2 April 1993, p.A12.
18   Michael Parks, 'Russia Urges End of Nuclear Arms Alerts', *Los Angeles Times*, 13 February 1992, pp.A10,11.
19   D. Paul, M. Intriligator and P. Smoker (eds), *Accidental Nuclear War*, Toronto: Stevens and Co., 1990; Thomas Coakley (ed.), *C³I: Issues of Command and Control*, Washington, DC: National Defense University, 1991, pp.3–104; C.E. Zoppo, 'Accidental Nuclear War and the Demise of the Soviet Union', unpublished manuscript, April 1992.
20   Joshua Handler, 'Submarine Safety – The Soviet/Russian Record', *Jane's Intelligence Review*, July 1992, pp.328–32; 'Declassified Documents Describe 1960 ICBM Accident', Moscow: ITAR-TASS, 24 October 1995; *FBIS-SOV-95-206*, p.34; 'Details of Nuclear Bomber Crash 20 Years Ago', Moscow: ITAR-TASS, 18 September 1992; *FBIS-SOV-92-182*, p.16.
21   Carol J. Williams, 'Yeltsin Cedes Some Power Before His Bypass Surgery', *Los Angeles Times*, 11 September 1996; pp.A10,11.
22   U.S. Senate, 'Testimony of Bruce Blair', Washington, DC: GPO; Hearings, 22 August 1995, p.34; 'Strategic Missile Forces Program Viewed', *FBIS-SOV*, 3 April 1995, p.22.
23   Bent Natvig, 'Accidental Nuclear War Considered from the Area of Reliability of Large Technological Systems', in Estonian Academy of Sciences, *Implications of the*

Dissolution of the Soviet Union for Accidental/Inadvertent Use of Weapons of Mass Destruction, Tallinn: Estonian Academy of Sciences, 1992, pp.134–5.

24   Ibid.
25   Michael Parks and Viktor K. Grebenshikov, 'Further Splintering of Soviet Army Seen', *Los Angeles Times*, 19 February 1992, p.A4; Carey Goldberg, 'Yeltsin Takes Direct Control of Russian Military', Los Angeles Times, 17 March 1992, pp.A6,7.
26   *FBIS-SOV*, 9 February 1995, pp.14–17; Ioury E. Federov, 'Russia's Nuclear Policy after the USSR', Chapter 12 of the present volume.
27   Bruce Blair and Henry Kendall, 'Accidental Nuclear War', *Scientific American*, **263**, (6), December 1990; John R. Harvey and Stefan Michalowski, 'Nuclear Weapons Safety: The Case of Trident', *Science and Global Security*, 4, (3), 1994, pp.261–338.
28   *FBIS-SOV*, 9 February 1995, pp.14–16.
29   'Testimony of Bruce Blair', pp.34–5.
30   An in-depth analysis of this problem is in Dietrich Schroeer, 'The Future of High Technology in Military Affairs', Chapter 1 of the present volume.
31   *FBIS-SOV*, 29 January 1992, p.2.
32   Ioury E. Federov, 'Russia's Nuclear Policy after the USSR', Chapter 12 of the present volume.
33   A technical discussion of ballistic missile guidance systems is David G. Hoag, 'Ballistic missile guidance', in B.T. Feld, T. Greenwood, G.W. Rathjens and S. Weinberg (eds), *Impact of New Technologies on the Arms Race*, Cambridge, MA: MIT Press, 1971, pp.19–106.
34   For a very informative discussion of verification technology and some projection of developments in this field, see Bruce Blair and Garry Brewer, *Verifying SALT Agreements*, ACIS Working Paper No. 19, Los Angeles, CA: Center for International and Strategic Affairs, University of California at Los Angeles, January 1980; also a review article on the literature of verification is Seong Cheon and Niall Fraser, 'Arms Control Verification: an Introduction and Literature Survey', *Arms Control Today*, **9**, (1), May 1988, pp.38–50.
35   U.S. House of Representatives, Committee on Armed Services, 'Missile Defenses', Washington, DC: GPO, 18 February 1992; also U.S. Department of Defense, 'New Strategic Defense Initiative Program Focus: Global Protection Against Limited Strikes [GPALS]', Washington, DC: Office of the Assistant Secretary of Defense for Public Affairs, 30 January 1991; Andrei Kokoshin *et al.*, 'Questions of Collaboration between Russia and the USA in the Area of Strategic Defenses', Moscow: Center of Scientific Research of the Committee of Scientists for Global Security, February 1992; A. Kokoshin and Y. Velikhov, 'Space Shield: Made in Russia and U.S.A.', *Moscow News*, 22 March 1992, *FBIS-SOV* of March 1992.

6 Nuclear Disarmament: The View from Russia

Anatoli S. Diakov

Introduction

The last decade of the 20th century has been characterized by tremendous changes in international relations, most importantly by the sharp reduction of nuclear weapons of the two major nuclear weapon states, Russia and the United States. But this positive and long-awaited process in Russia, in which all of its political and economic structures are in transition, is being carried out with certain difficulties. In order to ensure a positive outcome for the security of the world, the process of nuclear weapons reduction just started must be conducted in such a way that it will not compromise the efforts already undertaken by the two countries in that area. At the same time it should create conditions for further progress.

It is unrealistic to expect that nuclear weapons could be completely eliminated in the near future, therefore nuclear deterrence will continue to be a key element of security for all nuclear weapon states. At the same time, the continuation of the process of nuclear weapon reductions, and the realization of the declared strategic partnership between Russia and the United States, require revision of the mutual nuclear deterrence doctrine left over from the Cold War. A general task of the Russian–US relationships for the next several years should be a transition from 'mutual assured destruction' to 'mutual assured safety'. One condition necessary for solving this task is strengthened support of strategic stability. To achieve mutual assured safety, it is not only necessary to remove the opportunity for both sides to work towards superiority, but also to remove the motivation to achieve such superiority. That in turn will require a further reduction of nuclear weapons of both states, the transformation of their military–political doctrines and the introduction into their mutual relations of measures of trust and predictability of behaviour. It is clear that this will be no simple task. This is particularly true when we take into account the fact that the realization of agreements that have already been reached on nuclear weapons reduction has raised several problems which could prevent further progress unless properly resolved.

Progress in Nuclear Weapons Reductions

The nuclear arms build-up started in the 1940s and reached its maximum in the middle of the 1980s. At that point the two superpowers between them had accumulated over 60 000 nuclear warheads. The share of the former Soviet Union (FSU) amounted to about half of the total: 6612 nuclear warheads were deployed on 1398 ICBMs; 2804 nuclear warheads were deployed on 940 SLBMs carried by 62 nuclear-powered submarines; and 162 heavy bombers were equipped with 855 warheads. The total number of deployed strategic nuclear warheads thus reached a maximum of 10 271.

The total number of the tactical nuclear warheads in the FSU reached a maximum of about 17 000, which included about 5000 ground-based battle-field warheads (artillery shells, battlefield missiles, mines), about 2000 short- and intermediate-range ballistic missiles, about 2500 anti-aircraft missiles, about 4000 air-delivered bombs and tactical missiles, and about 3600 sea-based tactical warheads.

In May of 1989, the President of the Soviet Union informed the US Secretary of State Baker that the FSU had made a unilateral decision to withdraw 500 tactical nuclear warheads from the territory of its allies. When asked what kind of warheads would be withdrawn, the response was that they included 166 tactical air-launched bombs, 50 artillery shells and 284 warheads for tactical missiles. This may have been the first time that such information was revealed by the Soviet Union. During the period from 1989 to 1991, all tactical nuclear weapons were removed from the territory of states who had been members of the Warsaw Treaty Pact. The last train loaded with tactical warheads left the German Democratic Republic during the summer of 1991. During the same period, all nuclear tactical weapons were removed to the Russian territory from former Soviet republics such as the Baltic republics, Central Asia and Transcaucasus. By the end of 1991, tactical nuclear weapons remained only in the Ukraine and Belarus, and by May of 1992 these also had been transferred to Russia. All these measures were undertaken unilaterally by the Soviet Union.

At that time both Moscow and Washington realized that the loss of control of such huge nuclear arsenals represented a greater threat than the potential use of those weapons against each other. Bypassing long negotiations, unilateral initiatives on tactical nuclear weapons were undertaken by

Presidents Gorbachev and Bush. They decided to remove from the front lines all nuclear warheads for ground-based tactical missiles, artillery shells and land mines, air-launched tactical bombs and sea-based nuclear weapons, and to place these warheads in central storage. It was announced that all FSU nuclear warheads for various tactical weapons would be eliminated by the end of the 20th century. This was to include warheads for ground-based tactical missiles, artillery shells, mines, half of the tactical bomb inventory of the air force, half of the nuclear anti-aircraft missiles and one-third of sea-based weapons.

After the disintegration of the Soviet Union, Russia as the successor state received most of the nuclear weapons and practically all of the huge nuclear weapon production complex. Of course, it also received all of the problems related to their existence. Strategic nuclear weapons of the FSU had also been deployed in three other former Soviet republics, Belarus, Kazahkstan and Ukraine. These accepted the obligation to accede in the shortest possible time to the Nonproliferation Treaty as non-nuclear weapon states. In accordance with the Lisbon Protocol of 23 May 1992, they obligated themselves to eliminate all nuclear weapons located on their territories. The withdrawal of these strategic nuclear weapons from Belarus, Kazakhstan and Ukraine to Russia was started some time later and was completed by June 1996.

The implementation of the START-I and the START-II Treaties, Russia's unilateral reductions of tactical nuclear weapons and the decision of Belarus, Kazakhstan and Ukraine to become non-nuclear weapon states, will result in the elimination of 75 per cent of all FSU strategic nuclear warheads and more than half of all FSU tactical warheads. As has been stated by Russian officials, the process of elimination of nuclear warheads is going much faster than had been programmed. More than 3500 tactical and strategic nuclear warheads have been withdrawn from the Ukraine, and dismantling has been completed in Russia of about 2000 warheads for short- and intermediate-range missiles, and about 4500 warheads for anti-aircraft missiles, tactical bombs and ground- and sea-based tactical weapons.

Problems

Of course, the task of eliminating huge numbers of nuclear warheads in a limited period of time has generated a complex set of problems. These problems are related to non-proliferation policy, maintaining the momentum of nuclear reductions and making this elimination process irreversible. In general, these problems fall into three categories, but are all closely related and mutually reinforcing. Some of these problems have been solved relatively quickly, but others will require more time.

Warheads and Weapon Fissile Material Protection and Safety

It soon became evident that the safe transportation, with no losses, of thousands of nuclear warheads in a short period to the central storage facilities demanded a well-functioning organization, much technical equipment and large financial expenditures. During 1995–6, $200 million were spent by Russia to arrange the transportation of nuclear warheads. It is true that this transportation problem facing Russia was quickly realized by the world community and that essential help was provided by the United States, the United Kingdom and Germany to help solve it. Specially designed supercontainers and vehicles for safe and well-protected transportation of nuclear weapons were supplied by the United Kingdom. Special equipment for emergency response teams was delivered by the United States. This was intended to respond to any emergency which might occur during the transportation and handling of dismantled nuclear weapons and weapons-grade materials. It included armoured blankets made of Kevlar to protect containers with dismantled nuclear weapon components. Germany supplied heavy-duty manipulators for remote handling of high-level and toxic radioactive materials as well as of nuclear warheads. Thanks to this assistance, all transportation processes were accomplished without incidents or loss of nuclear warheads.

Other problems are created by the weapons-grade materials which will become 'surplus' as a result of nuclear arms reductions. It is necessary to store this surplus in a safe and secure manner to foil any attempts to steal it. This task should be carried out as soon as possible since, if stolen, the material could be used to make a nuclear weapon that could threaten any country in the world. In this context, the construction of a storage facility for the fissile material released in the elimination of nuclear warheads was begun by Russia at the Mayk site with assistance from the United States. The capacity of this storage facility is 50 thousand containers and it will accommodate about 40 per cent of the Russian weapons-grade plutonium. This facility will satisfy all modern international requirements and Russia is planning to place it under IAEA safeguards. Also under way in Russia is the development and implementation of the national nuclear material protection, safety and accounting system (MPS&A). Close collaboration with Western countries has been set up to establish this system. For example, a so-called joint Russian-US 'lab-to-lab' programme has been launched. In this programme nuclear material security experts from US nuclear laboratories have started to collaborate with their Russian counterparts on introducing into Russia modern Western techniques and equipment for detection of any attempts to steal nuclear materials.

One additional problem requires prompt action. This is the halting of the production of weapons-grade plutonium. Three plutonium-production reactors continue to operate in Russia. While these reactors are operating principally to supply heat to the cities of Tomsk and Gzeleznogorsk (the former Krasnoyarsk-26), they continue to produce weapons-grade plutonium at the rate of about 1.5 tonnes a year. The Russian government committed itself as of 1 October 1994 to using none of this new plutonium in weapons. It has also committed itself to shut down all these reactors by the year 2000, even though, because of financial problems, it is clearly unrealistic to expect that replacement power sources can be put into operation by that date. Currently, the most promising option for quickly halting the production of this weapons-grade plutonium is to redesign the reactor cores to produce only non-weapons-grade plutonium. If this option were realized, the reactors could continue to operate without producing such dangerous plutonium. Russian and US nuclear reactors experts are conducting joint work to resolve this issue.

Transparency and Irreversibility

A second group of problems is related to the transparency and irreversibility of the nuclear weapons reduction process. During the Moscow Summit of January 1994, Presidents Yeltsin and Clinton agreed to establish a working group to consider steps to ensure the transparency and irreversibility of the ongoing nuclear weapons reduction process. These steps are to include monitoring by the IAEA of parts of the surplus fissile material removed from nuclear weapons. In March 1995, the Secretary of the US Department of Energy and the Russian Minister of Atomic Energy agreed to host reciprocal inspections to confirm the stockpiles of plutonium and highly-enriched uranium that have been removed from nuclear weapons. Moreover, during the summit of September 1994, the US and Russian presidents agreed to exchange detailed information about stockpiles of nuclear warheads, stocks of fissile materials, and safety and security measures. But, in spite of many consultations and negotiations within the working group, there has so far been no significant progress on these issues.

It had been thought during these summit meetings that four agreements could be achieved during the first stage of cooperation:

1   an agreement concerning the shutdown of the three remaining Russian plutonium-production reactors and a halt in the further production of weapons-grade plutonium;
2   an agreement on reciprocal exchanges of detailed information on aggregate stockpiles of nuclear warheads and stocks of nuclear materials;
3   an agreement on the monitoring of facilities containing weapons-grade materials removed from weapons and declared as 'surplus';

4   an agreement for cooperation which would allow the exchange of classified and sensitive information about fissile materials.

At this moment only the first agreement, to shut down the three Russian
plutonium-production reactors, has been signed by both sides, and it has not
yet come into force. Because the two sides have different interpretations of
the agreement for cooperation, progress on other agreements has been considerably delayed. The United States wanted to achieve a comprehensive
agreement which would cover a very broad list of problems related to
nuclear weapons reductions. The Russian side insisted that the cooperation
should be related only to data exchanges, the shutdown of the production
reactors and the monitoring of storage facilities.

Finally, in October 1995, the two sides reached a mutual understanding
within the working group based on the joint presidents' statement of 10 May
1995. At that point, a Russian draft of an agreement for cooperation was
presented to the US negotiators. However, changes in high Russian governmental circles delayed further progress on this agreement. According to a
private communication with an official within the Russian Foreign Ministry,
the Prime Minister Victor Chernomyrdin refused to make a decision about
this draft agreement and passed it on to the president. The president in turn
took no action, with the justification that it was not necessary to hurry with
this issue. There are several possible reasons for this non-decision. These
may include the fact that NATO decided to bomb the Bosnian Serbs while
ignoring the Russian attempts to stop the bombardments, the enlargement of
the NATO membership, the debate within the United States about reinter-
preting the ABM Treaty and approaching elections in Russia. Unfortunately,
there has been no further progress on this agreement since October 1995.

The disposition of the huge quantities of weapons-grade nuclear materials removed from eliminated warheads presents other significant tasks requiring combined political, scientific, technological and economic efforts.
The ongoing dismantling in Russia and the United States of the thousands
of nuclear weapons retired under START treaties and unilateral reductions
will result in over 100 tonnes of excess weapons-grade plutonium and 700
tonnes or more of excess highly-enriched uranium. The existence of these
materials in weapons-usable form prevents making the nuclear weapon
reduction process irreversible, and increases the risk of nuclear proliferа-
tion. Therefore the overriding objective of Russian and US nuclear dismantling initiatives is to dispose of excess nuclear fissile material in such way
that it cannot be reformed into nuclear weapons in the country of origin or
stolen by terrorist groups.

The most obvious disposal method for weapons-grade uranium is to
blend it with natural uranium to produce fuel for nuclear power reactors.

Such disposition of HEU is technically straightforward and potentially profitable as long as the supplies do not greatly exceed the demand. In February 1993, governmental Russian–US agreements were signed, according to which 500 tonnes of Russian uranium recovered from dismantled warheads will be mixed with low-enrichment uranium and sold to the United States as the raw material for fabricating reactor fuel. This agreement is being implemented. In 1995, Russia delivered to the United States low-enrichment uranium (LEU) derived from 6.1 tonnes of HEU, and in 1996 will deliver more LEU derived from 12 tonnes of HEU. In each case the HEU was obtained from dismantled nuclear weapons.

The disposition of plutonium from dismantled nuclear weapons is more complex. It is impossible to eliminate its potential use in reconstituted weapons quality by simple dilutions or by other chemical processes. Although civilian plutonium is currently recycled for use in civilian nuclear power reactors in Europe, neither the United States nor Russia has the technological experience and appropriate facilities to start plutonium disposal on a larger scale in the near future. The development and deployment of technologies for such large-scale plutonium disposal involve an expenditure of several billion dollars and will require a substantial period of time to implement (25–40 years).

Therefore both countries will need to store their weapons-grade plutonium for a long period, and it is urgent and essential that an agreement be reached which ensures that fissile materials, declared to be excess to military needs, will never be reused in weapons. Placing the material under international safeguards could provide the international community with confidence that the elimination of this material for use in nuclear weapons is irreversible.

Problems Faced by the START-II Treaty

In spite of significant progress in the reduction of nuclear weapons, and even after the obligations of the START-II Treaty have been satisfied, Russia and the United States will each continue to possess several thousand strategic and tactical nuclear warheads. It is hoped that, in the long run, they will cut their nuclear arsenals even further. Meanwhile, it is clear that, not only are any further nuclear arms reductions beyond START II very uncertain, but progress on those agreements that have already been reached will require special efforts. The START-II Treaty has not yet been approved by the Russian Parliament and there are numerous criticisms of this treaty.

The arguments of Russian opponents of the START-II Treaty can be summarized in three major points: (1) the asymmetry of the Treaty; (2) a possible US break-out from the ABM Treaty; and (3) the potential expansion of the North Atlantic Treaty Organization (NATO). The asymmetry arguments run as follows. In accordance with the START-II Treaty, Russia should implement the prescribed reductions by eliminating the core of its strategic forces, namely intercontinental ballistic missiles (ICBMs) with multiple independently targeted reentry vehicles (MIRVs). Specifically, Russia should eliminate 154 silo-based SS-18 ICBMs, each with 10 warheads; 50 silo-based SS-19 ICBMs, each with six warheads; and 46 silo-based or mobile SS-24 ICBMs, each with 10 warheads. The Treaty does permit conversion of a further 105 SS-19s by downloading them to one warhead each, and permits the conversion of 90 SS-18 silos. So, under START II, the core component of the Russian nuclear triad should be reduced from 6612 to 400 warheads. This is not only in complete contradiction to the strategic concepts and the military operation plans adopted in Russia, but also contradicts the Russian understanding of strategic stability and parity. To reach the limits of 3000–3500 warheads imposed by START II, and to maintain the structure of her strategic forces, Russia would need to retain her 300 single-warhead SS-25 ICBMs and deploy about 1000 additional single-warhead ICBMs, which are extremely expensive to produce and deploy.

At the same time, the United States can implement its START-II reductions without changing the structure of its strategic forces, and with minimal economic costs. Under the Treaty, the United States would reduce all three components of its strategic triad in equal proportions. At the same time, the Treaty gives the United States a superiority in break-out capabilities. The core of the US strategic nuclear triad are the submarine-launched ballistic missiles (SLBMs). The level of 1700–1750 SLBM warheads imposed by START II could be reached simply by downloading three warheads from each missile and transferring them to a central storage facility, and all these removed warheads could be moved back to the missiles without a major effort. The same situation holds for the 500 *Minuteman*-III intercontinental ballistic missiles. In accordance with the Treaty, each of these missiles will be downloaded to one warhead and the two other warheads will be placed in storage. As for the 50 10-warhead MX (*Peacekeeper*) ICBMs, only the first stage of these missiles is to be eliminated. But these ICBMs could also be restored, taking into account that the second and third stages of the MX will not be destroyed, and that the silos for the *Minuteman*-II, *Minuteman*-III and MX are all the same.

The ABM problem runs as follows. The Anti-Ballistic Missile Treaty of 1972 is one of the 'cornerstones' of the nuclear weapons reduction process. That is why the US decision to move ahead with the 'development for deployment' of a national missile defence by 2003 has stimulated broad discussions among Russian military experts, particularly related to the START-II Treaty ratification. The House Senate conference bill passed in

December 1995 by the US Congress was seen in Russia as aiming towards the deployment in the long run of a national missile defence, and as a threat to the ABM Treaty. The concern was expressed that a nationwide ABM system combined with lower levels of strategic offensive arms would give the United States a substantial strategic advantage over Russia and destabilize strategic relations. The recent move by Senator Jesse Helms, in introducing legislation calling for the United States to withdraw from the ABM Treaty, made these concerns much deeper and the situation on ratification much worse.

Of course, despite these arguments by Russian opponents of the Treaty, there are also some reasons for Russia to ratify it. But even if the START-II Treaty is ratified by the Russian Duma, the reaction to the US move towards a nationwide missile defence will probably be a unilateral statement that Russia will consider a break-out from the ABM Treaty as a threat to its national interests and as providing a reason to withdraw from the START-II Treaty. If it did so, this would result in the breakdown of the whole system of treaties which currently regulates the Russian–US strategic relationship, and would make questionable further reductions in nuclear weapons.

The problem of NATO expansion runs as follows. There is no direct link between ratification of the START-II Treaty and NATO enlargement, but some individuals in foreign and defence policy circles in Moscow consider the NATO enlargement a potential threat to Russian security. The superiority in conventional weapons of NATO over Russia, combined with the resulting possible move of some NATO airbases to the borders of Russia, and the development in Eastern countries of high-accuracy weapons, are considered by them as a threat to the strategic balance. Even if these arguments are sometimes mostly emotional, they could, if used at a critical moment, poison the atmosphere in which the START-II Treaty is being considered.

In the context of these three points, a framework agreement between Russia and the United States to continue the process of reduction of their strategic nuclear forces could be essential to improve the prospects for Russian ratification of the START-II Treaty. If Russia is assured that, shortly after the year 2003, both sides would reduce to much lower strategic levels, to something like 2000 warheads, then Russia would not be so concerned that, by the year 2003, instead of 3000 warheads, it might have much smaller numbers, because it would know that within a short period both sides would reduce stocks to those same much smaller numbers. However, in spite of the US administration's interest in warhead elimination, the current official US position is based on an unwillingness to discuss in any detail further steps on nuclear weapons reduction until after the START-II Treaty enters into force.

Conclusion

Early in the 1990s, Russia (the former Soviet Union) and the United States began a process of changing their strategic relationships based on a mutual reduction of their nuclear offensive forces. Both countries will be unable to continue this process unless both of them believe themselves secure. A key component of that security is a parity in strategic nuclear forces. This is especially true for the current stage of disarmament because the measures to ensure the transparency and irreversibility of the recently started nuclear reduction process have not yet been implemented.

However, during the past several years, through the collaboration of the Russian Federation with the United States and other Western countries, a solid base has been created for implementation of these disarmament measures. Working jointly on the issues of safe transportation of nuclear warheads, safe storage of fissile materials removed from weapons and disposition of the excess fissile materials, both sides have demonstrated an ability to find answers to problems that may arise. Also, during that period, Russia and the United States have constructed an agenda to introduce first steps in transparency and irreversibility. All this gives grounds to be optimistic. Of course, the progress on this agenda is slowed down by elections in both countries, so at present the first task is to preserve this agenda as a base for future progress.

7 Implications of the Comprehensive Nuclear Test Ban for Nuclear Modernization and Proliferation

Eric Arnett

Introduction

This chapter examines the continuing relevance of the Comprehensive Nuclear Test Ban (CTB) that has been negotiated at the Conference on Disarmament in Geneva. After more than three decades of on-again, off-again negotiations, the CTB has finally been accepted by the international community.[1] It has been approved by a 156 to three vote in the United Nations.[2] Only India, Bhutan and Libya voted against the Treaty, which is now open for ratification by individual nations. Unfortunately, in order to go into force, it must be accepted by all six acknowledged nuclear states, and India has so far refused to accept it. However, this long-awaited accomplishment is already falling victim to rising expectations and attendant cynicism occasioned by the end of the Cold War: critics claim the CTB will no longer meaningfully constrain nuclear weapon programmes in the nuclear weapon and threshold states because knowledge about nuclear weapons is widespread and some relevant technologies are relatively simple, while states of proliferation concern could produce and use a nuclear weapon without testing it, as the United States did at Hiroshima.

The chapter describes the effects the CTB will have on nuclear programmes and decision making in the nuclear weapon states, the threshold states and non-nuclear weapon states of proliferation concern.[3] It concludes that, while some states will indeed maintain their nuclear weapon arsenals and options under the CTB and one or two may even undertake some modernization, the CTB will foreclose a number of technologies to all three groups of states and will probably be signed and ratified by all of them with few exceptions. Further, the CTB will help create a norm against nuclear modernization and strengthen the norm against nuclear proliferation in a way that reinforces other efforts to restrict nuclear activities. The former is particularly important, because modernization in the nuclear weapon states could support new nuclear doctrines based on the concept of regional nuclear deterrence or war fighting. Foregoing these programmes and doctrinal shifts is desirable both in itself and because it decreases the incentives for states fearful of Western intervention to seek a nuclear deterrent, whether or not they sign the CTB themselves.

The CTB does ban all nuclear weapon tests and other nuclear explosions – including 'peaceful nuclear explosions' – without thresholds or exceptions, but it does not ban preparations to test, first use of nuclear weapons in war, computer simulations or new types of nuclear weapons. Compliance with the Treaty will be verified by national, international and private means, including a treaty-mandated international system of seismic, atmospheric, hydroacoustic and perhaps infrasound monitoring stations. Detection and identification of tests below about one kiloton will require that human intelligence be used in some cases.[4] In cases of suspected non-compliance, any state party will be permitted to request an inspection that should begin promptly. The Treaty is expected to cost less than $100 million annually, to be paid by a modified UN scale of assessments roughly proportional to gross national product.

Likely Effects of the CTB on Modernization

Some critics who believe the Comprehensive Test Ban does not do enough for the cause of nuclear disarmament have stood a traditional hawks' argument on its head. Where the hawks used to claim that the CTB would not contribute to nuclear non-proliferation because states did not consider the CTB when deciding whether or not to develop nuclear weapons or to keep a nuclear option, now these critic doves say that the nuclear weapons states want the CTB because they no longer need to test.

In fact, the CTB will significantly inhibit undesirable modernization projects, as summarized in Table 7.1 and detailed below, as well as giving opponents of modernization projects that do not rely on testing a political tool to use against them. This section summarizes what is known about modernization plans and capabilities in the openly nuclear states, describes

Table 7.1   Effects of the comprehensive test ban on existing and possible nuclear weapon programmes

Country	Weapon	Status	Direct effect of CTB
United States	third-generation warhead	unlikely	prevents development
	low-yield warhead	unlikely	prevents weaponization
	D-5 follow-on	expected	must use existing warhead
Russia	third-generation warhead	unlikely	prevents development
	low-yield warhead	unlikely	prevents development and weaponization
	SS-NX-28 SLBM follow-on	expected	must use existing warhead
	SS-X-27 ICBM variant	planned	must use existing warhead
	S-400 air defence missile	planned	must use existing or non-nuclear warhead
United Kingdom	low-yield warhead	unlikely	prevents development without US advice
France	low/variable-yield warhead	unlikely	prevents development
	ASMP-A missile follow-on	expected	must use existing warhead
	M 51 SLBM	expected	must use existing warhead
	M 45 SLBM	planned	warhead certified before CTB
China	more accurate RV, MIRV	suspected	must use existing warhead
	DF-31, DF-41 and JL-2	planned	warhead certified before CTB
Israel	cruise missile	unlikely	must use existing warhead
India	thermonuclear warhead	suspected	prevents development
	missile warhead	unlikely	prevents certification
Pakistan	missile warhead	unlikely	prevents certification
Other states	more advanced warheads	unlikely	prevents development
	first-generation warhead	suspected	prevents certification

the effects of the CTB on these plans and consequent effects on doctrine and elucidates the ability of each state to ensure that it enjoys the benefits of the CTB in exchange for its costs. For this reason, each state's ability to detect and respond to non-compliance promptly is assessed.

China

China is developing three new strategic nuclear missiles, the *Dongfeng* (East Wind) DF-31 and DF-41 ICBMs and the *Julang* (Great Wave) JL-2 SLBM. All three missiles are expected to use the same 200- to 300-kiloton warhead.[5] The new systems will combine higher throw-weight with reduced vulnerability. The greater throw-weight of the new missiles would allow them to be MIRVed if China can develop that technology, which has thus far proved to be beyond its capabilities. At present, China deploys seven ICBMs, 10 to 20 'long-range' (4750km) land-based missiles and 12 SLBMs in its strategic nuclear force, and an unknown number of tactical nuclear weapons.[6]

China is thought to be developing more accurate re-entry vehicles and MIRVs. If these are developed under the CTB, they will have to use the DF-31 warhead, another existing warhead, or they will have to be deployed untested. More accurate warheads would make it possible for China to move away from what is thought to be its current doctrine of massive retaliation against cities to more carefully aimed strikes on other targets, potentially fuelling formal requirements for more weapons under different political conditions. The CTB would act as a brake on this trend if it prevented testing and certification of a new warhead yielding under 100 kilotons. The People's Liberation Army of China might create a requirement for MIRVs if strategic missile defences were deployed by a perceived adversary at a time when relations were deteriorating. The MIRVed missile (possibly the DF-41) would have to use an existing warhead if designed under the CTB.

China's ability to modernize is likely to be severely curtailed by the CTB. China has done fewer nuclear tests than any of the other nuclear weapon states, with the exception of Israel, and has already begun to disband its cadre of nuclear weapon designers after achieving the immediate goals set out in the initial years of the Deng era.[7] While China appears likely to continue its strategic modernization plans for at least another decade or two, further efforts will necessarily focus on delivery systems for existing warheads. The testing programme is more likely to be revived in response to the deployment of significant strategic defences in Russia or the United States than to counter another state's violation of the CTB. Covert Russian or US nuclear testing is likely to be detected[8] and, even in conditions of deteriorating relations, would not necessarily create a need for new Chinese testing unless it led to a change in China's nuclear doctrine in favour of war fighting, precisely the shift that the CTB is designed to inhibit.

France

France is in the midst of interrupted modernization. The warhead for the soon-to-be-deployed M 45 SLBM has just been certified. Another new SLBM, the M 51, is expected by 2010. The year 2010 is also the expected date for entry into service of a longer-range follow-on to the ASMP air-launched missile for the *Rafale* (Squall) multi-role aircraft. If, as has been speculated, the ASMP-A follow-on features a variable-yield warhead, it will require extensive testing.[9] France operates five nuclear-powered ballistic-missile submarines (SSBNs), each capable of carrying 16 six-warhead SLBMs, 87 land- and sea-based nuclear bombers and 18 land-based long-range missiles.[10] France also has 30 medium-range (480km) missiles in storage, which could be deployed should there be a reason.

France is also in the midst of a strategic debate that will determine whether it retains its traditional Gaullist all-or-nothing nuclear doctrine or revises it in favour of one encompassing regional war fighting.[11] At present, the military and nuclear establishments appear to favour continuing the traditional approach,[12] despite contrary signals from some politicians.[13] After the CTB Treaty enters into force, France will be constrained not to develop the war-fighting weapons, even if its policy is reversed. The possible closure of the Pacific test range at Mururoa would make such a reversal even less likely.

As in the case of China, a French decision to resume modernization and testing is more likely to stem from the sort of doctrinal change that the CTB is meant to inhibit than from another state's non-compliance. The decision to move towards a regional nuclear war-fighting posture from the traditional Gaullist doctrine would not necessarily stem from a potential adversary's nuclear programme, but might be stimulated by a political realignment in Paris. France's force posture has already been adjusted to account for Russia's limited ABM deployment around Moscow, although a broader ABM deployment might create an impetus for new systems, especially if relations with Russia were deteriorating. While France can be confident that non-compliance would be detected under the CTB Treaty, it is unlikely that French nuclear testing would be the appropriate response to any such violation, whether in Russia or elsewhere.

Russia

Russia is developing the SS-X-27 variant of the SS-25 ICBM and is thought to be developing a new SS-NX-28 SLBM, a follow-on to the SS-N-20 deployed on *Typhoon* SSBNs.[14] Russia's strategic forces numbered 8527 warheads on 1452 delivery systems at the beginning of 1995, but will be reduced to fewer than 3500 warheads under START II.[15] Little is known publicly about Russian tactical nuclear forces, but they are thought to number in the thousands, despite the destruction of approximately one-half of those withdrawn from Ukraine and one-third of those once deployed on warships and submarines.[16] Russia retains the option of redeploying tactical nuclear weapons aboard warships and recently revised its nuclear doctrine to allow first use of nuclear weapons under certain circumstances.[17] Russia probably continues to deploy at least part of the Soviet Union's force of nuclear-armed air defence and ABM missiles, and is developing a new air defence missile, the S-400, said to be similar in performance to the US Theater High Altitude Area Defense (THAAD) interceptor. Some S-400s may be nuclear armed.[18]

As in France, there are indications of Russian interest in the possible role of nuclear weapons in regional conflicts.[19] It is difficult to assess the effect of the CTB on Russia's ability to shift its doctrine in that direction, since the details of its tactical nuclear forces are not adequately known. It seems likely that the Soviet Union, like the United States, had already done some design and testing work on low- or very low-yield nuclear weapons. The USSR continued to deploy nuclear air defence and anti-ballistic missile systems after they were phased out in the West, for example. Russia would have inherited that Soviet technology and possibly operational systems. If so, they might nevertheless be seen as inappropriate for regional contingencies by the Russian armed services, just as US very low-yield designs developed during the Cold War are different from those advocated for future regional contingencies.[20] It is likely that Russia would have to develop new very low-yield weapons for regional roles, or at least repackage and recertify an existing design, if they were required by a new doctrine. This is exactly what the CTB is meant to prevent.

As in the case of France, a hypothetical decision to resume testing is more likely to stem from changes in doctrine than another state's violation of the CTB. Unlike China, Russia could respond to ABM deployments in conditions of deteriorating relations with existing weapons by simply reMIRVing its heavy missiles or producing more. No new warhead designs or testing would be needed.

United Kingdom

The United Kingdom has postponed any decision about nuclear modernization indefinitely by temporarily eliminating the military requirement for a follow-on to the WE-177 nuclear bomb, but it is probable that an air-launched missile will be developed early in the next century. The current British arsenal comprises about 100 gravity bombs and some 200 SLBM warheads. When the *Trident* procurement programme is completed, the SLBM force is likely to number 64 missiles, each with four to six warheads.[21] These missiles could be uploaded if Russia expanded its strategic missile defences and relations soured.[22] The United Kingdom's considerable experience with designing nuclear weapons without testing during the tripartite moratorium (observed by the UK, the USA and the USSR during November 1958 to September 1961) and a unilateral moratorium under the Labour government (during 1965 to 1974), gives it advantages under the CTB. Nevertheless, maintaining an experienced weapon design staff may be more difficult for Britain than for other countries,[23] and the option of resuming the test programme unilaterally is practically non-existent.[24]

As in France and Russia, there has been some interest expressed in the United Kingdom in shifting its doctrine towards regional war fighting.[25] Britain's inability to test without another state's complicity already limits its ability to develop new systems, so the discussion has focused more on regional uses of the existing air-delivered weapons or *Trident* missiles with a small number of warheads. All of these weapons have yields on the order of 100 kilotons,[26] reflecting the simplicity and single-mindedness of existing doctrine. The UK would not be able to develop very low-yield warheads without testing or US advice, so the CTB thereby constrains any new doctrine to use these high-yield weapons.

As with Russia, the United Kingdom would not need to test to respond to violations of the CTB, or an expansion of a potential adversary's missile defence system, given the emphasis on defeating Soviet defences that informed the design of the existing force. A hypothetical Russian expansion of strategic or tactical missile defence could be countered by increasing the number of warheads carried by each D-5 SLBM without additional testing.

United States

The United States has stopped designing new types of nuclear warheads and ICBMs, stopped nuclear weapon testing and stopped producing fissile material, although it has a large and increasing surplus. It has no official military requirements for new delivery systems, although there has been some discussion of a follow-on to the *Trident*-II programme, which encompasses the *Ohio*-class submarine and the D-5 missile, that would be designed with arms control limits in mind. *Trident*-II and the B-2 *Spirit* bomber modernization programmes use warheads that are already in the stockpile, and procurement will be completed not long after the CTB Treaty enters into force. In early 1995, US strategic forces numbered 7770 warheads on 1134 delivery systems, but will be reduced under START-II. Thenceforth, the United States will have six to 10 types of warhead in its arsenal of approximately 3500 deployed strategic weapons, and a few hundred tactical weapons, most of which will continue to be held in storage for possible crisis deployment. The United States retains the capability to deploy nuclear bombs to US and friendly air bases and nuclear land-attack cruise missiles aboard its submarines. The US Department of Energy will maintain the expertise to remanufacture existing warheads as they age and the ability to design and test new types should the United States no longer be bound by the Treaty.

US nuclear doctrine was reviewed by the Clinton administration in 1993 and 1994. The option of a unilateral no-first-use declaration was ruled out, and there is some interest in expanding the range of scenarios under which nuclear weapons could be used in regional contingencies. Many of these would not require new types of nuclear weapons, but some would: for example, very low-yield weapons to reduce the area subject to blast, fire and radiation effects.[27] For the remainder of the Clinton administration, it is unlikely that a military requirement for such very low-yield nuclear weapons will be issued. If a future president were persuaded by those who would like to see very low-yield nuclear weapons developed and deployed, the CTB would prevent her or him from doing so, unless the Congress acquiesced in a decision either to withdraw from or covertly to violate the Treaty.

US doctrinal thought continues to include scenarios in which nuclear weapons are seen as deterring or responding to non-nuclear threats, and 'predevelopment' programmes for very low-yield and third-generation nuclear weapons are promoted as appropriate for non-nuclear contingencies.[28] As in the case of France, the decision to create a formal military requirement for such weapons and to conduct attendant nuclear tests would more likely be the response to a change in doctrine than to a violation of the CTB Treaty. Hypothetical Chinese or Russian violations, which might signify a souring of relations and be the most difficult to detect given the area of the countries and their opacity to human intelligence, would not necessarily lead to new US nuclear weapon requirements or tests. Nuclear tests in, say, Iraq or North Korea, would be simpler to detect, likely leading to renewed efforts to contain the consequences for nuclear proliferation and the norm of not testing, rather than to retaliatory US tests.

Likely Effects of the CTB on the Threshold States

Three states occupy a region of political ambiguity most often referred to as 'the nuclear threshold': India, Israel and Pakistan. Although they inhabit very different places in this region, their concerns in the CTB negotiations were similar. First and foremost, they sought to preserve their carefully constructed postures of nuclear ambiguity. All three are long-time supporters of the CTB and are eager to get the good publicity sure to be associated with signing it after years of bad publicity stemming from their nuclear activities and refusal to sign the Nonproliferation Treaty (NPT). Since none of them is party to the NPT, none has had to accept any but the most rudimentary inspections of its nuclear facilities. None of these states has shown much interest in nuclear testing for at least 15 years and none is thought to be on the verge of important modernization. As a result, the CTB will have relatively little effect on their current plans beyond codifying and reinforcing the norm against testing. But India has refused to accept the final version of the CTB Treaty.[29]

India

India had produced enough plutonium for between 65 and 105 nuclear weapons by the end of 1995.[30] Although some facilities related to the nuclear electricity fuel cycle may have partial safeguards, those associated with the nuclear weapon programme have not been subject to inspection. India has conducted one test of a nuclear explosive device, has used the threat of additional tests as a political instrument during the Indira Gandhi administration,[31] and is thought to be able to deploy weapons at short notice. The Indian military has had little interest in the nuclear weapon programme and has not established a formal requirement for nuclear delivery or a strategic bombardment mission. If India were to deploy nuclear weapons in a crisis, it seems likely that they would take the form of gravity bombs to be delivered by the bomber force of the Indian Air Force, rather than other systems.[32] If India's confidence in the bombers' ability to reach their targets in Pakistan is eroded by improvements in the Pakistan Air Force's aerial combat and command and control capabilities, this perception could drive them towards a missile force, but at present the services have shown little interest in the *Prithvi* battlefield support missile and none in the *Agni* intermediate-range missile test bed.[33]

India is likely to try to maintain its nuclear infrastructure and its weapon option even if it ever signs the CTB Treaty. If the production of fissile material is terminated, it appears that India has already produced enough for a major arsenal. There is little reason for India to test, even if it decides to weaponize its capability, but a decision to move ahead with fusion weapons would require testing.[34] The CTB will reinforce the effect of India's observation of the current norm against testing and thereby foreclose the fusion bomb option. A clear national commitment against testing and development of new generations of nuclear weapons might lead to demoralization among Indian nuclear weapon designers. If combined with a decreasing willingness to fund nuclear research, this might lead to the collapse of the Indian nuclear option unless a commitment were made to a 'stockpile stewardship' programme similar to that of the United States.[35] The likelihood of such a collapse is difficult to judge, given the Indian commitment to nuclear power for generating electricity in the face of serious teething problems of that industry.

India sees itself surrounded by potentially hostile powers, but relations with all of them are improving, if not cordial. More importantly, there is little reason for India to fear that any of them could covertly test to India's disadvantage, whether the state of concern is China, Pakistan or the United States. Despite having relatively poor intelligence on the former two, India can be confident that they will be watched closely by Russia, the USA and several other states and private organizations in addition to the Treaty's implementation authority. The USA, which has never really been a military, much less nuclear, threat to India, will also be watched closely and is an easier subject for intelligence collection than China or Pakistan.

Israel

Israel had produced enough plutonium for between 55 and 95 nuclear weapons by the end of 1995.[36] Israel has allowed US personnel to make a small number of partial inspections at its Dimona facility, but has otherwise not allowed inspections. Israel has had access to French and US nuclear weapon design and test expertise, may have conducted one full-yield nuclear test, and is thought to deploy a force of boosted fission and fusion weapons for air and missile delivery.[37]

Although Israel has called for the states of the Middle East to conclude an agreement to banish nuclear weapons from the region, it is unlikely that it will give up its nuclear option in the near future. In the longer term, progress in the peace process might well bring about the conditions for such a zone free of nuclear weapons and perhaps other 'weapons of mass destruction', which is a high negotiating priority for other states of the region as well, having been endorsed by Egyptian, Iraqi and Palestinian negotiators in various fora. In the meantime, Israel will retain its large and advanced arsenal and the capability to modernize without additional testing. Given the sophistication of the current arsenal, other pressures not to test, and the age of the Dimona facility, it seems unlikely that Israel will have much reason to test, modernize or produce much more fissile material or many more nuclear weapons. Even the decision to deploy a hypothetical nuclear cruise missile would not require testing. The future of Israel's nuclear weapon designers is as difficult to discern as their past, but it is likely that a core of skilled professionals will be retained, regardless of Dimona's future. Perhaps an engineering approach to stockpile maintenance will be adopted.[38]

Although Israel's unilateral human intelligence collection capabilities in states of concern for its national security have deteriorated in recent decades, there is every reason for Israeli decision makers to be confident that the technical means available to it will minimize the risk of an adversary developing and testing a nuclear device for the foreseeable future. Not only Israeli technical means and those of the CTB implementing authority, but also Russian, US and other national technical means and private stations[39] monitor states of concern in the Middle East. Nor is there any reason to think that any data suggesting non-compliance in any of these states would be suppressed once acquired by the possessors of advanced national technical means (NTM). The two states of highest concern, Iran and Iraq, are under extraordinary scrutiny; Iran is seen by the United States as one of the two threats on which it bases its military planning and as a determined seeker of nuclear technology, and has invited the International Atomic Energy Agency (IAEA) to inspect any time, anywhere for evidence of a nuclear programme; while Iraq will remain under special obligations and safeguards, even if the current IAEA–UN special inspection regime is concluded.

Israel is very sensitive to treaty provisions regarding inspection of nuclear facilities. The magnitude of this concern has been such that Israel's observer delegation to the Conference on Disarmament at one point tabled an influential paper on consultation and clarification[40] suggesting that inspections should occur only rarely, only in the event of physical evidence similar to a nuclear test of the order of kilotons, and be essentially voluntary or invited. Israel resisted for a long time stronger proposals by others, even when they were promoted or supported by Russia, the other nuclear weapon state taking a conservative line on the issue.[41]

Pakistan

Pakistan had enough highly-enriched uranium (HEU) for six to 10 nuclear weapons when the programme was capped under President Benazir Bhutto. If Pakistan resumed production of HEU, it could produce enough for about three weapons each year.[42] Pakistan has resisted all attempts to open its nuclear facilities to inspection. Pakistan may have had access to Chinese nuclear weapon design and test expertise and is thought to be able to deploy nuclear weapons at short notice, although Bhutto has affirmed that Pakistan does not have an assembled explosive device. If Pakistan were to deploy nuclear weapons in a crisis, there is strong reason to believe that they would take the form of gravity bombs to be dropped by some of the Pakistan Air Force's 34 US-built F-16 *Falcon* aircraft, despite the importance of the F-16 in conventional air-to-air and air-to-ground roles. Pakistani military leaders have high confidence in this system, and are unlikely to develop similar confidence in other delivery systems for the foreseeable future.[43]

Pakistan will maintain its nuclear infrastructure and posture of deterrence and ambiguity under the Comprehensive Test Ban. It will retain an inherent ability to deploy first-generation weapons and to produce more fissile materials should its policy change. Pakistan has not felt a need to test in order to maintain its capabilities. In fact, it seems unlikely that Pakistan would test even without a CTB. Testing might facilitate overt weaponization, but if the regional situation required such a strong response, Pakistan would just as likely withdraw from the Treaty in any case. In short, the CTB reinforces many pressures keeping the lid on Pakistan's programme, but will not fundamentally alter its shape.

On the other hand, Pakistan has every reason to be confident that any attempt on India's part to violate the CTB would be detected and reported. India is a relatively open target for Pakistani human intelligence and is monitored closely by the United States. Additional monitoring measures negotiated for the CTB Treaty will only increase this confidence.

Likely Effects of the CBT on Proliferation

Western governments have emphasized the role of the CTB in preventing horizontal proliferation. Conservative critics say that this effect of the CTB is exaggerated. This section examines the effects of the CTB on the nuclear programmes and contexts for decision making in five states thought in the West to be of proliferation concern: Algeria, Iran, Iraq, Libya and North Korea.[44] It identifies areas in which the CTB contributes to non-proliferation beyond the traditional concerns with the NPT's Article VI, namely verification, certification of first-generation weapons and other political effects, significant as these are. Most importantly, it shows how the CTB reassures states that might seek a nuclear capability to deter Western intervention or nuclear use that the Western states will not be able to develop new types of weapons for regional war fighting doctrines. While some states may seek nuclear weapons for other reasons, a more decisive move towards regional war fighting in France, Russia, the United Kingdom or the United States would likely act as a goad to regional nuclear programmes. This holds particularly for Iran and North Korea, where interest in nuclear weapons apparently stems directly from concerns about intervention and deterrence. This effect is particularly important because it is obtained even if these states do not sign the treaty.

For each of the countries under consideration, this section summarizes what is known about their ability to produce fissile material and the likely means of delivering a first-generation nuclear weapon. It then considers their expressed or likely attitudes towards CTB provisions, particularly inspection, organization and verification, and specifically their confidence that their potential adversaries would comply. Interestingly, the direct effect of the CTB is found to be slight on the nuclear programmes of these states, primarily because they are already observing the norm of not testing and only North Korea is expected to have a nuclear weapon to test for the foreseeable future. In contrast, the indirect political effect of the CTB in reassuring these states could be quite significant, but might require further unilateral, bilateral or international measures to be fully effective.

Algeria

Algeria is building a reactor capable of producing enough plutonium for a nuclear weapon every three years.[45] Algeria has signed a safeguards agreement with the IAEA and is a state party to the Nonproliferation Treaty. There is no sign that a reprocessing facility is being built, and few observers believe that Algeria is of proliferation concern. Continuing political instability in the country leaves lingering doubts, nonetheless.[46]

Iran

Iran does not have the infrastructure to separate more than a few grams of fissile material.[47] Nevertheless, the Israeli and US governments consistently claim that statements of Iranian officials and patterns of imports and scientific recruitment indicate an intention to acquire nuclear weapons, a charge Iran consistently denies. Iran is not known to have done any experiments relevant to the design of nuclear weapons. Its arms industry, built up during the 1980s to offset the effects of the war with Iraq and the international arms embargo, produces only simple systems, but has created a cadre of engineers familiar with high explosives. Iran is a state party to the Nonproliferation Treaty, and all Iranian nuclear facilities are under IAEA safeguards. Iran has taken the additional step of inviting the IAEA to inspect any site on its territory at any time in order to counter the US charge that it is trying to produce nuclear weapons. The first such inspection in February 1992 revealed that a suspect site in the Elbruz mountains was in fact a retreat and study centre. The second, in November 1993, discovered that a suspected centrifuge facility near Isfahan was actually a refrigerator warehouse. However, Iran has not allowed the IAEA to implement the more rigorous 93+2 safeguards until they are universally accepted.[48]

Iran's air force is inferior to those of all its potential enemies, having suffered attrition during the war with Iraq and an unreliable supply of spare parts.[49] Delivery of a hypothetical nuclear weapon is more likely to rely on means that stand a better chance of surviving the trip to target, for example missiles or submarines.[50] Given the creativity and influence (albeit somewhat diminished) of the *Pasdaran* Revolutionary Guard, unconventional means of delivery might also be of concern.

Iran has been very active in the Conference on Disarmament. The tenor of its public positions indicates a commitment to a strict CTB meant to relieve its feelings of threat from US and, to a lesser extent, Israeli nuclear capabilities. As a result, Iran's positions have been towards the maximalist end of the spectrum (its invitational inspections and membership in the Chemical Weapons Convention and the Nonproliferation Treaty make it less concerned about intrusive verification than some others) and insistence that all states in the region must join the regime. Iran stuck by these positions even when they threatened to result in delays in completing the Treaty,[51] given that the CTB is not as high on its disarmament agenda as regional denuclearization, security guarantees and transparency in armaments, especially US deployments to the Gulf. These considerations are ameliorated slightly by Iran's efforts to reassure European trading partners and to engage the Gulf Co-operation Council states in confidence-building consultations, goals to which constructive participation at the Conference on Disarmament can only contribute. In the end, Iran voted for the CTB in the United Nations.[52]

Iran's confidence that others are complying with the Treaty's provisions will be highest in the case of Iraq, where nuclear activities either have been halted or are being strictly regulated. Iran's ability to collect and interpret open-source human intelligence in the West is better than that of most other states in the region, given its history of commercial, military and scientific contact and continued access to a sizeable expatriate community.

Iraq

Iraq's infrastructure for producing nuclear weapons has been eliminated and it will remain under unprecedented international supervision for the foreseeable future, but concerns linger about remaining expertise relevant to nuclear weapon design.

Iraq is eager to play a positive role in negotiations such as those for the CTB in hopes of building a consensus that UN sanctions be lifted; this is its highest foreign policy priority.[53] Iraq is not likely to share some other states' concerns about intrusive verification, because it is already subject to the most intensive inspection regime imaginable and cannot expect to assemble the wherewithal to mount any activity that might be perceived as non-compliant with the CTB.

The Iran–Iraq war and the Kuwait crisis would appear to demonstrate some weaknesses in Iraqi intelligence gathering and assessment in neighbouring states and the United States. Nevertheless, there is every reason for the Iraqi government to be confident that non-compliance in Iran would be detected and made public through US national technical means, CTB and NPT verification provisions, and Iran's invitation to the IAEA for additional 'anytime anywhere' inspections. Concerns about possible British, French, Israeli or US non-compliance are more likely to be relieved through monitoring open-source information.[54]

Libya

Libya has operated a small research reactor since 1981. Libya is a state party to the Nonproliferation Treaty and is subject to IAEA safeguards. As in the case of Iran, concerns about Libya arise from official rhetoric and attempts to import sensitive technology, rather than from actual progress in the nuclear programme.[55]

As in the case of Iraq, Libya's foreign policy establishment sees the lifting of UN sanctions as its highest goal, with concerns such as negotiation of and accession to the CTB important in mainly serving to support that effort.

North Korea

North Korea operates a reactor capable of producing enough plutonium for about one nuclear weapon a year and has done so long enough to have produced between four and seven weapons by the end of 1995, had the programme not been frozen. A larger reactor under construction, and originally planned to be started up in 1995, would have increased this production capacity tenfold. Another reactor, originally scheduled for completion in 1996, would have brought total plutonium production in North Korea to the equivalent of about 50 nuclear weapons a year.[56] North Korea has been reluctant to allow inspections of its facilities, in particular special challenge inspections. North Korea has a large and variegated military;[57] its paramilitary forces are sufficiently influential for them to be capable of retaining control of nuclear weapons and responsibility for their delivery, perhaps through unconventional means.

Although North Korea denies that it is attempting to produce nuclear weapons, officials also justify interest in the technology on the basis of their perception of a continued threat from within and outside the region. Nuclear weapons might provide a counter to fears of conventional or nuclear attack from Japan, South Korea or the United States, all of which North Korea sees as past and possibly future enemies. Any reduction of Chinese commitment to North Korea's security can only reinforce the perception that nuclear weapons are needed.

Under these circumstances, the CTB could play a minor but significant role in North Korea's nuclear diplomacy. Signing the Treaty could give the country a chance to make a positive contribution to balance its arms control record, while constraining the nuclear forces arrayed against it.[58] North Korean intelligence on Japan, South Korea and the United States apparently does not take into account widely available open sources of information. Suspicions that enemies are not complying with the Treaty may not be alleviated by international verification means or inspections, given the North Korean world view.

Specific provisions, however, made a big difference in the national position. Since the scope and inspection procedures of the Treaty make it appear likely that sensitive installations will be vulnerable to inspection, North Korea is likely to reject them. This is especially true if the Treaty is to be administered by the IAEA or if the Executive Council's deciding whether an inspection will be allowed is perceived as stacked against North Korea. North Korea was absent when the United Nations voted on the CTB.[59] Of all the states considered in this discussion so far, only North Korea has not signed the Chemical Weapons Convention or accepted any similar verification regime. Like Iraq, but perhaps more so, North Korea sees the IAEA and the United Nations, with which it fought a brutal war that is still not entirely resolved, as pawns in an international conspiracy against it. North Korean mistrust is not allayed even by the elaborate system for international verification of the CTB.

Conclusions

At first blush, there would appear to be merit in the argument made by opponents of the Comprehensive Test Ban that the Treaty will not have a major effect on the nuclear programmes of threshold and non-nuclear weapon states. Closer examination shows that the CTB will make significant contributions in some, but by no means all, cases.

First, and perhaps most importantly, the CTB demonstrates that the United States will not develop new types of nuclear weapons for regional contingencies. Although President Clinton and the US Congress have already foreclosed this possibility, continued commentary and reporting from anonymous sources in the Energy and Defense Departments stoke fears that nuclear modernization might resume, perhaps after Clinton leaves office. The fact that very low-yield nuclear weapons or those of the third generation (electromagnetic pulse or microwave weapons) cannot be developed without testing should reassure some states that the threat posed to them by US nuclear forces will get no worse. Although there remains a potent conventional threat to Iran, Iraq and North Korea (the explicit objects of US nuclear planning) as well as a residual nuclear threat in the form of strategic forces and older tactical forces that can be deployed to their regions, this cap on US capabilities removes one incentive for them to pursue a nuclear option. The CTB's capping effect is all the greater on France, Russia and the United Kingdom, since they have not renounced modernization, as the United States has done.

Notes

1 Some of the areas of contention that had to be resolved are discussed in two SIPRI publications: E. Arnett, 'The comprehensive nuclear test ban,' in *SIPRI Yearbook 1995: World Armaments, Disarmament and Security*, Oxford: Oxford University Press, 1995; and E. Arnett (ed.), *Implementing the Comprehensive Test Ban: New Aspects of Definition, Organization and Verification*, Oxford: Oxford University Press for SIPRI, 1994. This section draws on these two sources.
2 Barbara Crossette, 'U.N. Endorses a Treaty to Halt All Nuclear Testing', *New York Times*, 11 September 1996, p.A3.
3 For our purposes, a nuclear weapon state is one that is known to have nuclear weapons: China, France, Russia, the United Kingdom and the United States. A threshold state is one with an ambiguous nuclear capability, either an unacknowledged nuclear arsenal like Israel's or the ability to assemble nuclear weapons on short notice, such as India and Pakistan. Much of this chapter is derived from E. Arnett (ed.), *Nuclear Weapons after the Comprehensive Test Ban: Implications for Modernization and Proliferation*, Oxford: Oxford University Press for SIPRI, 1996.
4 Human intelligence includes monitoring open sources, such as government documents, parliamentary hearings and private publications, private communications and, in some cases, espionage. Some of these, however, are not allowed to trigger an on-site inspection.
5 J.W. Lewis and D. Hua, 'China's ballistic missile programs: Technology, strategies, goals', *International Security*, 17, (2), Fall 1992, pp.5–40; J.W. Lewis and L. Xue, *China's Strategic Seapower: The Politics of Force Modernization in the Nuclear Age*, Stanford, CA: Stanford University Press, 1994; E. Arnett, 'Military technology: The case of China', in *SIPRI Yearbook 1995*, pp.356–88. The JL-2 is to be deployed aboard a new SSBN, the 09-4.
6 Arnett, 'Military technology'; David Albright, William M. Arkin, Frans Berkhout, Robert S. Norris and William Walker, 'Inventories of fissile materials and nuclear weapons', in *SIPRI Yearbook 1995*, pp.356–88 and pp.317–36; International Institute for Strategic Studies, *Military Balance 1996–1997*, Oxford: Oxford University Press, 1996, pp.179–80.
7 Deng sharply curtailed military R&D and procurement upon coming to power in the

late 1970s, focusing scientific efforts on the 'Three Grasps': the ICBM, the SLBM and a communications satellite. Government support of military R&D efforts was further curtailed as these goals were achieved in the 1980s: Arnett, 'Military technology'.

8   US testing would be detected by open-source intelligence, if nothing else, and Russian testing would likely be detected and publicized by the United States, even if it were not detected by international means. The mechanisms of such detection are discussed in E. Arnett, 'The complementary roles of national, multinational and private means of verification' in Arnett (ed.), *Implementing The Comprehensive Test Ban*, pp.65–85.

9   R.L. Garwin, R.E. Kidder and C.E. Paine, *A Report on Discussions Regarding the Need for Nuclear Test Explosions to Maintain French Nuclear Weapons under a Comprehensive Test Ban*, Washington, DC: Federation of American Scientists and Natural Resources Defense Council, 1995, p.19. The variable-yield warhead is said to offer more flexibility for use in regional contingencies, but runs counter to traditional French doctrine. There is not yet a formal requirement for either the ASMP follow-on or the variable-yield warhead.

10 Only four sets of SLBMs were bought, so the total number of warheads in the SLBM force is estimated to be 384: Arkin *et al.*,'Stockpiles'.

11 Garwin *et al.*, *Report*; and D.S. Yost, 'Nuclear debates in France', *Survival*, **36**, (4), Winter 1994–5, pp.113–39.

12 J. Bouchard, the current director of the Directorate for Military Applications of the Atomic Energy Commission, acknowledged that France did not seek a variable- or low-yield warhead: Garwin *et al.*, *Report*, p.20. The only military figures to advocate such a role are Col. H. de Roquefeuil, Deputy Chief of Operations of the Strategic Air Force, and Gen. V. Lanata, Air Force Chief of Staff: Yost, 'Nuclear debates', p.120; and D. Garraud, 'Nuclear weapons: The strategic quarrel behind the tests', *Libérátion*, 29 October 1993, p.8. See also H.M. Kristensen and J. Handler, *Changing Targets: Nuclear Doctrine from the Cold War to the Third World*, Washington, DC: Greenpeace International, 1995, pp.15-21.

13 R. Galy-Dejean *et al.*, *La Simulation des Essais Nucléaires*, Paris: Commission de la Défense, Assemblée Nationale, Rapport d'Information 847, 1993.

14 D. Lockwood, 'Nuclear weapons developments', in *SIPRI Yearbook 1994*, Oxford: Oxford University Press, 1994, p.285. Russia flight-tested an all-Russian variant of the SS-25 ICBM in December 1994: Arkin *et al.*, 'Stockpiles'.

15 Arkin *et al.*, 'Stockpiles'.

16 There are probably between 2000 and 6000 Russian tactical nuclear weapons, making Russia's total nuclear holding between 11 000 and 15 000: Arkin, *et al.*, 'Stockpiles'; F. Berkhout, O. Bukharin, H. Feiveson and M. Miller, 'A cutoff in the production of fissile material', *International Security*, **19**, (3), Winter 1994/5, pp.167–202.

17 Russia subsequently signed a bilateral no-first-use agreement with China.

18 A. Arbatov, 'Theatre missile defence and the ABM Treaty', in *SIPRI Yearbook 1995*.

19 Those advocating such a doctrinal shift include Gen. P. Grachev, Minister of Defence, and Col.-Gen. I. Sergeyev, Commander of the Strategic Missile Forces: 'Interview with Army General Pavel Grachev, Minister of Defence', *Nezavisimaya Gazeta*, 9 June 1994; I. Baychursin, 'Russia's nuclear missiles are not targeted anywhere, but the Strategic Missile Forces are on combat duty', *Nezavisimaya Gazeta*, 15 December 1994; Kristensen and Handler, *Changing Targets*, p.28. Russia's recent doctrinal adjustment from unconditional no-first-use to a conditional no-first-use policy almost identical to NATO's was apparently meant primarily to provide an incentive for Ukraine to join the Nonproliferation Treaty (NPT). It is difficult to construct a scenario in which Russia would see value in using nuclear weapons, and even more

difficult if the non-nuclear weapon states party to the NPT, the group that Russia has vowed not to use nuclear weapons against, are excluded from the list of potential adversaries.

20 R.K. Wallace, *Hydronuclear Experiments as Related to the Comprehensive Test Ban Treaty*, Washington, DC: US Department of Energy, 1994; Arnett, *Nuclear Weapons*.

21 Lockwood, 'Nuclear weapons developments', p.299.

22 Russia maintains 100 strategic anti-ballistic missile interceptors around Moscow and its anti-tactical ballistic missile systems are seen as more capable against strategic missiles than the controversial US THAAD (Theater High Altitude Area Defense) system's interceptor: A. Arbatov, 'The ABM Treaty and theatre ballistic missile defence', in *SIPRI Yearbook 1995*, pp.681–96.

23 P.M. Lewis, 'The United Kingdom', in Arnett, *Nuclear Weapons*, pp.99–115. Lewis bases this conclusion mainly on the deep administrative separation between the nuclear weapon and civilian scientific establishments.

24 The United Kingdom has always tested in Australia or the United States.

25 The most direct public discussion of this possibility came from M. Rifkind, UK Secretary of State for Defence: M. Rifkind, House of Commons, *Statement on the Defence Estimates 1994*, London: Her Majesty's Stationery Office, 1994, pp.19,20; Kristensen and Handler, *Changing Targets*, p.22.

26 Arkin *et al.*, 'Stockpiles'.

27 The Nuclear Posture Review that was concluded in 1994 identified no requirement for a 'new design nuclear warhead', but did not bar introducing warhead designs that were already on the shelf in new systems. The United States developed very low-yield warheads for use in Central Europe during the Cold War, but they are not in the stockpile at present: Wallace, *Hydronuclear Experiments*; Office of the Assistant Secretary of Defense, International Security Policy, *Nuclear Posture Review*, Washington, DC: Department of Defense, 1994; Office of the Assistant Secretary of Defense, Public Affairs, *Press Conference with Perry, Shalikashvili, Deutch and Bacon*, Washington, DC: Department of Defense, 1994.

28 W.M. Arkin, 'Agnosticism when real values are needed: Nuclear policy in the Clinton administration', *Federation of American Scientists Public Interest Report*, September/October 1994; and Kristensen and Handler, *Changing Targets*.

29 Crossette, 'U.N. Endorses a Treaty'.

30 India has also been pursuing uranium enrichment technology, with unknown results. See D. Albright, F. Berkhout and W. Walker, *World Inventory of Plutonium and Highly Enriched Uranium, 1992*, Oxford: Oxford University Press for SIPRI, 1993, pp.161–2. There is reason to believe that India's inventory of fissile material is smaller than these conservative estimates, because Indian nuclear facilities have had a poor operating history: Arnett, 'Military technology', p.359.

31 Arnett, 'The comprehensive nuclear test ban'.

32 India operates 88 *Jaguar*, 20 *Sea Harrier*, 154 MiG-21 MF, 54 MiG-23 and 148 MiG-27 attack aircraft; 35 *Mirage* 2000, 170 MiG-21 bis, 26 MiG-23 MF and 65 MiG-29 fighters; and 8 *Kilo* 4 T-209/1500 and 7 *Foxtrot* submarines which could be used for nuclear delivery: International Institute for Strategic Studies, *Military Balance 1996–1997*, pp.160–61. In addition, India is working to develop indigenous ballistic missile, aircraft and submarine designs, but progress has been slow: Arnett, 'Military technology'. There is no public evidence of a major cruise missile programme. For an elucidation of the nuclear potential of aircraft, missiles and submarines, see E. Arnett, 'Choosing nuclear arsenals: prescriptions and predictions for new nuclear powers', *Journal of Strategic Studies*, **13**, (3), September 1990, pp.152–74.

33   Arnett, 'Military technology'. The *Agni* programme has since been frozen.

34   Because of suspicious imports, the US government believes India is researching fusion weapons: Arnett, 'Military technology'.

35   This is the argument of G. Deshingkar in 'India', in Arnett, *Nuclear Weapons*, pp.41–54.

36   Albright *et al.*, *World Inventory*, p.157. Some observers believe Israel has also imported HEU from South Africa, which produced between 200 and 525kg before halting its nuclear weapon programme.

37   Most sources speculate that nuclear warheads are to be carried by intermediate-range *Jericho* 1 and 2 ballistic missiles and some of Israel's 206 F-16 Falcon multi-role aircraft. Some may also be carried by short-range *Lance* ballistic missiles. Israel will soon receive the F-15I variant of the US F-15E *Strike Eagle*, which would also be capable of nuclear delivery. There has been speculation to the effect that Israel is interested in deploying nuclear-armed cruise missiles on submarines to increase the effective range and decrease the probability that pre-emption would succeed, but the status of such a programme, if it exists, is unknown.

38   The *engineering* approach contrasts with the *science-based* approach.

39   Additional IRIS seismic stations are to be deployed in and near the region, for example.

40   Conference on Disarmament, 'Nuclear Test Ban Treaty', Working Paper 102, 7 June 1994. See discussion in Arnett, 'The comprehensive nuclear test ban'.

41   E. Arnett, *Implementing the Comprehensive Test Ban*, pp.65–85; P.M. Lewis, 'Organization for effective implementation', in Arnett, *Implementing the Comprehensive Test Ban*, pp.86–102.

42   Albright *et al.*, *World Inventory*, p.167.

43   Pakistan also operates 18 *Mirage* III, 56 *Mirage* 5 and 49 A-5 *Fantan* attack aircraft; 100 F-6 and 79 F-7 fighters; 4 *Atlantic* ASW aircraft; and 2 *Agosta* and 4 *Daphné* submarines which could be used for nuclear delivery. The Pakistani Army may be in the process of incorporating domestically developed *Hatf*-1 and -2 short-range ballistic missiles into their force structure: International Institute for Strategic Studies, *Military Balance 1996–1997*, p.166.

44   This section focuses on these five because the debate concerns Western security perceptions. It must be acknowledged that some observers doubt that all of these states are really of concern, while other states are of proliferation concern to other observers. For example, North Koreans are very concerned about possible nuclear proliferation by Japan and South Korea.

45   Albright *et al.*, *World Inventory*, p.178.

46   Algeria's air force operates 10 Su-24 and 40 MiG-23 attack aircraft and 70 MiG-21, 20 MiG-23 and 10 MiG-25 fighters. Algeria's navy owns two *Kilo* submarines, but they are in Russia at present for refit: International Institute for Strategic Studies, *Military Balance 1996–1997*, p.128.

47   Albright *et al.*, *World Inventory*, pp.176–7.

48   Safeguards under the 93+2 programme include, for example, atmospheric monitoring near reactors.

49   The Iranian air force operates some 60 F-4, 60 F-5 and 30 Su-24 attack aircraft and 60 F-14, 25 F-7 and 30 MiG-29 fighters; International Institute for Strategic Studies, *Military Balance 1996–1997*, p.133. Rumours that Iran might receive Tu-22M *Backfire* bombers from Russia or Ukraine cannot be substantiated.

50   The Iranian army operates an estimated 10 *Scud* and about 25 CSS-8 short-range missile launchers. Indigenous missiles are said to be in development; International

Institute for Strategic Studies, *Military Balance 1996–1997*, pp.132–3. The navy has taken delivery of two *Kilo* submarines, but has little operating experience. These submarines could theoretically be used to transport a nuclear explosive device to installations in the Gulf or the US base at Diego Garcia. See E. Arnett, *Gunboat Diplomacy and the Bomb: Nuclear Proliferation and the US Navy*, New York: Praeger Publishers, 1989.

51 Some observers charged that Iran was intentionally undermining progress towards the CTB and the NPT extension in hopes of unravelling the nuclear non-proliferation regime. Such an interpretation is not necessarily demonstrated by recent Iranian diplomacy, which actually points up the ways in which large multilateral negotiations can be handicapped by differences in priorities and national interests.

52 Crossette, 'U.N. Endorses a Treaty'.

53 Details of Iraq's positions on the CTB are difficult to discover. Iraqi officials interviewed for this study were reluctant even to speculate without clear instructions from superiors. Public statements at the Conference on Disarmament have been limited to the issues of Iraq's membership, which is being blocked by the United States, and the lifting of sanctions.

54 Arnett, *Implementing the Comprehensive Test Ban*, pp.65–85. All four of these countries have made nuclear threats against Iraq within the last six years, whether explicitly or implicitly.

55 L.S. Spector and J.R. Smith, *Nuclear Ambitions: The Spread of Nuclear Weapons 1989–1990*, Boulder, CO: Westview Press, 1990, pp.177–8. Libyan delivery systems include 6 Tu-22 bombers; 55 MiG-23, 44 *Mirage* 5, 14 *Mirage* F-1, 6 Su-24 and 45 Su-20/22 attack aircraft, 80 *Scud* missile launchers and four *Foxtrot* submarines: International Institute for Strategic Studies, *Military Balance 1996–1997*, pp.139–40. None of these systems has been operated effectively in recent action, and the submarines may not be seaworthy.

56 Albright *et al.*, *World Inventory*, p.174.

57 North Korea operates 110 J-5/MiG-17, 160 J-6/MiG-19, 130 J-7/MiG-21, 46 MiG-23, 30 MiG-29, 18 Su-7 and 35 Su-25 aircraft, as well as 21 Type-031 *Romeo* and four *Whiskey* submarines which could be used for nuclear delivery. The army also operates a single independent regiment of some 30 *Scud* missiles: International Institute for Strategic Studies, *Military Balance 1996–1997*, p.187.

58 As in the case of Iraq, North Korean positions on specific Treaty provisions are difficult to confirm. Most public statements by North Korea at the Conference on Disarmament refer to other aspects of the nuclear issue in the region.

59 Crossette, 'U.N. Endorses a Treaty'.

8 A Nuclear Weapon-free World: Is it Desirable? Is it Possible? Is it Probable?

Francesco Calogero

Introduction

At the end of July 1995, the Annual Pugwash Conference was held in Hiroshima to mark the fiftieth Anniversary of the destruction of that city (on 6 August 1945) by the first use of nuclear weapons in war. Nagasaki was destroyed by another nuclear weapon on 9 August 1945, the last time – we hope the last time ever – a nuclear weapon was used to kill. Much of this chapter draws on the report I gave at that Conference, in my capacity as Secretary General of the Pugwash Conferences on Science and World Affairs, but talking of course in my personal capacity, as we always do in Pugwash.[1] The thrust of this chapter is to explore the desirability, possibility and probability of a nuclear weapon-free world. The end of the Cold War has changed part if not all of these parameters, and mostly in a positive direction.

At the opening of the Pugwash Conference in Hiroshima, the Pugwash Council issued a declaration, the 'Hiroshima Declaration'. Since this document is highly relevant to this presentation it is attached below as Appendix 1. And, because of its direct relevance, also attached below as Appendix 2 is the Communiqué of the Norwegian Committee announcing on 13 October 1995 the award of the 1995 Nobel Peace Prize to Joseph Rotblat and to the Pugwash Conferences on Science and World Affairs.

The Desirability of the Complete Elimination of Nuclear Weaponry

We begin with the question of the desirability of the *complete elimination of nuclear weaponry*. A multi-authored monograph on this topic, entitled *A Nuclear Weapon-Free World: Desirable? Feasible?*, was produced by Pugwash in 1993.[2] (This monograph is now also available in Russian, Chinese, Arabic, Japanese, Swedish, Spanish and French.) No attempt will be made here to cover again the material discussed in that Pugwash monograph, including the very question of what is meant by the 'elimination of nuclear weaponry', in light of the obvious fact that the technological feasibility of nuclear weapons cannot be forgotten. In fact, the main focus here will be to try and convince the reader that, even among those who were in the past the main supporters of the usefulness of nuclear weapons, the opinion is now gaining ground that nuclear weapons are in fact dangerous and obnoxious, and that it would therefore be desirable to eliminate them if at all possible. To do this, we will rely heavily on quotations, and will mainly use American sources, because indeed in the past the most articulate and influential advocacy of the thesis attributing to nuclear weapons an essential, and largely positive role came from America, or more generally from 'Western strategic thinking', hoping of course not to produce thereby a pro-nuclear weapon backlash among those who tend to have an anti-American or anti-Western bias.

It should be emphasized that the present writer does not agree with all the arguments which will be reported, especially when they are based on a viewpoint exclusively focused on the national security of the United States rather than on a less narrow view of international security. However, the 'change of paradigm' documented by the quotations used, is of paramount importance in supporting the idea that a transition is now in the offing. This is a transition in 'mainstream thinking', from considering the elimination of nuclear weaponry a dangerous notion promulgated by utopian idealists and devious propagandists, to recognizing that it is an achievement essential for the long-run survival of our civilization; an achievement whose immediate realizability is perhaps moot, but whose eventual feasibility deserves serious study. And a positive outcome of this study cannot and must not be excluded, unless we believe our civilization is in fact doomed.

Les Aspin was a professional analyst of nuclear weapon strategy and served for many years as chairman of the Armed Services Committee of the US House of Representatives. He was therefore in a very good position to talk about the nuclear weapon strategy of the United States, both as an expert and more importantly as someone who held for many years a key decision-making position. In February 1992, he published a study with the significant title *From Deterrence to Denuking: Dealing with Proliferation in the 1990s.* This study was the outcome of a process of elaboration involving a large cross-section of the expert community on nuclear matters in the United States and worldwide. Les Aspin was subsequently chosen by President Clinton as his first Secretary of Defense; he unfortunately had to resign after a few months in office, mainly for health reasons. As Secretary of Defense, he initiated an internal Review of the Nuclear Posture of the United States, which he probably hoped would question the basic premises of the reliance of the United States on nuclear weaponry; unfortunately, after he left the Department of Defense, that Review was taken over by bureaucrats steeped in Cold War thinking and was totally emasculated, producing a stale reformulation of nuclear deterrence doctrines, with only some cosmetic embellishments that were probably introduced only to muster support for the indefinite extension of the Nonproliferation Treaty by non-nuclear weapon countries. But this is what Les Aspin wrote after being for many years chairman of the Armed Services Committee of the US House of Representatives, and before becoming Clinton's first Secretary of Defense:

> During the Cold War, the United States and its NATO allies relied on nuclear weapons to offset the conventional superiority of the Warsaw Pact in Europe. Even a few years ago, if someone had offered the United States a magic wand that could have instantly wiped out all nuclear weapons and the knowledge to make more of them, the reality is we would have declined the offer.
>
> Nuclear weapons were the great equalizer that enabled Western capitals to deal with numerically larger Eastern Bloc forces. To have used the magic wand would have made the world safe for conventional war. This was not a desirable outcome when large Eastern Bloc conventional forces were deployed right up to the inner Germany border.
>
> Today, however, circumstances are dramatically different. With the disappearance of the Warsaw Pact and the fading of the threat posed by former Soviet forces, the United States is the biggest conventional force on the block. Nuclear weapons still have the same purpose – as a great equalizer. But it is the United States that is now the potential equalizee. ...
>
> Today, if offered that magic wand to eradicate the existence and the knowledge of nuclear weapons, we would very likely accept it. This radical change in our interests in nuclear weapons is the backdrop against which we must understand the evolving nuclear threats we face today.

A remarkably similar message was promulgated in the book, *Reducing Nuclear Danger*, published in 1993.[3] Its three co-authors have experienced deep involvement in the formulation of US nuclear strategies. McGeorge Bundy was Assistant for National Security to President Kennedy, William J. Crowe, Jr. served as chairman of the Joint Chiefs of Staff and Sidney Drell is a distinguished physicist, who served as president of the American Physical Society and also as chairman of the three-man committee that was mandated a few years ago by the US Congress to assess the safety and reliability of the American nuclear weapon arsenal. The committee issued the 'Drell Report',[4] which states that most of the nuclear weapons now deployed are not up to the safety standards mandated by Congress – a grave revelation to which nobody has unfortunately paid much attention except for those who tried to exploit it to argue the need to continue nuclear weapon testing. The sentences which are reproduced on the cover of *Reducing Nuclear Danger* – and which are evidently meant to convey its main message – are the following:

> From the beginning of the Cold War in 1946 to its end in 1990, the U.S. government would have rejected any offer from the gods to take all nuclear weapons off the table of international affairs. Today such an offer would deserve instant acceptance; it would remove all kinds of risks of catastrophic destruction, and it would leave us and our friends quite safe from Russian expansion. We should be free to enjoy two extraordinary strategic advantages: first, as the least threatened of major states and second, as the one state with modern conventional forces of unmatched quality. Unfortunately no one knows how to abolish nuclear weapons, but the dramatic change in what we now need from these weapons makes a great difference in the limits we can accept on the size and use of our own nuclear forces, and that difference in turn affects what others can decide.[5]

Our third quotation comes from a paper that Robert S. McNamara contributed to a Pugwash Workshop on Nuclear Forces held in December 1994 in Geneva. Robert McNamara served as Secretary of Defense under Presidents Kennedy and Johnson, and has probably contributed more than anybody else to shaping the original 'mainstream thinking' about nuclear weapons. That paper, bearing the significant title, 'A long-range policy for nuclear forces of the nuclear powers', is published in the October 1994 / January 1995 issue of the *Pugwash Newsletter.*[6] Its text essentially coincides with the concluding chapter of McNamara's recent, highly controversial book, *In Retrospect: the Tragedy and Lessons of Vietnam,*[7] as well as his op-ed article in the *International Herald Tribune* of 9 August 1995 on the fiftieth anniversary of the nuclear destruction of Nagasaki.[8] This is what McNamara writes (the extract excludes the footnotes, except for a very relevant one at the end):[9]

> The point I wish to emphasize is this: human beings are fallible. We all make mistakes. In our daily lives, mistakes are costly, but we try to learn from them. In conventional war, they cost lives, sometimes thousands of lives. But if mistakes were to affect decisions relating to the use of nuclear forces, they would

result in the destruction of whole societies. I believe, therefore, it can be predicted with confidence that the indefinite combination of human fallibility and nuclear weapons carries a high risk of potential catastrophe.

Is there a military justification for continuing to accept that risk? The answer is no.

In *Nuclear Weapons After the Cold War,* Carl Kaysen, George W. Rathjens and I pointed out that proponents of nuclear weapons 'have produced only one plausible scenario for their use: a situation where there is no prospect of retaliation, either against a non-nuclear state or against one so weakly armed as to permit the user to have full confidence in his nuclear forces' capability to achieve a totally disarming first strike.' We added that 'even such circumstances have not, in fact, provided a sufficient basis for the use of nuclear weapons in war. For example, although American forces were in desperate straits twice during the Korean War – first immediately following the North Korean attack in 1950 and then when the Chinese crossed the Yalu – the United States did not use nuclear weapons. At that time, North Korea and China had no nuclear capability and the Soviet Union only a negligible one.'

The argument which Kaysen, Rathjens and I made leads to the conclusion that the military utility of nuclear weapons is limited to deterring one's opponent from their use. Therefore, if our opponent has no nuclear weapons there is no need for us to possess them.

Partly because of the increased understanding of how close we came to disaster during the Missile Crisis, but also because of a growing recognition of the lack of military utility of the weapons, there has been a revolutionary change in thinking about the role of nuclear forces. Much of this change has occurred in the past three years. Many military leaders, including, for example, two former Chairmen of the Joint Chiefs of Staff, a former Supreme Commander of Allied Forces in Europe, and a senior US Air Force officer currently on active duty, are now prepared to go far beyond the Bush/Yeltsin agreement. Some go so far as to state, as I have, that the long-term objective should be a return, insofar as practical, to a non-nuclear world.

That is, however, a very controversial proposition. A majority of Western security experts – both military and civilian – continue to believe the threat of the use of nuclear weapons prevents war. Zbigniew Brzezinski, President Carter's National Security Adviser, argued that a plan for eliminating nuclear weapons 'is a plan for making the world safe for conventional warfare. I am therefore not enthusiastic about it.' A report of an advisory committee, appointed by former Defense Secretary Richard Cheney and chaired by former Air Force Secretary Thomas Reed, made essentially the same point. Clearly the current Administration supports that position. However, even if one accepts their argument, it must be recognized that their deterrent to conventional force aggression carries a very high long-term cost: the risk of a nuclear exchange.

Unbeknownst to most people, John Foster Dulles, President Eisenhower's Secretary of State, recognized this problem in the mid-1950s. In a highly secret memorandum only recently declassified, Dulles proposed to 'universalize the capacity of atomic thermonuclear weapons to deter aggression' by transferring control of nuclear forces to a veto-less UN Security Council. Dulles' concern has been echoed in recent years by other prominent security experts. As I have said, I doubt that the public is aware of their views. They have been reflected in three reports and numerous unclassified, but not widely disseminated, statements.

The three reports have all been published since 1990:

1. In 1991, a committee of the US National Academy of Sciences, in a report signed by retired Joint Chiefs of Staff Chairman General David C. Jones, stated: 'nuclear weapons should serve no purpose beyond the deterrence of ... nuclear attack by others.' The committee believed US and Russian nuclear forces could be reduced to 1,000–2,000 warheads.

2. The Spring 1993 issue of *Foreign Affairs* carried an article co-authored by another retired Chairman of the Joint Chiefs of Staff, Admiral William J. Crowe, Jr., which concluded that by the year 2000, the U.S. and Russia could reduce strategic nuclear forces to 1,000–1,500 warheads each. The article, later ex-panded into a book, added: 'Nor is 1,000–1,500 the lowest level obtainable by the early 21st Century.'

3. In August 1993, General Andrew Goodpaster, former Supreme Allied Com-mander of NATO Forces in Europe, published a report in which he said the five existing nuclear powers should be able to reduce nuclear weapons stockpiles to 'no more than 200 each' and 'the ultimate would be *a zero level*' [emphasis in the original].

These three reports should not come as surprises. For nearly 20 years more and more Western military and civilian security experts have expressed doubts about the military utility of nuclear weapons. This is what they have said:

By 1982, five of the seven retired Chiefs of the British Defence Staff had expressed their belief that initiating the use of nuclear weapons, in accordance with NATO policy, would lead to disaster. Lord Louis Mountbatten, Chief of Staff from 1959–1965, said a few months before he was murdered in 1979: 'As a military man I can see no use for any nuclear weapons.' And Field Marshall Lord Carver, Chief of Staff from 1973–1976, wrote in 1982 that he was totally opposed to NATO ever initiating the use of nuclear weapons.

Henry Kissinger, speaking in Bruxelles in 1979, made quite clear he believed the US would never initiate a nuclear strike against the Soviet Union, no matter what the provocation. 'Our European allies,' he said, 'should not keep asking us to multiply strategic assurances that we cannot possibly mean or if we do mean, we should not execute because if we execute we risk the destruction of civilization.'

Admiral Noel Gaylor, former Commander-in-Chief of US air, ground, and sea forces in the Pacific, remarked in 1981: 'There is no sensible military use of any of our nuclear forces. The only reasonable use is to deter our opponent from using his nuclear forces.'

Former West German Chancellor Helmut Schmidt stated in a 1987 BBC interview: 'Flexible response [NATO's strategy calling for the use of nuclear weapons in response to a Warsaw Pact attack by non-nuclear forces] is non-sense. Not out of date, but nonsense. ... The Western idea, which was created in the 1950s, that we should be willing to use nuclear weapons first, in order to make up for our so-called conventional deficiency, has never convinced me.'

Melvin Laird, President Nixon's first Secretary of Defense, was reported in *The Washington Post* of April 12, 1992 as saying: 'A worldwide zero nuclear option with adequate verification should now be our goal. ... These weapons ... are useless for military purposes.'

General Larry Welch, former U.S. Air Force Chief of Staff and previously Commander of the Strategic Air Command, recently put the same thought in these words: 'Nuclear deterrence depended on someone believing that you would commit an act totally irrational if done.'

And in July 1994, General Charles A. Homer, chief of the U.S. Space Command, stated: 'The nuclear weapon is obsolete. I want to get rid of them all.'

In the early 1960s, I had reached conclusions similar to those cited above. In long private conversations, first with President Kennedy and then with President Johnson, I had recommended, without qualification, that they never initiate, under any circumstances, the use of nuclear weapons. I believe they accepted my recommendations. But neither they nor I could discuss our position publicly because it was contrary to established NATO policy.

Today, given the totally contradictory views regarding the role of nuclear weapons held by the Administration and the Brzezinskis and Reeds on the one hand and the Lairds and Schmidts on the other – but with the recognition by all that initiation of the use of nuclear weapons against a nuclear equipped opponent would lead to disaster – should we not begin immediately to debate the merits of alternative long-term objectives for the five declared nuclear powers?

We could choose from three options:

1. A continuation of the present strategy of 'extended deterrence', the strategy just reconfirmed by the Administration. This would mean limiting the U.S. and Russia to approximately 3,500 strategic warheads each, the figure agreed upon by Presidents Bush and Yeltsin;

2. A minimum deterrent force – as recommended by the U.S. National Academy of Sciences committee, and supported by General Jones and Admiral Crowe – with the two major nuclear powers retaining no more than 1,000–2,000 warheads each; or

3. As General Goodpaster and I strongly advocate a return, by all five nuclear powers, insofar as practicable, to a non-nuclear world. (*Footnote*: 'Insofar as practicable' refers to the necessity of maintaining protection against 'breakout'. The elimination of nuclear weapons could be accomplished in a series of steps, as both General Goodpaster and I have suggested.)

If we dare break out of the mindset that has guided the nuclear strategy of the nuclear powers for over four decades, I believe we can indeed 'put the genie back in the bottle'. If we do not, there is a substantial risk that the 21st Century will witness a nuclear holocaust.

Our last quotation comes from a speech by President Clinton at the US Air Force Academy commencement ceremony in Colorado Springs on 1 June

1995: 'As horrible as the tragedies in Oklahoma City and the World Trade Center were, imagine the destruction that would have resulted had there been a small nuclear device exploded there.'

Indeed, the tremendous risk that nuclear explosive devices might be acquired or manufactured by terrorist groups, by criminal gangs or by crazy sects, is evidently concrete in a world awash with tens of thousands of nuclear weapons, and with inadequately guarded stocks of weapon-grade nuclear materials, sufficient to manufacture tens of thousands of nuclear explosive devices. Against this threat, the possession of nuclear weapons provides absolutely no protection.

Current Actions on Nuclear Disarmament

Recently, over 170 countries confirmed their commitment never to acquire nuclear weapons as they accepted the unlimited extension of the Nonproliferation Treaty on 11 May 1995. Nuclear weapons are now excluded from a fair portion of the Earth and its environment through treaties which are largely or fully in force: in Latin America, the South Pacific, and Antarctica, in space, on the sea bed and ocean floor, and on the moon and other celestial bodies. The creation of additional nuclear weapon-free zones is in the offing, for instance in Africa and South East Asia. Such regional agreements, in the context of peaceful arrangements to defuse ongoing conflicts, offer a natural way to address and eliminate the main remaining risks of nuclear weapon proliferation in the Middle East and South Asia; in the only other serious case of Korea, this process of containment seems well on its way. All five nuclear weapon states have committed themselves to the Comprehensive Test Ban Treaty; the two major nuclear weapon powers have already chosen to observe self-imposed moratoria on nuclear weapon testing for some years, and they are engaged now in the dismantling and elimination of their nuclear weapons at what is allegedly the fastest pace technologically feasible – approximately 2000 warheads dismantled a year both in the United States and in Russia. And the commitment to get rid of chemical weaponry altogether, which is now being implemented by the world community, demonstrates that the desirability and feasibility of the goal to eliminate at least this category of weapons of mass killing are now – for the first time in history – almost universally accepted.

The intention to eliminate nuclear weapons completely is not yet wholeheartedly supported by the leaders of the nuclear weapon countries, although it is entailed by commitments they have undertaken. In any case, for the immediate future the most important task for them – which does not require an immediate commitment to get rid of nuclear weapons altogether

– is active pursuance of the nuclear disarmament programme. This programme includes immediate ratification by Russia and speedy implementation by both Russia and the United States of the START-II Treaty, progress towards a START-III involving reductions beyond those mandated by START-II (also to avoid certain of these reductions causing new deployments), universal acceptance of a Comprehensive Test Ban Treaty effectively banning any further tests of nuclear weapons and thereby excluding any further development of these weapons, the cut-off of any further production of weapons-grade fissile material, effective transparency and maximal security with respect to all nuclear weapons and all weapons-grade fissile materials (numbers, quantities, storage sites, deployments – of course, no data useful for targeting need be revealed), elimination of nuclear weapons at the fastest pace technologically feasible and, last but not least, immediate transition to a zero-alert nuclear posture, implying the physical impossibility of using any nuclear weapon without a substantive delay of at least days. This delay can be achieved by the systematic separation of warheads, or some essential component of them, from launchers, and it would greatly improve the overall security of the world.

Many years ago, Presidents Gorbachev and Reagan agreed that '*A nuclear war cannot be won and must never be fought*'. It is now becoming evident that the logical corollary of that obvious statement is that nuclear weapons have no reason to exist: they should be phased out. Indeed, it is evident that, *in the long run* – but on a time scale of decades, not centuries – the stark question is whether our civilization manages to eliminate nuclear weapons, or the opposite happens and our civilization is wiped out by nuclear weapons, which sooner or later will fall into irresponsible hands, unless we find a way to get rid of them altogether.

The Possibility of Complete Nuclear Disarmament

A graphic image of human folly is the obscene size attained by the nuclear weapon arsenals. The explosive power of nuclear weapons can be compared to that of all the bombs dropped during World War II. The firepower of World War II was three megatons. For the 1980s, the explosive power of nuclear weaponry was 18 000 megatons or the firepower of 6000 World War IIs. The idea that the nuclear arsenals contain the explosive yield of 6000 World War IIs is truly mind-boggling.

Just 20 years ago, or even 10 years ago, the claim that such a picture was a clear demonstration of collective lunacy was considered inappropriate, if not wrong; certainly, it tended to disqualify anyone making it from being taken seriously within the fraternity of experts – even well-meaning ones –

in nuclear weapon matters. That never prevented me from making this point. Today, one still often hears that 'nuclear weapons cannot be disinvented, hence we must be prepared to live with them forever', with the implication that this justifies such a huge arsenal.

Many experts said for a long time that it would be impossible to lift off the ground a machine heavier than the air, or that it would be impossible for a man to set foot on the moon, or ... one could continue with a long list of so-called 'impossibilities' which were in fact realized. Few imagined that it would be possible to eliminate certain diseases, such as smallpox, so completely that the question of whether it makes any sense to preserve the corresponding vaccines is now debated. Yet humankind has been able to achieve such a goal.

It is impossible to disinvent the idea of hijacking aeroplanes, yet this has not eliminated civilian air traffic, it has just forced the introduction of cumbersome and costly controls. Our civilization, faced with the prospect that the risk of aeroplane hijacking might eliminate the convenience of civilian air traffic, has found a way to reduce the practice of hijacking, with an effectiveness adequate to cope with the problem. The same will happen with nuclear weapons. The point, surely, is not whether this will happen; it is when. It is our task to make this happen soon. The only question really is whether it will happen before, or after, a nuclear catastrophe. It is our task to make this happen before such a catastrophe.

The analogy with hijacking is a useful one to bear in mind. A real risk in the future is the actual or threatened use of nuclear explosive devices by subnational groups, which cannot be deterred because their strength depends on the intrinsically clandestine mode of their operations. It will not be easy to cope with this danger, but one thing is absolutely clear and – obvious as it is – needs repeated reiteration: the possession of nuclear weapons provides absolutely no protection against this danger, if anything, it contributes to increasing the probability that it will materialize.

The threat of acquisition of nuclear weapons by a state, even a rogue state, is easier to cope with. First of all, only the acquisition of a deliverable nuclear arsenal makes any sense for a state; and this is much more difficult to acquire secretly than a single primitive nuclear device. Thus, against the potential nuclear weapon capability of a state, verification has a fair chance of working, especially if combined with global measures to reduce secrecy and impose societal verification. Moreover, a state can be deterred even by conventional means; modern technology provides the capability to inflict enormous damage even without using any 'weapon of mass destruction', such as nuclear, chemical or bacteriological weapons.

This very remark implies that our ultimate goal should not be limited to the elimination of weapons of mass destruction: it should aim at eliminating war as an instrument for settling international disputes. This goal must be achieved because modern technology has made wars, even if fought with only 'conventional' means, horrendously destructive. Moreover, all wars should be eliminated because, once nuclear weaponry is done away with, it is likely it might be reintroduced in the context of some war involving the major powers. In this last respect, the argument that 'nuclear weapons cannot be disinvented' has indeed its cogency, as clearly explained over 40 years ago in the Russell–Einstein Manifesto that originated Pugwash:[10]

> [This] hope that perhaps war may be allowed to continue provided modern weapons are prohibited ... is illusory. Whatever agreements not to use H-bombs had been reached in time of peace, they would no longer be considered binding in time of war, and both sides would set to work to manufacture H-bombs as soon as war broke out, for, if one side manufactured the bombs and the other did not, the side that manufactured them would inevitably be victorious.

But fortunately, and perhaps contrary to what is still a widespread opinion, the possibility of eliminating war altogether as a social institution is achievable, as clearly demonstrated by the fact that this goal has now been realized in certain parts of the world, such as North America and Western Europe. In Western Europe, where both world wars originated, the concept of solving by going to war international disputes which affect crucial interests of the citizens of these countries, for instance the introduction of a common currency or the enforcement of common agricultural policies, is now quite ridiculous. Equally laughable is the idea that the two West European nuclear weapon countries could utilize their nuclear capabilities to any effect whatsoever in the context of such disputes. This underscores very evidently the essential uselessness of nuclear weaponry and the lack of wisdom of those who continue to squander their resources in order to develop and maintain such useless arsenals, which constitute a threat primarily against those who possess them.

A first, short-term but important goal is to promote universal acceptance of the proposition that *the only purpose of nuclear weapons is to deter the use of nuclear weapons by others*. This notion is not too far from attaining the status of conventional wisdom even among 'mainstream' nuclear weapon experts. It logically entails, once it has been universally accepted, that nuclear weapons *may well disappear;* hence, by all means, they *must quickly disappear*, even without any other 'paradigmatic change' in strategic thinking. Because everybody now agrees that having nuclear weapons around is unsafe, unless there are strong justifications for their existence.

In the context of the Cold War, it was relatively easy to convince large numbers of people, in certain countries having the ambition to be 'great powers' (whatever that really means in the modern world), that the possession of nuclear weapons was the best guarantor of their security and of their status, or at least an indispensable one. But with the end of the Cold War, even in those countries, more and more people are now asking themselves the simple question: is the availability of nuclear weapons an asset or a liability? Does it provide advantages or risks? And the politicians and decision makers are also beginning to ask themselves these same questions, and to wonder whether the choice which in the past appeared so obvious and profitable for them – to engage in nationalistic breast beating by brandishing a nuclear arsenal – is now losing, not only practical utility, but political appeal as well. Perhaps the best way to deal with those who are still affected by this syndrome is not with aggressive confrontation, but with compassionate pity, and a fair amount of ridicule.

Many might find it distasteful that the matter of nuclear weapons should be treated lightly, with ridicule rather than horror. Yet ridicule may be a more potent deterrent to nuclear proliferation than confrontation and fear. Personally, it is the approach that comes more natural to me whenever I look at the remarkable situation in Europe, where for some reason Great Britain and France possess a nuclear arsenal, and Germany and Spain and Italy and Sweden and others do not. Are the countries who do not possess a nuclear arsenal at some disadvantage? Do those who possess nuclear weapons enjoy some privileges? And if not, why do they cling to their nukes at a considerable risk, and at a considerable cost? Of course many explanations may be concocted: for instance, that it is precisely those nuclear weapons which have prevented war from breaking out in Europe. It is, of course, difficult for anyone to disprove such an argument, but the following story, whose authenticity cannot be vouched for, seems well to the point. On the train now travelling underground between London and Paris a gentleman was noticed who every few minutes would open the window to throw out some white powder. When asked the reason for this behaviour, he explained he did so in order to keep the elephants away from the tracks. And when someone pointed out to him that there were no elephants at all around, he replied, 'Of course, this shows how very effective my powder is.'

But in any case, the dispute whether nuclear weapons were or were not essential to prevent war in Europe during the years from 1945 to 1990 is an argument about the past, of little relevance to the completely changed circumstances of the present and, we must hope, of the future. When one is thinking about the future, terms such as 'hope' come naturally to mind, as well as the natural objection, 'What if things take a turn for the worse instead?' This is indeed the basis for arguing – as was amply done, for instance, in the context of the American Nuclear Posture Review – that a robust nuclear weapon capability must be maintained to *hedge* in the face of an uncertain future.

However, what seems not to be taken into adequate consideration is two thoughts. First, by hedging one not only prepares for an eventual future turn for the worse; one also makes such a development more likely, by emphasizing the more confrontational aspects. Indeed, it is a well known phenomenon that the hawks inside two conflicting camps tend to reinforce each other's influence. Second, the wise way to hedge against a turn for the worse in the future is to achieve in the meantime as deep and complete a disarmament as possible, of course not unilaterally, so that, should relations worsen again, the immediate outcome will be at worst a bout of nuclear rearmament, rather than an immediate nuclear confrontation.

The Probability of Complete Nuclear Disarmament

With regard to the questions raised by the title of this chapter, an important development is the creation of the 'Canberra Commission', with the specific task of planning the transition to a nuclear weapon-free world (NWFW). The creation of this international commission was announced, by the Labor government of Australia then in office, in November 1995. We were told that it was a follow-up to the Pugwash monograph mentioned at the beginning of this chapter; and perhaps also a spin-off of the announcement in October 1995 of the award of the 1995 Nobel Peace Prize to Joseph Rotblat and to Pugwash, an award that refers explicitly to the realization of a NWF world (see Appendix 2 below). A commitment to support the work of the commission was then reiterated by the Conservative government that assumed office in Australia following the elections held in March 1996.

The Canberra Commission includes a remarkable cross section of internationally eminent personalities and security experts, including, among others, Joseph Rotblat, President of Pugwash, Robert NcNamara and Michel Rocard, former prime minister of France. It completed its report in August 1996, and presented it to the 1996 General Assembly of the United Nations. We may be justifiably optimistic that this report will provide a blueprint for assessing the best way to make a transition to a NWF world.

It is clear in any case that a NWF world will rest on two main pillars. In the first place, there should be an international treaty banning the possession of nuclear weapons by all and having effect *erga omnes,* binding everyone in the world, with an adequate mechanism of enforcement; in the second place, there should be a stringent verification system, relying on all kinds of technological and societal monitoring mechanisms.

Of course the underpinning of the viability of such a regime will be the universal recognition that the only alternative to it is 'universal death'. Indeed, while I would like to end this chapter by reiterating that it expresses my personal opinions and does not pretend to present here the view of the Pugwash Conferences, I also wish to quote in conclusion the closing sentence of the 1955 Russell–Einstein Manifesto, from which Pugwash originated. This sentence is most topical today, inasmuch as the dangers it spells out, as well as the opportunities to eliminate them, have now become more concrete and more imminent:[11]

> There lies before us, if we choose, continual progress in happiness, knowledge and wisdom. Shall we, instead, choose death, because we cannot forget our quarrels? We appeal, as human beings, to human beings: remember your humanity, and forget the rest. If you can do so, the way lies open to a new Paradise; if you cannot, there lies before you the risk of universal death.

Notes

1   An analogous text has appeared in the *Proceedings of the Sixth Castiglioncello Conference 'Fifty Years of Nuclear Weapons'*, Milan: USPID, 1996; and may also appear in the *Proceedings of the Second Sakharov Conference*, held in Moscow, 20–25 May 1996, as well as in those of the International Symposium, 'Science and Society: History of the Soviet Atomic Project (40s and 50s)' (HISAP '96), held in Dubna, Russia, 14–18 May 1996.
2   J. Rotblat, J. Steinberger and B. Udgaonkar (eds), *A Nuclear Weapon-Free World: Desirable? Feasible?*, Boulder, CO: Westview Press, 1993.
3   McGeorge Bundy, William J. Crowe, Jr. and Sidney Drell, *Reducing Nuclear Danger: The Road Away from the Brink*, New York: Council on Foreign Relations, 1993.
4   Sidney Drell, John S. Foster, Jr. and Charles H. Townes, *Report of the Panel on Nuclear Safety, Committee on Armed Services, House of Representatives, 101st Congress of the US, 2nd Session, December 1990*, Washington, DC: US GPO, 1990.
5   Bundy *et al.*, *Reducing Nuclear Danger*, pp.5–6.
6   Robert S. McNamara, 'A long-range policy for nuclear forces of the nuclear powers', *Pugwash Newsletter*, October 1994/January 1995.
7   Robert S. McNamara, *In Retrospect: the Tragedy and Lessons of Vietnam*, New York: Random House, 1995, pp.342–6.
8   *International Herald Tribune*, 9 August, 1995.
9   Robert S. McNamara, 'A long-range policy for nuclear forces of the nuclear powers'.
10 For instance, in J. Rotblat, *Scientists in the Quest for Peace – A history of the Pugwash Conferences*, Cambridge, MA: MIT Press, 1972, pp.137–40.
11 Ibid.

Appendix 1   Hiroshima Declaration of the Pugwash Council, 23 July 1995

Fifty years ago, two American atomic bombs destroyed the Japanese cities of Hiroshima and Nagasaki. Those two mushroom clouds – and the horrific devastation beneath them – marked the end of the most destructive war in history and, at the same time, the beginning of a new era dominated by the danger that global nuclear war would wreak more havoc in six hours than World War II had wrought in six years.

Civilization is fortunate to have survived the half-century since 1945 with no such nuclear war and, indeed, no further explosion of a nuclear weapon in anger. This may have been partly the result of sensible restraint and good management, but it has also been partly the result of good luck.

In these 50 years, the number of nations declaring themselves possessors of nuclear weaponry increased from one to five; the number possessing them without declaring so increased from zero to three or more; and the total number of nuclear weapons on the planet grew to a peak of 70 000 before beginning a gradual decline.

During this period, the use of nuclear weapons was explicitly threatened occasionally, implicitly threatened continuously, seriously contemplated more often than will ever be admitted, and narrowly averted, more than once, by the last-minute quenching of crises that had careened to the brink of nuclear war. A close review of this history offers little basis for complacency that a nuclear-armed world will succeed in refraining indefinitely from using these weapons again.

On the contrary, there can be no real safety against nuclear destruction until the weapons themselves have been destroyed, their possession forsworn, their production prohibited, their ingredients made inaccessible to those who might seek to evade the prohibition. Indeed, real safety will require still more. Because the knowledge of how to construct nuclear weapons cannot be erased from human memory, and because, in the extremity of war, nations that previously forswore them may race to produce them anew, it will be necessary to eliminate war itself as a means of resolving disputes among nations.

This view may appear utopian, but to reject it is to accept not only the possibility but the inevitability that someday, somewhere, immense numbers of people will again perish under nuclear mushroom clouds like those that obliterated Hiroshima and Nagasaki 50 years ago. It could be hundreds or thousands of mushroom clouds in the mindless spasm of a large nuclear war, it could be one mushroom cloud here, a few there, in scattered acts of nuclear violence committed by warring nations, or by the factions in civil wars, or by terrorists.

Wherever, whenever, however many mushroom clouds it may be, we say such an outcome is unacceptable and must be prevented. It can only be prevented if nuclear weapons and, ultimately, war itself are banned from this planet.

The end of the Cold War, and the beginning of deep reductions in the huge nuclear arsenals that the Cold War spawned, have provided an unprecedented opportunity for the world to take further decisive steps toward achievement of these ends. The opportunity must be seized, or it will be lost ... and civilization may be lost.

In this fiftieth year after the nuclear destruction of Hiroshima and Nagasaki, therefore, we, the Council of the Pugwash Conferences on Science and World Affairs, rededicate ourselves to the goals of the *Russell–Einstein Manifesto* of 1955 that initiated the Pugwash movement, that is, to the abolition of nuclear weapons and the abolition of war. We invite all of humankind to join us in this effort.

Appendix 2   The Norwegian Nobel Committee Communiqué 13 October 1995

The Norwegian Nobel Committee has decided to award the Nobel Peace Prize for 1995, in two equal parts, to Joseph Rotblat, President of Pugwash, and to the Pugwash Conferences on Science and World Affairs, for their efforts to diminish the part played by nuclear arms in international politics and in the longer run to eliminate such arms.

It is fifty years this year since the two atomic bombs were dropped on Hiroshima and Nagasaki, and forty years since the issuing of the *Russell– Einstein Manifesto*. The Manifesto laid the foundations for the Pugwash Conferences, which have maintained a high level of activity to this day. Joseph Rotblat was one of the eleven scientists behind the Manifesto, and has since been the most important figure in the Pugwash work.

The Conferences are based on the recognition of the responsibility of scientists for their inventions. They have underlined the catastrophic consequences of the use of the new weapons. They have brought together scientists and decision-makers to collaborate across political divides on constructive proposals for reducing the nuclear threat.

The Pugwash Conferences are founded in the desire to see all nuclear arms destroyed and, ultimately, in a vision of other solutions to international disputes than war. The Pugwash Conference in Hiroshima in July this year declared that we have the opportunity today of approaching those goals. It is the Committee's hope that the award of the Nobel Peace Prize for 1995 to Rotblat and to Pugwash will encourage world leaders to intensify their efforts to rid the world of nuclear weapons.

9   Post-Cold War Weapons Reduction: The Role of NATO

Lamberto Zannier

Introduction

In the past decade, more dramatic and profound changes have occurred in the international security environment than during any other period since World War II. While marking the end of a long period of confrontation, the post-Cold War era has also brought with it a degree of uncertainty and instability in many areas, with a number of implications for international security. These new problems, however immediate, should not be allowed to overshadow the fact that the political transformation in Europe has provided unique new opportunities to build a lasting and stable security environment based on cooperation rather than on confrontation. A fundamental task, for the states and institutions concerned, is to make use of these opportunities to advance a process of cooperation that will result in more security for all.

One of the areas in which we can achieve more substantial results is disarmament and arms control. In fact, over the last few years, we have already witnessed the conclusion and implementation of a number of far-reaching agreements, which have resulted in dramatic reductions in the fields of nuclear and conventional weapons. This chapter will highlight the specific contributions that the North Atlantic Treaty Organization (NATO) has made to this process.

Nuclear Arms Control

Several nuclear arms control agreements came with the end of the Cold War, rather than after it. One of these is the 1987 Intermediate-range Nuclear Forces (INF) Treaty, which led to the elimination of an entire category of nuclear weapons systems. Similarly, the START-I Treaty came relatively early in the Cold War thaw; with the end of the Cold War, the implementation of the START-I Treaty is proceeding successfully, well in advance of the target date. A major problem for the entry into force of this treaty was, at the beginning of the post-Cold War period, the issue of the succession to the former Soviet Union by a number of new independent states and their accession to the Nonproliferation Treaty (NPT) as non-nuclear weapons states. The Western allies conducted intense dialogue, both individually and collectively, within the framework of the existing cooperative structures of the NATO alliance, with all parties involved in order to promote a satisfactory resolution of these issues. In this context, Belarus, Kazakhstan and Ukraine should be given credit for their accession to the Nonproliferation Treaty as non-nuclear weapon states and for the transfer of virtually all nuclear weapons on their territories to Russia. In particular, NATO ministers have welcomed the recent announcement that all nuclear weapons have been transferred from the territory of the Ukraine for dismantling, in accordance with the US–Russia–Ukraine trilateral statement signed in Moscow in January 1994.

The successful entry into force of the START-I Treaty, and the significant progress in its implementation, paved the way for the ratification of the START-II Treaty by the US Congress in January 1996. NATO allies are confident that ratification of the START-II Treaty by Russia can also be achieved in the near future, so as to allow for a further dramatic reduction of the strategic nuclear weapons of the United States and Russia to a level of 3000 to 3500 each. This would be another extremely important step forward in the process of reduction of the huge nuclear arsenals accumulated in the long years of the Cold War.

These achievements have had a profound impact on the international strategic situation and have created a sound basis for stability and cooperative security for the 21st century. The new strategic environment has made it possible to reduce NATO's reliance on nuclear weapons as a deterrent against aggression. Hence the circumstances in which the use of nuclear weapons might need to be contemplated are considered very remote. As spelled out in the Alliance's *Strategic Concept*, nuclear forces retain only a fundamentally political role: to preserve peace and prevent coercion.

NATO's initiatives for lowering the levels of its nuclear forces go well beyond what has been agreed in the framework of formal treaty stipulations.

The alliance has rapidly reduced and adapted its nuclear posture following the end of the Cold War. In 1991, NATO decided to reduce its nuclear stockpile in Europe by over 80 per cent. As a part of these reductions, which were completed in 1993, all ground-launched systems, including nuclear artillery, surface-to-surface missiles and surface-to-air missiles, have been removed from Europe for elimination; all nuclear weapons for surface ships and tactical submarines assigned to NATO have also been eliminated. These systems have been removed entirely from NATO inventories and the United States is dismantling all the associated warheads. Further reductions will be made by 1998, with the withdrawal and elimination of US nuclear bombs from Europe. France has also announced the elimination of all its intermediate- and short-range missile systems and the postponement of a new submarine-launched missile system. NATO's only nuclear weapons remaining in Europe are bombs for dual-capable aircraft. These have also been substantially reduced in number and are stored in a reduced number of locations in highly secure conditions. The dual-capable aircraft associated with them have been reduced in readiness and reoriented to conventional roles.

NATO members also believe that, in the present strategic situation, there exist no immediate military threats against the alliance. While NATO does have an obligation to prevent current risks from developing into threats to its members, the present nuclear posture will, for the foreseeable future, continue to meet the requirements of the alliance, even in case of its future enlargement. There is, therefore, no need now to change or modify any aspect of NATO's nuclear posture or policy. On the other hand, nuclear forces, even at a reduced level, will continue to fulfil an indispensable and unique role in alliance strategy and to provide an essential and enduring political and military link between the European and North American members of the alliance. These roles are sufficient to serve the fundamental purpose of contributing to the preservation of peace and security, which is one of the central objectives of the Washington Treaty establishing NATO.

Disposal of Nuclear Weapons

A prominent example of NATO's practical contribution to reducing the risks inherited from the Cold War has been the establishment, at the beginning of 1992, of a working group for the exchange of information on national assistance projects that support the elimination of nuclear weapons in Russia and other new independent states. Following the demise of the Soviet Union, the safe and secure dismantling of former Soviet nuclear weapons became a matter of highest international priority. Several NATO member countries launched a number of individual programmes to assist Russia and the new independent states in their efforts in this area. The United States alone has invested over $1.5 billion in programmes of assistance.

In addition to weapons dismantling, these national assistance programmes are mainly focused on ensuring safe transportation and protection for fissile material, providing emergency-response equipment, constructing storage facilities and helping with the conversion of weapons-grade nuclear material. These activities also cover areas such as the establishment of effective export controls, support for the creation of science and technology centres in Moscow and Kiev, and the retraining, resettlement and housing of personnel involved. A further important part of these efforts is the agreement between Russia and the United States on the purchase and conversion of Russian highly-enriched uranium into low-enriched uranium as fuel for nuclear power stations. The main objective of these activities is to ensure that the dismantling of nuclear weapons is carried out under conditions of safety and security, and that it does not result in any loss of control or proliferation of nuclear materials, equipment and technology.

Proliferation Control for Weapons of Mass Destruction

In spite of all these efforts, the road to achieving lasting and stable security conditions is not without dangers, and new risks and challenges lie ahead. One of the most serious threats faced by the international community today is the risk posed by the proliferation of weapons of mass destruction (WMD) and their delivery means, including the illicit trade in fissile material.

Some two dozen countries have ongoing programmes to develop weapons of mass destruction and/or the means to deliver them. In some cases, such programmes have been developed to advanced levels, and would be helped greatly by the acquisition of weapons-related material, delivery means or related technology. At the NATO summit in January 1994, the alliance's heads of state and government stated that WMD proliferation constitutes a threat to international security and is a matter of concern to NATO. They therefore decided to intensify and expand the alliance's political and defence efforts against proliferation, taking into account the work already under way in other international fora and institutions. The primary objective of this initiative is to consider how to strengthen ongoing non-proliferation efforts and develop new efforts to reduce the proliferation threat and to protect against it. In so doing, NATO wants to avoid duplicating or substituting for efforts taking place in other international fora; rather it wants to reinforce and supplement existing non-proliferation regimes. As an important element in this approach, NATO has initiated consultations with its North Atlantic Cooperation Council (NACC) partners, in order to foster a joint approach to the proliferation problem.

Members of NATO are actively supporting the disarmament and non-proliferation efforts taking place in a number of international fora. In particular, they gave their full support to the unconditional and indefinite extension of the Nonproliferation Treaty, which they view as the cornerstone of the international nuclear non-proliferation policy. They also support the work of the Conference on Disarmament in achieving a truly comprehensive and sufficiently verifiable global ban on all nuclear testing, and in initiating negotiations on a fissile material cut-off treaty.

As a defensive alliance, NATO must also address the military capabilities needed to discourage the proliferation of weapons of mass destruction and consider how to protect NATO territory, populations and forces against them. While WMD proliferators will probably lack the capability to threaten the destruction of NATO member states, any crisis involving such proliferators could carry the risk that nuclear, biological and chemical (NBC) weapons might be used. It is important to ensure that NATO's military posture demonstrates the cohesion of the alliance, and that it provides reassurance and maintains NATO's freedom of action in the face of proliferation risks. NATO's military posture should show to any potential aggressor that the alliance cannot be coerced by the threat or use of NBC weapons and has the ability to respond effectively to such threats to its security if they emerge. NATO's defence efforts that address proliferation risks are an integral part of the continued adaptation of the alliance to the new security environment after the Cold War. They will play an important role in the enhancement of NATO's capabilities and will improve the alliance's overall capacity to accomplish all of its required missions.

NATO and Conventional Arms Control

There have been many recent developments in arms control of conventional weapons as related to NATO. In the autumn of 1995, an unprecedented process of reductions in five categories of conventional armaments in Europe was completed under the 1990 Conventional Forces in Europe (CFE) Treaty. This resulted in a drastic reduction of the total quantity of military equipment in both NATO and the former Warsaw Pact countries. This process, with its conditions of full transparency, has also led to the development of an enhanced pattern of cooperation between armed forces of the former Warsaw Pact nations. Members of NATO, who had been the main promoters of the conclusion of this landmark treaty, have launched a cooperation programme in the field of verification with the other treaty signatories. This has contributed to the establishment of a more cooperative military relationship between them. Over 50 on-site inspections have already been conducted by joint multinational teams with the participation of non-NATO states parties.

As a result of the overall successful implementation of the CFE Treaty, the capability of launching a surprise attack and the danger of large-scale offensive action in Europe as a whole have been diminished substantially, although risks and challenges still exist in some parts of Europe. Even though not all treaty obligations have been fully complied with by all the states who are parties to it, the resolution of the so-called 'Russian flank' issue in the context of the CFE Review Conference at the end of May of 1996 has substantially improved the overall implementation record. It is now time to look ahead and consider new efforts to preserve the achievements of the treaty and to enhance its viability and effectiveness.

To this effect, the states who are parties to the CFE Treaty are working within the framework of the Joint Consultative Group in Vienna to address operational issues based on recommendations by the Review Conference. These include enhancements in the areas of information exchange and notifications, verification and arms limitations. The other main task for negotiators in Vienna will be to consider the scope and parameters of a process that could improve the operation of the treaty in a changing environment. This should include considerations of measures and adaptations that could help achieve the objectives of the treaty, and enhance its viability and effectiveness. Progress in this work will be reported to ministers at the time of the Organisation for Security and Cooperation in Europe (OSCE) Lisbon summit in December 1996.

NATO and Regional Arms Control

Other than adapting the CFE Treaty to new circumstances, the next challenge in the area of conventional arms control is the application of confidence- and security-building measures and arms limitations on a regional scale. The primary goal should be to contribute to the settlement of international crises or conflicts that are on a regional scale but threaten to expand. An example of such a contribution has been the successful conclusion of agreements on confidence- and security-building measures, and on regional arms limitations, within the framework of the Dayton peace process. The challenges for the adaptation of traditional arms control to a regional crisis are manifold. For example, one of the criticisms of the CFE Treaty is that it has proved unable to contribute to the settlement of such regional crises as the one in Chechnya or the conflict in Nagorno-Karabakh.

This specific criticism is valid. However, we must keep in mind that the objective of conventional arms control continues to be the creation of stability at lower levels of armaments and under conditions of full transparency. Arms control cannot be used by itself as a tool for crisis management. Instead, arms control can contribute by providing the necessary framework of military stability, in order to allow a broader political effort to settle a conflict.

The conclusion of arms control agreements in the former Yugoslavia has been the result of strenuous efforts by the OSCE states and, in particular, the witness states, to bring all relevant parties to the negotiating table, and to assist them throughout the complex and difficult process of negotiation. The implementation of these agreements, and in particular of the agreement described in Article IV – which will entail substantial reductions of military equipment – will be no easy challenge. Its success will be closely linked with the overall progress in the implementation of the peace process and, in the first instance, with the successful outcome of the elections in Bosnia–Herzegovina. NATO has been fully supportive of the goals of these negotiations and has provided the respective chairmen with liaison officers to ensure appropriate coherence between the arms control process and the implementation of the Dayton peace plan. NATO has also put at the disposal of the OSCE its expertise in the area of implementation and verification, and has invited representatives of the parties to a number of visits and training courses on inspections and arms reduction procedures. This has been a way in which the experience built up throughout the process of implementing the CFE Treaty can be shared with the States who are parties to the process of arms control in the former Yugoslavia.

An important corollary to this process will be an expanded arms control process on the broader basis provided for by Article V of Annex 1B of the Dayton Peace Agreement. That article asks for the establishment of a regional balance in and around the former Yugoslavia. It asks that this should be accomplished by increasing the transparency of military forces, and the predictability of their operations, at lower levels of forces on a regional basis. At the same time a clear dispute resolution process should be established under the aegis of the OSCE for direct and continuous discussion of regional security problems among the states most immediately involved. Article V negotiations will thus result in a mix of traditional arms control, regional measures and political dialogue, with a view to simultaneously preventing conflicts and enhancing stability, in specific regions. It may involve both CFE states and non-CFE countries, which could result in a coordination of their respective obligations in the area of arms control. But, perhaps even more importantly, it will also result in establishing a permanent mechanism within the OSCE for the purpose of facilitating the resolution of any disputes that may arise.

Conclusions

It is clear that, with the end of the Cold War, there is no longer a unidirectional threat to European security. As the discussions above have pointed out, different instruments are now needed to address the very diverse security risks that are emerging in this post-Cold War world. NATO has shown that it is ready to do its part to contribute to an ongoing process aimed at improving security and stability in Europe. Yet no single country or institution can resolve any of these complex issues by itself. On the contrary, there is the need to further enhance those patterns of cooperation that are already well developed, both bilaterally and in the framework of our institutions. In order to increase its ability to cope with the new challenges, NATO, for one, is ready to take on this task and to continue acting decisively towards the improvement of security conditions in Europe.

10 The New Verification Game and Technologies at our Disposal

Patricia Lewis

Introduction

Since the end of the Cold War, multilateral arms control negotiations have taken a more central role. Whereas, in the past, the two nuclear superpowers had well-defined attitudes to verification and compliance – attitudes that they sometimes changed in reaction to each other's proposals – today other states are also defining the approach to verification. Examples include the Chemical Weapons Convention (CWC), the IAEA's '93+2' programme to strengthen safeguards and the debate in Geneva on verifying a comprehensive test ban treaty.

Technology has also changed. While some states may wish to turn the clock back and prevent, for example, satellite images being used in the verification regime of a treaty, non-governmental organizations and the news media – anyone with a few thousand dollars at their disposal – are able to commission commercial satellites or buy 'off the shelf' data. Although the spatial resolution of these data is not yet as good as that of superpower military satellites, much of it tells experienced analysts exactly what they want to know.

This chapter looks at the development of negotiations and of technology, and examines the 'democratization' of verification, particularly the role for academia, non-governmental organizations and the media.

Verification

Verification is a process which establishes whether all parties are complying with their obligations under an agreement.[1] The process of verification consists of multiple steps that can be either unilateral or cooperative in nature, or both. It includes monitoring, collection of relevant information, analysis of the information and judging compliance.

Verification cannot provide total certainty that all parties are complying with a treaty. Each agreement will have its own standard of verification. For example, the requirements for the verification regime of a treaty banning all nuclear weapons will be far more stringent than, say, those for the Conventional Forces in Europe Treaty. There is a general understanding that verification regimes should be designed so that violations are detected in time for appropriate action to be taken. The important role of verification is to ensure that a party contemplating cheating on a treaty realizes that it cannot do so without running a substantial risk of being found out. The design of verification regimes determines whether the likelihood of catching significant cheating is very high (say, 80 to 100 per cent) or is low (say, below 50 per cent). Generally, the more effort, money and resources put into verification, the higher the probability of detecting cheating.

There is a synergy between verification of arms limitation agreements and intelligence gathering for national security. Both processes include collecting information, collating information from a number of sources, analysing the information and distributing the information or analysis to interested parties.[2] Both verification and intelligence activities lead eventually to decisions on national and international security. The key difference between verification and intelligence gathering is that the former is carried out entirely in the open with the consent of all participating states, whereas the latter is a highly secretive operation. Intelligence agencies, however, play a role in verification, often by providing background information or by making suggestions for on-site inspection targets. The verification process also feeds information into the intelligence agencies, such as 'ground-truthing' (establishing if the information on the ground supports the information gleaned from satellites).

Confidence-building measures are activities which are designed to build trust between parties. They are self-contained in the sense that they constitute an agreement between parties to carry them out. Verification, on the other hand, relates to an undertaking between the parties which could stand without verification per se. Verification can often play a confidence-building role, for example in the process of election monitoring, verification of arms reductions and so on.

Verification in the Past

USA–USSR (Russia) Bilateral Treaties

From the end of World War II and the beginning of nuclear weapons until the rise of Mikhail Gorbachev in the USSR, the role of verification in USA–USSR arms control treaties was greatly dependent on the technology available to carry out monitoring at a distance. Throughout the bilateral negotiations, until the 1987 Intermediate-range Nuclear Forces (INF) Treaty, the issue of intrusive on-site inspections for verification purposes was guaranteed to stall or even halt negotiations. The United States pursued the concept of 'anytime, anywhere' inspections,[3] whilst the USSR viewed such proposals with intense suspicion, believing inspections to be a cover for espionage. The stand-off was so well established that it was said that 'verification is becoming a shield for those not interested in arms control to hide behind'.[4]

The Strategic Arms Limitation Treaties and the Anti-Ballistic Missile Treaty all relied for their verification on 'national technical means' which, in the arms control context, meant monitoring by intelligence satellites. The Threshold Test Ban Treaty and the Peaceful Nuclear Explosions Treaty were not ratified for many years, partly because of the issue of verification. In 1991, when agreement was reached on intrusive verification, the treaties finally entered into force.

The breakthrough in intrusive verification between the two superpowers came when USSR General Secretary Gorbachev introduced the policy of *Glasnost* (openness) and offered to open up sensitive military sites for inspections. The first bilateral agreement that took advantage of this change in policy was the 1987 INF Treaty, which not only included on-site inspections of INF bases, but also allowed monitoring of production facilities and of missile reductions. Since then the United States has back-tracked,[5] and the military and commercial agencies have raised concerns over the intrusiveness of on-site inspections and the cost of the verification regimes.

Multilateral Treaties

The main multilateral treaties in the field of arms control and disarmament are the Geneva Protocol (1925, entry into force (eif) 1928); Antarctic Treaty (1959, eif 1961); Partial Test Ban Treaty (1963); Outer Space Treaty (1967); Tlatelolco (1967, eif 1968); Nonproliferation Treaty (1968, eif 1970); Seabed Treaty (1971, eif 1972); Biological Weapons Convention (1972, eif 1975); Environmental Modification (Enmod) Convention (1977, eif 1978); Inhumane Weapons Convention (1981, eif 1983); Rarotonga (1985, eif 1986);

Stockholm Accord (1986); Conventional Forces in Europe (1990, eif 1992); Vienna Document (1990); Open Skies (1992, eif outstanding); Chemical Weapons Convention (1992, eif outstanding).

Although East–West tensions were played out in multilateral negotiations (for example, in the Chemical Weapons Convention (CWC)), their effects were often mitigated by states not participating in the Cold War. As a result, the arguments over intrusive verification in multilateral negotiations were of a different calibre from those in bilateral negotiations.

Treaties such as the 1968 Nonproliferation Treaty (NPT) and the 1959 Antarctic Treaty have provisions for on-site inspection, although the 1963 Partial Test Ban Treaty (PTBT) and the 1972 Biological Weapons Convention (BWC) have no verification provisions at all. Adherence to the NPT is monitored by the International Atomic Energy Agency (IAEA) in Vienna through bilateral safeguards agreements between the Agency and each member state. However, IAEA membership is not the same as NPT membership.

Before the end of the Cold War, but during the Gorbachev thaw, the highly significant Stockholm Accord was agreed between the participating states of the CSCE (Conference on Security and Cooperation in Europe, now called OSCE – Organisation for Security and Cooperation in Europe). This was a series of confidence-building measures designed to increase transparency over military exercises in Europe. From the beginning of the Accord, states carried out challenge inspections of military exercises and exercise calendars and data on the exercises were exchanged between the states.

The execution of the Accord was very successful. The trust that built up between the CSCE countries as a result of the Stockholm Accord had a number of effects, including (1) the formation of friendly relationships between East and West inspectors; (2) a reduction in the perception of 'the other side' as an 'enemy', so that there developed a sense of common purpose, (3) a pride in the inspection process itself, which led to friendly rivalry in, for example, seeing which team could offer the best food and wine; and (4) a reduction in the numbers and scales of the military exercises (partly as a result of lessening tension and partly as a result of attempting to reduce the cost of observation and inspection).

Thanks to the success of the Stockholm Accord, further treaties on conventional forces in Europe were negotiated (the Vienna Accord, the Conventional Forces in Europe Treaty (CFE) and the Open Skies Treaty). All of these treaties have met with success, although the CFE Treaty has inherent structural problems due to the break-up of the Warsaw Pact.

At the Conference on Disarmament, the Chemical Weapons Convention was successfully negotiated, but with less stringent on-site inspection requirements than first postulated. As it is yet to come into force, it is not possible to say how the verification provisions will be viewed in practice.

The Biological Weapons Convention is undergoing a process whereby confidence-building measures and verification provisions are being worked out, and they will be integrated into the Treaty in the next few years.

Verification in the Present

Strengthening IAEA Safeguards: '93+2'

The Nonproliferation Treaty was severely undermined by the discovery of (1) Iraq's nuclear weapon programme, (2) the suspicion over the capabilities and intentions of North Korea (DPRK) and the long refusal of North Korea to fulfil its safeguard obligations, and (3) the protracted dispute over the ownership of ex-Soviet nuclear weapons on the territory of the Ukraine.

If the International Atomic Energy Agency is to detect undeclared illegal activities in the future, safeguards need to be strengthened and reinforced. The IAEA has embarked on a programme (called '93+2') to evaluate the technical, financial and legal aspects of a wide set of safeguard measures. Proposals for new measures are extensive. They include new techniques, new types of on-site inspection and much more information to be provided by states parties.

There is clear emphasis on obtaining more information. This includes early provision of design information about the construction of and modification to nuclear facilities, and information on nuclear material and nuclear equipment transfers and on relevant non-nuclear material and equipment. A key component to obtaining information is an 'Expanded Declaration' in which a state would provide information on all nuclear-related processes (including past and future facilities), production, research and development, and training. The thinking behind the Expanded Declaration is to make the total nuclear programmes of states more transparent.

A significant part of the new techniques aimed at increasing access to information is the procedure called 'environmental monitoring'. This is a technique which takes samples from the air, soil, water, vegetation or exposed buildings' surfaces in the vicinity of the facility under investigation. The IAEA's studies thus far indicate that environmental monitoring is indeed a powerful tool. Isotopic signatures can be extremely specific and, the nearer to the facility the sample is taken, the easier it is to identify signatures of certain activities. Even past activities can be detected through this technique. Environmental monitoring thus has a significant deterrent effect. Even if inspectors are not allowed access to a building and even if an illegal activity was in the past, there is still a significant chance of a clandestine nuclear weapons programme being discovered.

Coupled with a greater degree of access to information and with environmental monitoring is a greater degree of physical access to nuclear and nuclear-related facilities. Increased physical access falls into two categories. The first is the concept of broad access which includes managed access. The second is the underutilized provision for no-notice inspections. Broad access means (1) access to any location on a site containing a safeguarded facility, (2) access to nuclear-related locations listed within an Expanded Declaration which are specifically declared as not containing nuclear material, and (3) access to other locations of interest to the IAEA on a voluntary basis. Managed access – a concept stemming from the negotiations for the Chemical Weapons Convention – is a process by which transparency is negotiated on site so that inspectors can have necessary access while valid, sensitive information can be protected, for example, by shrouding. Managed access is applicable to all three types of broad-access inspections and has been shown to be a practical approach to on-site inspections in commercially sensitive facilities.

In the case of no-notice inspections, states receive no advance warning of the inspection. The state and the facility know of an inspection only when the inspectors arrive at the facility gate. No-notice inspections are intended, in the main, to be for use at locations with declared nuclear material. In the future, however, it may be that a large number of states will opt for 'anytime, anywhere', no-notice inspections within an Expanded Declaration in exchange for a reduction in routine inspections.

Fundamental to many of the proposed new measures is the intention to increase the IAEA's cooperation with states and state systems of accounting and control (SSACs). Although there is a variation in the technical capabilities of the SSACs, there is nonetheless a common core of capabilities which would allow the IAEA to make use of the SSACs' activities and thereby reduce effort and costs. In the case of certain SSACs, cooperation with the IAEA is already established. In other cases – owing to history, capabilities and transparency concerns – the relationships between SSACs and the IAEA are underdeveloped. However, the IAEA is clearly making increased cooperation with SSACs a priority in its drive to reduce costs for routine inspections and thus make money available to carry out environmental monitoring and no-notice inspections.

Because there is going to be a large increase in the amount of information flowing into the IAEA, and this information is going to come from a variety of sources, it is vital that the procedures for analysis be improved. In addition to the already extensive computerized system in existence, the IAEA is developing a model to describe the known paths for nuclear weapons proliferation. The model will employ all types of information, including the potential uses of dual-use technology, non-nuclear materials and information from no-notice inspections and from environmental monitoring. The model is helping to determine the type of information required and how the information should be collected. It is thus an interactive part of the whole 93+2 process.

There are problems, however, with the implementation of the 93+2 process. Because some of the measures require a new legal agreement between the IAEA and each state, the implementation of 93+2 has been divided into two parts. The implementation of the Part 1 measures which do not require any new agreement began in 1995. The Part 2 measures which do require new agreements have yet to be implemented. The Part 2 measures include information on nuclear-related research and development not involving nuclear materials at research centres and universities; information on all buildings at nuclear plants and at other relevant locations; lists of domestic manufacturers of nuclear equipment; development plans; inspections at locations other than the 'strategic points' at which inspections are already carried out; inspection access to other locations of interest; and no-notice inspections beyond the 'strategic points' and other locations.

Comprehensive Test Ban Treaty

The mainstay of the verification regime for the Comprehensive Test Ban Treaty (CTBT) will be an International Monitoring System (IMS) comprised of four basic technologies: seismic, radionuclide, infrasound and hydroacoustic detector networks. This monitoring system will comprise 50 primary and 120 auxiliary seismic stations, a network of 11 hydroacoustic monitors, 60 infrasound stations and 80 stations for measuring atmospheric radionuclides. It is likely that 40 of the 80 stations for increasing radioactive particles will also monitor the presence of noble gases such as xenon and argon. There are provisions for the 'improvement of the verification regime', which allow electromagnetic pulse (EMP) detection, satellites or other technology to be incorporated in the IMS, subject to the consensus of the Executive Council, without requiring the full process of an Amendment Conference. The International Data Center under the technical secretariat will process raw data from the IMS stations and send it to states parties.

On-site inspections and how to decide whether to carry one out had been a constant source of tensions within the negotiations. The final text allows an on-site inspection to be triggered by any relevant kind of information 'consistent with generally recognized principles of international law', including national technical means but excluding espionage. The Executive Council must decide to carry out an inspection by a 'majority of all members'. There was an extensive argument between the United States and China on this issue: China insisted that the majority be two-thirds and the US wanted a simple majority of those present and voting.

A decision on the on-site inspection has to be taken by the Executive Council within 96 hours of receiving a request and an inspection team has to arrive within six days of the receipt of the request. The timeframe for an inspection is 60 days, with the possibility of extending it by up to 70 days, subject to a majority decision of the Executive Council. Also included in the on-site inspection provisions are overflights and managed access. States are allowed to protect sensitive facilities and information unrelated to compliance with the treaty. The inspection should move from less intrusive to more intrusive procedures. For a specific country, inspectors and access points have to be identified to the CTBT office within 30 days of the treaty's entry into force, and updated as appropriate.

The treaty also includes penalties if the Executive Council deems a request to have been 'frivolous or abusive'. Failure to comply with treaty obligations or abuse of the treaty's provisions can result in penalties ranging from suspension of membership rights to collective measures in conformity with international law, and the taking of urgent cases to the United Nations.

Verification in the Future

Going to Zero

The destruction of South Africa's nuclear weapons demonstrated that, while it may not be possible to 'disinvent' nuclear weapons, it is possible to dismantle a nuclear weapon arsenal and to verify the dismantling of the whole programme.

There are two approaches to reductions in existing nuclear weapons arsenals, and both are needed, operating in parallel, if reductions are to be successful. The traditional approach is that of 'top-down' reductions, that is to let the United States and Russia decrease their arsenals first, eventually bring in China, France and the United Kingdom, and hope for cooperation from Israel, India and Pakistan. The regional approach seeks to establish regional nuclear weapons-free zones through treaties such as the Treaty of Tlatelolco and the Treaty of Rarotonga.

Both of these approaches require stringent verification. The first requires the type of verification regime set in place by the INF and START Treaties with the addition of verifying warhead dismantling and cessation of fissile material production, then bringing other nuclear weapon states into the structure as and when necessary. The second approach needs a confidence-building approach as the states in the region build trust in each other through a sequence of agreements and confidence-building measures.

The regional approach could follow on to the two nuclear weapon-free zones in existence (South Pacific and Latin America) and build from there. For example, the next step could be the establishment of a sub-Saharan nuclear free zone in Africa. The regions of South Asia, the North Pacific/ East Asia, the Middle East, North America, the Commonwealth of Independent States and Europe could all be involved in a process of confidence building, transparency and, where appropriate, nuclear weapons reductions in parallel with the 'top-down' reduction process.

Much of the technology for verifying global nuclear weapon elimination is well known and has been used in the context of treaties to reduce nuclear-tipped missiles. However, the technologies required for verifying warhead dismantling are unproven within that context and there will have to be a period of preparation and practice inspections to ascertain and correct the problems and pitfalls associated with that verification process. Achieving a world free of nuclear weapons will also require the successful implementation of the comprehensive nuclear test ban and a ban on the production of fissile material for weapons purposes.

Getting to zero nuclear weapons will not be the whole story. Sustaining a nuclear weapons-free world indefinitely will be challenging. The verification regime will be intrusive and expensive. For how long will a high degree of intrusion be required or accepted? For how long will states be willing to fund such a verification regime and for how long can the world maintain its enthusiasm for such a process?

Regional Confidence Building and Sub-state Conflicts

A mechanism for reducing tension between groups within states before it reaches the point of conflict is needed within the international security system. In the first place, a mechanism is required for alerting the international community to tension that may escalate to violent conflict. Second, we should have a process of mediating between the hostile parties. Third, a set of tried and tested verification and confidence-building measures, appropriately chosen for the individual situation, should be put into operation.

The application of verification and confidence-building measures to sub-state conflicts has received very little attention until now, and it is this new task that provides the biggest challenge for the future. The main difficulty in applying confidence-building measures to sub-state and trans-border conflicts is that the situation is not one of state-to-state, but one of groups within states. Often, one of the groupings will be the government of the state, or one of the groupings may inhabit a region crossing state boundaries. There may be many vested interests in not allowing a mediation and confidence-building process to begin. These include an unwillingness to share power, a fear of exposure, deeply held prejudices and so on. Therefore there has to be a procedure whereby a group, or groups, who feel under threat can approach the international community directly and be accorded some status so that they may be recognized and heard internationally.

During the process of mediation and negotiation, there are steps that can be taken to increase confidence in the intentions of the parties and to increase the likelihood of success for subsequent agreements. These range from building trust between local communities to providing data on levels of military equipment held by the state and by paramilitary organizations. Building trust through structured and agreed procedures between local communities or between the state and a minority group is called 'civilian confidence building'.

The application of verification and confidence building to sub-state and trans-border conflicts, such as ethnic or religious conflicts, is a new idea.[6] Such measures could include (1) the setting up of youth organizations that include representation from all sections of the population; (2) establishing an independent newspaper that is mandated to take the concerns and aspirations of all sections of the population into account, and to help build bridges between minorities and majorities, and which is monitored by an independent agency; (3) establishing locally based committees, on which UN representatives also sit, to act as a forum for low-level complaints to lessen the risk of escalation into violent conflict; and (4) setting up, if appropriate, visits from communities in neighbouring states that have overlapping ethnic or religious communities to facilitate the exchange of ideas, information and solutions.

In the case of sub-state violent conflicts where there are military, paramilitary or militia (as in the case of Northern Ireland, for example), the military capabilities of all the groupings need to be known and monitored, and that information must be made available to all parties. Independent observers could be allowed to observe the military capabilities of each party so that each side has more confidence in the numbers they are given. During a negotiation, it is unlikely that parties will wish to give highly detailed data on the location, configuration and command and control of their military capabilities. However, once agreement has been reached, a detailed data exchange and verification regime could be established through an independent organization, such as the UN or the OSCE, and reductions, withdrawals, repositionings and reconfigurations could then be verified to everyone's satisfaction.

As in the case of state-to-state trust building, such measures would not solve major problems by themselves and they are no panacea. However, they could help to reduce tensions and improve the climate for negotiations and long-term agreements. For example, in a long-running dispute, there can be agreement that neither side wishes to enter into a violent conflict with the other and they may be able to identify a number of confidence-building measures to relieve tension. Such measures can be reinforced if there is a degree of verification built in, for example through on-site inspections and aerial overflights. Tensions within negotiations are then reduced and parties may find that they reach agreement much more quickly – or they find that there is still disagreement, but that it is no longer so critical.

This process has been dubbed 'agreeing when we can – negotiating when we can't'. It requires the realization that, although confidence-building measures cannot solve a problem, they do help to reduce tension and increase understanding, and thereby facilitate creative discussion. This principle could be the foundation for experimenting with a range of new civilian and military confidence-building measures which could set the scene for a more peaceful and prosperous 21st century.

Environmental Agreements

The role of verification in environmental agreements is now an established field of study and it is recognized as an important activity for future security. The effect that environmental degradation has on international security, in terms of poverty, migration, conflict over resources and so on, is becoming increasingly apparent. It is in the interests of all states that environmental agreements are complied with, just for the sake of the survival of the planet as we know it. For this reason, the implementation review processes and verification mechanisms are crucial in determining the success of environmental agreements. For example, it is in the interests of all states that competing industries in other countries are not gaining monetary advantage by ignoring their obligations under environmental agreements.

The countries with most to gain from checking that states are complying with their environmental obligations are often those which are most severely affected by the environmental degradation; these are frequently the poorer countries. It is very much in their interests that polluting states – in many cases the wealthier industrially developed states – are truly reducing their polluting emissions. This is particularly the case for climate changes and trans-boundary pollution.

However, some states, particularly those that are less industrialized, are generally suspicious of verification. One of the most important tasks facing the international community is to promote the values of implementation and verification and to point out the very real advantages that verified, meaningful treaties hold for disadvantaged states. This is particularly true for the ways in which appropriate technologies and methodologies could be used to implement the treaties. Industrially developing nations could make a significant contribution to the techniques being developed to monitor environmental agreements and, in doing so, they could shape the process more to their liking. Grand declarations and statements of intent on environmental issues are no longer enough. Environmental agreements must be backed up by strong implementation and checks on that implementation – the environment is an issue that concerns all.

The verification of environmental agreements has some overlap in the methodologies and technologies with the verification of arms control treaties, but there are also a number of differences. First, although some key environmental agreements have hard targets and timetables (such as the Montreal Protocol) and some ban explicit activities (such as the Whaling Convention), some agreements are much less quantitative than those in the field of disarmament.

Second, the measurable environmental data are very different from the data counting specific pieces of military hardware. There are often large margins of error and so there is much reliance on comparisons and consistencies of self-reported data with other variables. In addition, many of the baseline data are unknown. For example, with the Biodiversity Convention, it is impossible to know how many species there are in the world.

Third, even when there are individual items that can be measured, such as endangered animal species or species of plant life, they are subject to other forces in addition to malignant human activities that can destroy them. Trying to separate the activities that can be controlled and monitored from those that cannot is difficult, particularly when they are entangled. On the other hand, by far the greatest threat to animals and plants is the destruction of their natural habitat by humans. In addition, such destruction is relatively easy to measure accurately, and there is a large body of reliable data to support the monitoring of forest, marshlands and desert areas and so on.

The security picture is becoming more complex. In many cases environmental degradation, such as water shortages or water pollution, are forming part of the backdrop to violent conflict. Building confidence in environmental agreements via effective implementation will become an increasingly important part of global and regional security regimes.

Environmental agreements, particularly those which aim to protect plants and animals, often cover complex issues which states may have neither the resources nor the inclination to address properly. To a large extent, the implementation and monitoring of such agreements is provided by non-governmental and intergovernmental organizations (NGOs and IGOs).[7] This is an increasing trend in all international agreements with large and small NGOs and IGOs playing crucial, and sometimes leading roles.

The Role of NGOs

In the fields of arms control/disarmament, conflicts, human rights, the environment and so on, non-governmental organizations are playing an increasingly central role. The increasing importance of NGOs is due to a number of factors: (1) the deliberate move towards professionalism within NGOs, (2) the quality of research that NGOs carry out, (3) the quality of information that NGOs give to the media and general public, and (4) the reduction in expenditure by government ministries in industrial states which has led to a reduction in the quality of the research and information and of the decisions made within them. Cost cutting has also led to a reordering of priorities within governments so that there are a number of issues about which a government may have very little knowledge and there are many places in the world where a government may have no representation – there NGOs may be running significant operations.

There are both advantages and disadvantages to this situation. NGOs can be more flexible than governments and can therefore act quickly if necessary. NGOs are often more in touch with widespread public opinion (since they are largely funded by voluntary subscriptions) and they tend to see human rights as their main priority. Because they are not government, people often trust NGOs more readily, and NGOs are therefore often the best mediators and reconciliators.

However, not all NGOs are worthy of trust. Some may set out deliberately to worsen a situation, although more likely such an outcome will be the result of incompetence, lack of discipline and overstretching of resources. There is widespread concern over the accountability of NGOs. Democratic governments are generally accountable to their parliaments and to the public. Censure can be shown through both avenues. NGOs, on the other hand, are accountable to their funders (membership or foundations, or both). In the end, to whom are the funders accountable? If the membership is very large and spread throughout the population and there are good processes of accountability to the membership, NGOs are subject to censure similar to that of democratic governments: members can vote with their feet and their wallets. However, NGOs which have limited membership, such as religious groups or small specialized organizations, are particularly vulnerable to the lack of checks and balances in their policy formation and action. Those organizations that entirely depend on foundations to fund them are aware that many of those funding bodies are highly unaccountable for their decisions and yet may be quite influential in their ability to affect policy.

There are no easy answers to these problems. Non-governmental organizations are playing a larger part in international negotiations, in conflict resolution and in verification. In this respect the world has changed rapidly over the last 30 years and new communications technology has been one of the major factors in that change. It is likely, therefore, that NGOs will continue to increase their roles in international politics, and accommodation in the international system must be made for them.

Notes

1   *Verification in All its Aspects: Study on the role of the UN in the field of verification*, United Nations General Assembly A/45/372, 28 August 1990.
2   Michael Herman, 'Intelligence and Arms Control Verification', in J.B. Poole (ed.), *Verification Report 1991*, New York: The Apex Press for VERTIC, 1991, p.187.
3   Article 10 of the US draft of the CWC, Conference on Disarmament Document CD/500, Geneva, 1984.
4   Sidney Graybeal, US Commissioner to the US–USSR Standing Consultative Commission, 1973–7, quoted in Richard Scribner, Theodore J. Ralston and William D. Metz, *The Verification Challenge: Promise and Problems of Strategic Nuclear Arms Control Verification*, Boston: Birkhäuser, 1985, p.21
5   See, for example, Gordon M. Burck, 'The Chemical Weapons Convention Negotiations', in J.B. Poole and R. Guthrie (eds), *Verification Report 1992*, London: VERTIC, 1992, pp.126–8.
6   Dennis Sammut, 'The CSCE and Russian Peacekeeping', in J.B. Poole and R. Guthrie (eds), *Verification 1995: Arms Control, Peacekeeping and the Environment*, Boulder, CO: Westview Press for VERTIC, 1995, p.291.
7   John Lanchbery, 'Reviewing the Implementation of Biodiversity Agreements', in *Verification 1995: Arms Control, Peacekeeping and the Environment*, p. 330.

Appendix   Treaties and Technologies

Nonproliferation Treaty
IAEA safeguards
Based on IAEA Information Circular 153 (1972)
Designed to detect the loss of a 'significant quantity' of nuclear material within a 'conversion time'
Significant quantities are Pu: 8kg; HEU: 25kg; LEU: 75kg; U-233: 8kg
Conversion times are: Pu: 7–10 days; HEU: 7–10 days; oxides: 1–3 weeks; nitrates: 1–3 weeks; spent fuel: 1–3 months; LEU: 12 months; natural U: 12 months
Nuclear weapons states do not have to accept safeguards
Verification is carried out by on-site inspections/data verification and locks, seals and recording equipment
IAEA membership is not the same as NPT membership

'93+2' Strengthened Safeguards
Environmental sampling is a powerful tool for detecting traces of material. It is done in two ways: bulk sampling which allows the presence of illegal quantities to be detected but does not always provide a 'smoking gun'; and particle sampling which allows tiny traces of illegal material to be detected unambiguously and thus does provide a 'smoking gun'.

Export Controls
Zangger Committee (nuclear technologies)
London Suppliers Club (nuclear technologies)
Australia Group (chemical technologies)
Wassenaar Agreement (conventional technologies)
Missile Technology Control Regime (missile technologies)
Trigger lists
Common export controls
Reliance on sharing intelligence

Nuclear Test Monitoring
Seismic detection
Radioactive debris monitoring
Hydroacoustic detection
Infrasound detection
On-site inspections
Aerial overflight
Satellite images
Data transmission; international data centres; remote sensing satellites

Nuclear Weapon Reductions (INF and START)
On-site inspections
National technical means (particularly satellites)
Radiation detectors
Imaging techniques
Seals
Linear measuring devices
Portal perimeter monitoring
Infra-red profiler
X-ray cargo scanner
Closed-circuit TV

Chemical Weapons Convention
Sampling equipment – leak-proof
Portable analytic equipment
X-ray equipment
Ultrasonic equipment
Mobile mass spectroscopy
Real-time x-ray fluorescence
Protective clothing/masks
Tags, seals, locks
Data transmission
Laboratory analysis
Gas–liquid chromatography
High-performance liquid chromatography
Mass-selective detectors
Infra-red spectroscopy
Nuclear magnetic resonance
Mass spectroscopy
Neutron activation analysis

Open Skies
Cameras, 30cm resolution
Video recorders, 30cm resolution
Sideways-looking synthetic aperture radar (SAR), 3m resolution
Infra-red line-scanning devices, 50cm resolution

Conventional Forces in Europe Treaty and Stockholm Accord
Training: language, and so on
Binoculars
Tape recorders
Communication equipment
Cameras – still and video
Helicopters for overflying exercises and CFE sites

11 The Open Skies Treaty: A Cooperative Approach to Confidence Building and Verification

Hartwig Spitzer

Introduction: History and Scope of the Open Skies Treaty

The Treaty on Open Skies, signed in Helsinki on 24 March 1992, represents the most wide-ranging multinational effort so far to enhance military transparency and confidence building through mutual aerial observation flights. Its origins and scope are representative of the last stage of the Cold War; it is a product of Cold War suspicion and of the attempt to overcome this suspicion by mutually agreed openness. It has been actively promoted by far-sighted and dedicated members of the governments of Canada and Hungary, but it would not have become reality without US initiative and substantial compromises on the part of both the US and the USSR/Russian governments.

In the spring of 1989, half a year before the revolutionary changes in Central Eastern Europe, President Bush was in the first 100 days of his presidency. His public approval ratings were meagre and he was looking for a foreign policy initiative which would allow him to gain ground and to test Gorbachev on his claim of the greater openness of *Glasnost*. He ordered his National Security Council Staff to prepare a wide-ranging review of arms control initiatives available to him. One of several such initiatives was 'Open Skies', which goes back to a proposal launched by President Eisenhower in 1955. Canadian officials became aware that Open Skies was being considered within the National Security Council in April 1989 and were attracted by the idea. They began to encourage their American counterparts to consider the subject sympathetically. During a visit to Washington in early May 1989, the Canadian prime minister, Mulrony and his foreign minister, Clark urged President Bush and his Secretary of State, Baker to respond positively to Open Skies.[1]

Bush took up the idea. On 12 May 1989, he proposed that an Open Skies initiative be considered by the states of the North Atlantic Treaty Organization (NATO) and the Warsaw Pact Organization (WPO):

> Now, let us again explore that proposal [Open Skies] but on a broader, more intrusive and radical basis – one which I hope would include the allies on both sides. We suggest that those countries that wish to examine this proposal meet soon to work out the necessary operational details, separately from other arms control negotiations. Such surveillance flights, complementing satellites, would provide regular scrutiny for both sides. Such unprecedented territorial access would show the world the true meaning of the concept of openness. The very Soviet willingness to embrace such a concept would reveal their commitment to change.[2]

The two main goals of the initiative have apparently been to increase mutual confidence through increased scrutiny of each other's activity and to test General Secretary Gorbachev's commitment to *Glasnost*. Obviously, the territories to be covered by overflights would have to include all of North America and Siberia, which are excluded from inspections under the Treaty on Conventional Forces in Europe (CFE).

For Canada, one of the main goals was to allow smaller states of the two alliances, which did not have reconnaissance satellites of their own, an opportunity to monitor events of interest. Canada also wanted to demonstrate to the European NATO countries that the North American allies were willing to share the burden of intrusive inspections of their territories.[3]

Unfortunately, these goals did not give the negotiators a sufficiently quantifiable set of criteria upon which to design the regime. It took almost three years of political manoeuvring, technical discussions and searching for compromise positions before the Open Skies Treaty could be signed, on 24 March 1992, in Helsinki. Since crucial technical details of sensor calibration and aircraft certification were not settled in time, the Open Skies Consultative Commission (OSCC) had to deal with them in the following years. As a result, the Open Skies Treaty is technically much more complicated than the CFE Treaty.

The negotiation history was marked by two major conferences in Ottawa (February 1990) and Budapest (April/May 1990), a stalemate until September 1991, and an intense negotiation period in Vienna from November 1991 to March 1992. The negotiations went through many ups and downs. Surprisingly, the dissolution of the Soviet Union on 31 December 1991 had little impact. Russia was understood to act as the successor of the Soviet Union in the negotiations. Other republics were invited to join. In fact, Belarus and the Ukraine joined the negotiations immediately. Georgia and Kyrgyzstan signed the treaty, but will not take part in the initial implementation phase. The former Soviet head of delegation Yevgeny Golovko continued as Russian Open Skies ambassador. Trial flights were arranged by Canada and Hungary as early as January and February of 1990 and the conclusion of the Hungarian–Romanian bilateral Open Skies Treaty in May 1991 (described below) had a stimulating effect on the negotiations. A lively account of the negotiation history is given by Peter Jones.[4]

Already in 1990 the states parties (that is, all NATO states and the states of the dissolving WPO) were able to agree on the initial objective of the treaty. The treaty was meant to enable participants to identify rapidly massing military formations by the generic types of vehicles within them. This required the ability to differentiate a tank from a truck, though not necessarily to identify exactly what type of tank or truck might be involved.[5] The states parties also agreed on a 24-hour all-weather sensor capability. This essentially paved the way for the choice of sensor types and capabilities of the treaty. In the end, the parties compromised on having 'imaging sensors' only, in particular (1) optical film and video cameras with a ground resolution of 30cm, and (2) thermal infra-red imaging sensors with a ground resolution of 50cm, and imaging radar with a ground resolution of 3m.

These capabilities are meant to match the initial intentions of the treaty, as stated in the preamble: (1) monitoring of compliance with existing or future arms control agreements, and (2) strengthening of the capacity for conflict prevention and crisis management in the framework of the Conference on Security and Co-operation in Europe and in other relevant international institutions.

Many other difficult issues had to be addressed. These included the ownership of the aircraft and the origin of the crew, data sharing, flight quotas, and territorial restrictions. These issues were eventually resolved in March 1992.

Treaty Provisions

According to the treaty, each state party has the right to conduct a certain number of observation flights (active quota) and is obliged to accept observation flights by other state parties over its territory (passive quota). The total active quota of a state shall not exceed its passive quota. Under the allocated passive quotas for each year, Russia (including Belarus) and the United States each have to accept 42 overflights; Canada, France, Germany, Italy,

Turkey, the Ukraine and the United Kingdom each have to accept 12 overflights; Norway has to accept seven overflights; Denmark, Poland, Romania and the Benelux group (Belgium, the Netherlands and Luxembourg) each have to accept six overflights; Bulgaria, Greece, Hungary, Iceland, Spain and the Czech and Slovak Republics together each have to accept four overflights; Portugal has to accept two overflights; while the passive quotas of Georgia and Kyrgyzstan will be decided by the first OSCC.[6] During the first three years of operation, an upper limit of 75 per cent of the ultimate quotas applies. When trying to allocate the individual active quota entitlements, problems occurred since almost every party wanted to overfly Russia and the Ukraine.

Finally, the parties agreed to an initial distribution of active quotas, which is considerably below the 75 per cent limit. Under this distribution, Russia, for example, has to accept inspection by Benelux (one inspection), Canada (2), Denmark (1), France (3), Germany (3), Italy (2), Norway (2), Poland (1), Turkey (2), the United Kingdom (3) and the United States (8). In turn it may inspect Benelux (two inspections), Canada (2), Germany (3), Greece (1), Italy (2), Norway (2), Turkey (2), the United Kingdom (3) and the United States (4).[7]

One important provision of the treaty is that the full territory of each state party can be overflown except for areas of hazardous airspace and a 10 km zone along the state borders. This implies that the vast territories of North America and Siberia which were hitherto 'off limits' to inspections will now be accessible to Open Skies flights.

Upon the insistence of Russia, each state to be overflown has the choice of either receiving the aircraft of the observing state or of providing an aircraft with full sensor equipment of its own for the observing state, the so-called 'taxi option'. This provision goes back to the Soviet hesitancy about fully opening its airspace to foreigners. Since Russia pushed the taxi option, the United States and others insisted that a Russian taxi aircraft would have to be equipped with all allowable sensors that are operating at the resolution specified by the treaty. Demonstration of that capability became an issue.

The treatment of sensor resolutions is indicative of the treaty's dual character between Cold War military thinking and a new openness. Whereas civilian remote-sensing practitioners would be happy if a sensor exceeded the design resolution, Open Skies negotiators have tried desperately to avoid this. A lot of effort has to be spent in proving that a sensor does *not* exceed the resolution specified by the treaty. This is to be accomplished in an initial seven-day certification of each Open Skies aircraft and by a short demonstration flight at the beginning of each Open Skies observation event. During these tests certain calibration targets (such as panels with black and white strips in the case of optical cameras) are displayed on an airfield and recorded by the sensors on board the overflying aircraft. Subsequent processing and analysis has to prove that the resolution goals have been met. It should be noted that the specified resolution of 30cm for photographic cameras is not defined as the standard photographic resolution, but rather as a type of pixel resolution.

Article IV of the Treaty limits the 'ground resolution' of optical cameras to 30cm. Ground resolution is defined in the Article II of Treaty as 'the minimum distance on the ground between two closely located objects distinguishable as separate objects.' This is a traditional definition. However, when describing that resolution in Decision III, the Treaty deviates from traditional photogrammetric practice and specifies that the 'value of the ground resolution shall be equal to the width of a single bar in the smallest group of bars [in a calibration target] which can be distinguished as separate bars, in centimeters.' Since ground resolution is most often explained in terms of Ground Resolved Distance (GRD), or the width of a bar and a space in a resolution target, 30cm ground resolution per Article II is, in reality, 60cm GRD. Many participants in Open Skies were disappointed to learn that. What they had thought the potential image quality to be, would be significantly less.[8]

However, this resolution will still allow the detection of regular military vehicles from their dimensions. For optical cameras, Decision III of the Treaty establishes the resolution and hence the minimum flight height H_{min}. H_{min} is the flight altitude at which the cameras achieve exactly 30cm of resolution. Decision III defines H_{min} as a function of at least five test points ($n = 5$) using pictures taken of a ground resolution target in the following equation:[9]

$$H_{min} = \frac{1}{n}\sum_1^n H_i \left[\frac{L_a}{L_2}\right]\left[\frac{K_1}{K_2}\right]^m$$

where n is the number of images being analysed; H_i is the height of the aircraft in metres at the moment the target was photographed; L_a is the agreed ground resolution of 30cm; L_2 is the measured ground resolution in centimetres; K_1 is the agreed modulation contrast of 0.4 at which the ground resolution is defined; K_2 is the effective modulation contrast (see the equation below); and m is the agreed corrected exponent value of 0.45,

$$K_2 = (C-1)/(C+2), \text{ and } C = 10^{\Delta \log E}.$$

where $\Delta \log E$ is the difference between the logarithms of the exposure response E from black and white bars of the calibration target.

One of the main tasks of certification and demonstration flights is to determine the minimum allowable flight altitude for each of the sensors. It has been pointed out that the above formula for the minimum flight altitude derived from Decision III might be insufficient since the actual ground resolution depends also on atmospheric conditions, such as the mean visibility and the aerosol content.[10] A more recent evaluation states that the above equation performs well under the set conditions of clear weather. Data taken by the US Open Skies team show that the above equation does model US camera resolutions.[11] Another important part of certification is the checking of film processing conditions required for achieving the treaty resolution.[12]

After considerable manoeuvring the states parties agreed on the sharing of the raw data. After an Open Skies observation flight any state party can request a first-generation copy of the raw data taken. In the case of photographic film, these raw data (a copy of the film negative) represent almost the full information in easy-to-analyse form. In case of thermal infra-red line scanners and synthetic aperture radar (SAR), much more systemic knowledge is necessary in order to transform the raw data into a useful product.

The option, and right, of data sharing is one of the most innovative features of the treaty, emphasizing its cooperative character. So far, data have been treated as 'government confidential' material, accessible to concerned government agencies, but not to the general public. Hence there are limits to openness. These limits, which date back to 1990, appear somewhat outdated in view of the upcoming commercial US photo-satellites which will provide black and white pictures with one-metre ground (pixel) resolution. Typical commercial pictures cover ground areas of about 10×10km, at a projected cost of a few hundred dollars.

Peter Jones describes the time sequence of observation events, which are analogous to on-site inspection procedures of the CFE Treaty.

The party requesting an overflight must inform the party to be overflown of its intention 72 hours before the arrival of its aircraft at a designated point of entry; the party to be overflown must acknowledge receipt within 24 hours and state whether it would allow the overflying country to bring its own aircraft or would exercise its right to provide an aircraft; after arrival, the aircraft and sensors might be inspected, and the proposed mission plan should be handed to the host country (this must be done no less than 24 hours before the overflight was scheduled to commence); once the overflight plan had been agreed, and the 24-hour period had elapsed, the flight would commence; the observing country would depart within 24 hours following the flight, and arrangement must be completed within this period; the entire time in-country should not exceed 96 hours. Attempts have been made to ensure that all of these time periods are flexible, however. Virtually any of them may be shortened by mutual consent.[13]

The Open Skies Consultative Commission

The treaty foresees the formation of an Open Skies Consultative Commission (OSCC). This body is responsible for the reallocation of active quotas on an annual basis. It will discuss any proposals for the upgrading of existing sensor types and the introduction of new sensor categories. As called for in Article VIII, the OSCC provides a forum within which disputes related to the treaty may be discussed if bilateral talks fail. The OSCC will discuss any technical questions arising from the accession to the regime of new states. The OSCC is also the forum to which bodies of the Organisation for Security and Cooperation in Europe (OSCE) or any other relevant international organization would address requests for extraordinary observation flights in times of tension.[14] The OSCC is mandated to meet at least four times a year in Vienna. In fact, its offices are next to the headquarters of the OSCE in the Vienna Hofburg.

The OSCC has established four working groups whose themes are costs, sensors and calibration rules, notification procedures and formats, and rules of procedure of the OSCC. On the basis of the results of the working groups, the OSCC establishes legally binding 'Decisions' to the Treaty. Such decisions can be further elaborated by 'Guidance Documents', which are open to continuing discussion.

The OSCC and its working groups started intensive work on 2 April 1992. A sizable number of questions related to sensor calibration, aircraft certification and other procedures had to be addressed. The OSCC also had to resolve the matter of Czech and Slovak flight quotas after the dissolution of Czechoslovakia. As a result of these meetings several decisions were taken concerning (1) how to calculate the minimum permissible flight altitude when using optical and video cameras; (2) how to calculate the minimum height above ground level at which each video camera with real-time display and each infra-red line-scanning device installed on an observation aircraft may be operated during an observation flight; (3) calibration activities; (4) the format in which data are to be recorded and exchanged on recording media other than photographic film; and (5) the mandatory time period for storing and sharing data recorded during an observation flight. These decisions were considered important milestones in the technical and procedural elaboration of the treaty provisions.[15]

The OSCC also held two seminars on the possible use of the Open Skies regime for environmental monitoring, on 3–4 December 1992 and on 11–12 July 1994. The seminars established the potential of Open Skies in the environmental area. In 1995, the work of the OSCC slowed down somewhat owing to outstanding treaty ratifications which prevented its entering into force. Work on drafting a Guidance Document for aircraft and sensor certification continues.

In summary, the OSCC has proved to be an efficient body when it comes to resolving outstanding technical questions. It is also a sounding board for potential future extensions of the treaty.

Trial Flights and Preparations for Implementation

The states parties have been quite forthcoming in arranging mutual trial flights in order to develop and test procedures and for training purposes. Pioneering and ground-breaking trial flights were carried out by Canada and Hungary in January and February 1990 and by Romania and Hungary on 29 June 1991. Germany and the United States were particularly active in subsequent years. For example, in 1995, Germany was involved in 12 test flights with Spain, Portugal, the Ukraine, the United States, Canada, Russia, Poland and Romania.[16] A short record of the overall trial flights undertaken in 1992–4 can be found in *SIPRI Yearbooks* for 1993–5.

Most of the signatory nations have established an active Open Skies operation centre even though the treaty has not entered into force. These active nations have pursued a training programme that is intended to prepare equipment and train personnel for treaty operations. Several nations have aircraft modified specifically for Open Skies use. These include Bulgaria: one operational AN30, a medium-sized twin-engine turbo-prop aircraft with a range of about 1200km; the Czech and Slovakian Republics: one operational AN30 (joint aircraft); Germany: one TU-154M in operation with an observation range of more than 3000km, plus one planned TU-154M; Hungary: one operational AN26; Romania: one operational AN30; Russia and Belarus: one AN30 in operation, two planned AN30 and one TU-154M under discussion; Turkey: two planned CN235 CASA twin-engined aircraft with a range of about 1200km; Ukraine: one operational AN30; United Kingdom: one operational Andover PR MK1, a twin-engined turbo-prop aircraft with a range of about 1200km; United States: one operational OC-135, two OC-135 in preparation, all with an observation range of over 3000km.

Belgium, Canada, France, Greece, Italy, Luxembourg, Netherlands, Norway, Portugal and Spain have jointly pursued the development of a sensor pod to be installed under a C-130 *Hercules* aircraft. This concept allows any similar model in the fleet of C-130s to be used for Open Skies observation missions, thereby saving the large expense of dedicating aircraft to the Open Skies mission. The pods are boxes initially containing optical and video cameras only.

All participating aircraft will be equipped with panoramic and framing photographic cameras. Germany, Russia and the United States are also testing or planning 'thermal infra-red line scanners', which can produce thermal images. However, infra-red line scanners can only be used for treaty applications three years after the treaty's entry into force. Germany and Russia are jointly developing a Russian-made synthetic aperture radar system (SAR), whereas the United States is refurbishing a rather ancient SAR system of its own.[17] As a rule, sensors used under Open Skies have to be unclassified and commercially available.

Because Open Skies observation missions are flown in all types of weather, most countries have more than one camera system and more than one type of film. The lower-resolution systems allow the aircraft to fly 'under the weather' and still abide by treaty resolutions, while the high-resolution systems allow for wide-area observation when the weather is good. Germany and the United Kingdom have introduced 'resolution degrading optics' to lower the resolution of their systems to achieve 'under the weather' capability without the expense of another camera system. Analogous to a low-pass filter, these degrading optics are intended to reduce the resolution in a way that cannot be reversed or enhanced later.[18]

Ratification Problems and Prospects

Most of the signatories have ratified the treaty and deposited the instruments of ratification with the two depository states of the treaty, Canada and Hungary. So far, treaty ratifications have been deposited by Belgium, Bulgaria, Canada, the Czech and Slovak Republics, Denmark, France, Germany, the United Kingdom, Greece, Hungary, Iceland, Italy, Norway, the Netherlands, Poland, Portugal, Romania, Spain, Turkey and the United States. The treaty has been signed but not yet ratified by Georgia and Kyrgyzstan; and it has not yet been signed by Belarus, Luxembourg, the Russian Federation and the Ukraine. However, the treaty can only enter into force when Belarus, Russia and the Ukraine have completed their ratification process. Here a major problem has arisen because the Russian Duma seems to be quite reluctant to take action on Open Skies, as well as on the ratification of the START-II Treaty and the Chemical Weapons Convention.

Critical voices within the Duma claim that the treaty is discriminating against Russia because the 16 NATO states have agreed not to overfly each other, so that a disproportionately higher fraction of data is being generated by overflights over Russia (initially 28 flights per year) than over any other state. For comparison, the initial passive quotas of Germany and the USA will be five and four, respectively. The Western European Union states reacted to this in July 1995 by offering Russia additional quotas on a voluntary basis. But some asymmetry remains.

The outlook for Open Skies Treaty verification by the Duma appears quite dim at present. For many Western states, ratification of START-II and the Chemical Weapons Convention is clearly higher on the agenda of political priorities and diplomatic efforts. In the Duma itself a substantial majority of parliamentarians is critical of the West and of anything which is perceived as weakening Russia's military strength. On the other hand, part of the Russian government and the military system seems to have accepted Open Skies as an endeavour of mutual benefit.

Ratification in the Ukrainian Rada failed on 16 January 1996 'for financial reasons'. It is unclear when another attempt at ratification can be made. It is assumed that Belarus will ratify the treaty once Russia has done so.

A Success Story: The Hungarian–Romanian Open Skies Treaty

Much more than any trial flight, the joint experience of Hungary and Romania has demonstrated convincingly the success of an Open Skies regime in confidence building between and within the states. The two countries have also demonstrated that an Open Skies Treaty can be executed in a very cost-effective way.

Treaty Provisions and Initial Experience

Soon after the Budapest Open Skies conference of May 1990, Romania proposed to Hungary to start negotiations for a bilateral Open Skies agreement.[19] Serious negotiations began in February 1991. After six days of negotiations, the main body of the agreement had been worked out. The aim of the two delegations was to create a simple and cost-effective regime, matching the financial and technical resources of the parties. It was agreed that, in the initial stage of the implementation of the agreement, both parties would use only those aircraft and sensors which they had at the time of the negotiations. According to the 'Quota Annex', Hungary and Romania will have the right to carry out four observation flights a year in each other's airspace. This figure may seem low, but it is quite substantial if one takes into account that the bilateral regime will continue functioning after the entry into force of a multilateral Open Skies agreement.

The 'Sensor Annex' permits the use of film and video cameras, without limiting their performance. Neither the focal length nor the ground resolution of the sensors is limited. This makes it possible for the parties to use the best equipment they have and to fly as low as they wish, without breaking the rules of flight safety. It also saves lengthy and costly procedures of sensor certification.

Information sharing is ensured by the use of dual cameras. The two negatives are developed in an established ground facility of the observed party. One negative is taken home by the observing party and the observed party retains the other. When video cameras are used, the videotape is copied. The original remains with the observed party and the observing party may take home the copy.

The treaty was signed in Bucharest on 11 May 1991. The first demonstration flight took place on 29 June 1991, using a Romanian aircraft, which was equipped with a French-made OMERA 35 dual camera. The camera has a focal length of 200mm and takes two identical black-and-white pictures at a time. The demonstration flight proved fully the confidence-building capability of Open Skies and the technical feasibility of a cost-effective cooperative procedure.

Operations in 1992–6 and Political Effects

The Hungarian–Romanian Open Skies Treaty has since been put into regular practice.[20] Each state performs four observation flights annually, still using the OMERA 35 dual camera and a video system mounted on AN26 and AN30 aircraft. As the result of careful planning – considering the weather conditions – 90 per cent of the pictures taken are of good or excellent quality. So far the full territories of both states have been mapped twice. Recent flights are being made to confirm that there is no change in the military postures. Four flights a year – one in each of the four seasons, if possible – have proved sufficient for that purpose. The costs of the flights are kept as low as possible. Aircraft crews use the Open Skies flights as part of their regular training. Hungary spends about DM10 000 per flight for aircraft operation costs (mostly fuel) and the *per diem* of two camera technicians. The film is surplus material from France that is close to its expiration date and is provided at no cost.

The political impact and success of the treaty have been enormous. The military and the political establishments of both countries are very pleased with the results. The treaty is regularly mentioned in speeches of key politicians when talking about Hungarian–Romanian relations. The treaty has received very good publicity through newspaper and television coverage aimed at the general public. Both to politicians and to men and women in the street, the mutual opening of the airspace of the two states for observation of military sites is probably the most convincing reassurance of their peaceful intentions. This is a non-trivial result, in view of the conflict potential around the Hungarian minorities in Romania and the scars left by past history. In fact, one might conclude that the mutual Open Skies flights have contributed considerably to the prevention of violence or military tension between the two states. They have also helped the general public in overcoming or retraining old perceptions of the enemy.

Possible Extensions of the Open Skies Treaty

The treaty holds an interesting potential for extension on several levels. It might be expanded to include additional state parties. After the treaty has entered into force, the Open Skies Consultative Committee can agree on the admission of additional states. Several of the so-called 'non-aligned states', such as Finland, Ireland, Sweden and Switzerland, have expressed strong interest. They have been attending the Open Skies and OSCC plenary sessions in an observer role. In addition, it would be a good idea to include the Baltic States, Croatia, Macedonia, Serbia, Slovenia and the three political camps of Bosnia in some kind of Open Skies regime.

The treaty might be expanded to include additional fields of application. Two of these fields of application, beyond military confidence building, are mentioned in the preamble of the treaty, namely crisis management in the framework of the CSCE/OSCE and protection of the environment. It seems to be a common understanding among most states parties, in particular most NATO states, that these issues can only be brought to the negotiation table after entry into force (that is full ratification) of the treaty. This position is debatable in view of the situation in Bosnia and the obvious need for confidence-building measures in the former Yugoslavia.

When it comes to environmental monitoring using Open Skies, a spectrum of interests emerges. Many NATO states have sufficient civilian infrastructure for remote sensing of the environment. In contrast, some of the Central and East European states, in particular Hungary, seem to be interested in making dual use of their Open Skies aircraft for environmental monitoring. Certainly, there is a sufficient number of environmental problems that cross borders, such as river pollution; these require a joint approach towards solutions. Observation flights for environmental purposes would probably have to be arranged separately from flights over military sites, in order to ease the open and free use of the pictures taken. On the sensor side, photographic cameras equipped with infra-red-sensitive false colour film and thermal infra-red line scanners are very useful tools for environmental monitoring.

The treaty allows for the inclusion of additional types of sensors at a later stage. Obvious candidates are multispectral imaging sensors for environmental monitoring and air probe samplers for monitoring radioactivity in case of reactor accidents.

Conclusions

In spite of the rapid changes in Europe since 1989, the architecture of the Open Skies Treaty still holds an important potential for military and political confidence building in unstable areas of Europe and beyond. The best proof of this capability has been presented by the experience with the Hungarian–Romanian bilateral Open Skies agreement. Open Skies can also support the verification of present and future arms control agreements. One area which has been neglected so far is the support of the verification of the Chemical Weapons Convention, of the Nonproliferation Treaty and of the Comprehensive Test Ban Treaty by airborne observation. Open Skies could play a role in each of these.[21]

Although the Open Skies Treaty still contains remnants of Cold War suspicion, it promotes confidence building and cooperative security structures in a powerful way. In particular, the elements of 'equity' (equal data access for all parties) and 'symbolic cooperative action' pave the way towards a more peaceful future. Both the military and the general public can learn how to prevent wars by mutual openness and cooperation. Many other areas of the world would profit greatly from Open Skies regimes that might be adapted to regional conditions.

Notes

1 Joe Clark, 'Open Skies', in M. Slack and H. Chestnutt (eds), *Open Skies – Technical, Organizational, Operational, Legal and Political Aspects*, Toronto: Centre for International and Strategic Studies, York University, Toronto, 1990, pp.vi–vii.
2 Peter L. Jones, 'Open Skies: a Review of Events at Ottawa and Budapest', in J.B. Poole (ed.), *Verification Report 1991*, New York: The Apex Press for VERTIC, 1991, p.73.
3 Clark, 'Open Skies'.
4 Jones, 'Review of Events'; Peter L. Jones and Marton Krasznai, 'Open-Skies: Achievements and Prospects', in J.B. Poole and R. Guthrie (eds), *Verification Report 1992*, London: VERTIC, 1992; Peter Jones, 'Open Skies: Events in 1993', in J.B. Poole and R. Guthrie (eds), *Verification Report 1993*, London: Brassey's, 1993.
5 Jones, ' Review of Events', p.74.
6 Jones, 'Events in 1993', p.150.
7 Ibid., p.152.
8 Douglas C. Armstrong, 'Technical Challenges under Open Skies', in *Proceedings of the First International Airborne Remote Sensing Conference and Exhibition, Strasbourg, 12–15 September 1994*, Ann Arbor, MI: ERIM, 1994; p.I-56.
9 Scott P. Simmons, 'When better resolution is not good: The Treaty on Open Skies', in *Proceedings of the Second International Airborne Remote Sensing Conference and Exhibition*, San Francisco, 24–27 June 1996, Ann Arbor, MI: ERIM, 1996, pp.I-403–410.
10 Armstrong, 'Technical Challenges'.

11   Simmons, 'When better resolution is not good'.
12   Ibid., p.I-409.
13   Jones, 'Events in 1993', p.149.
14   Ibid., p.155.
15   Stefanie Bailer, 'Appendix 20c, Treaty on Open Skies', in Stockholm International Peace Research Institute, *SIPRI Yearbook 1995*, Oxford: Oxford University Press, 1995, p.155.
16   'Implementierung von Rüstungskontrollabkommen durch die Bundeswehr im Jahre 1995', Bonn: Bundesministerium der Verteidigung, 15 April 1996.
17   K.R. Fortner and P.L. Hezeltine, 'The US Open Skies Synthetic Aperture Radar (SAROS)', in *Proceedings of the Second International Airborne Remote Sensing Conference and Exhibition*, pp.III-359–67.
18   Simmons, 'When better resolution is not good', p.I-406.
19   Jones and Krasznai, 'Open-Skies: Achievements and Prospects', pp.53–5.
20   Marton Krasznai, private communication, 1996. Krasznai represents Hungary on the OSCC.
21   F.R. Cleminson, 'Overhead Imaging. An underused but potentially effective asset in the process of ongoing monitoring and verification of multilateral arms control treaties', in *Proceedings of the Second International Airborne Remote Sensing Conference and Exhibition*, pp.382–91.

12   Russia's Nuclear Policy after the USSR

Ioury E. Federov

Introduction

The question which could and perhaps should be asked is whether it is important to analyse Russia's nuclear policy five years after the collapse of the Communist regime and of the Soviet Union. Are there any reasons to believe that Russian nuclear weapons may still present a threat to the rest of the world?

There was a lot of optimism immediately after the fall of Communism in Central and Eastern Europe and in the former Soviet Union. The resulting end of the Cold War has radically decreased the risk of large-scale military conflict both in Europe and in the wider global arena. Russian–American talks culminated in January 1993 in the START-II Treaty. Its implementation would drastically reduce the number of Russian and American strategic weapons and in particular would eliminate the most dangerous Russian 'heavy' ICBMs.

Most concerns at the beginning of the 1990s were related, not to the policies and intentions of the new Russian leadership, but to the possibility of nuclear proliferation, the uncontrolled export of nuclear technologies, materials and expertise from the Soviet successor states, and to the prospect of the further disintegration of Russia, leading to a collapse of centralized control over nuclear weapons. However, at this time there was a general understanding that the end of global ideological and military confrontations eliminated the very possibility that Russian nuclear weapons might be used as an instrument of deterrence or as a tool for achieving some political and military aims. Russian policy gave no grounds for such suspicions. The very notion of East–West deterrence was often regarded – at least in Russia – as losing its *raison d'être*. A perspective seemed to be emerging that Russia and the West were forming a strategic partnership.

Some of these concerns are no longer relevant, while others have become even more acute. Belarus, Kazakhstan and later the Ukraine joined the Nonproliferation Treaty, and have moved nuclear weapons deployed on their territories to Russia (with the exception of 18 SS-25 ICBMs which are still in Belarus). The disintegration of the Russian Federation does not seem likely. At the same time, the smuggling of nuclear materials, sometimes of weapons grade, is becoming a fact of life.

There is also growing evidence of new dangers coming from the post-Soviet area. Internal conditions in Russia are favourable to militant nationalistic groups and movements that are mostly anti-Western. Of equal importance could be a transformation of the present regime. There is clear evidence of imperialistic attitudes aimed at promoting the reintegration of the newly independent states into a single country and at establishing a zone covering the territory of the former Soviet Union where Russia has 'special responsibility' or 'vital interests' – a zone of economic, political and military domination, in fact. The Chechnya war demonstrated the readiness of Russia's government to use brutal force to achieve its goals, despite intense criticism from both inside and outside the country. The military doctrine approved by the Russian president in November 1993 establishes an active role for Russian military forces in the post-Soviet area, and considers nuclear weapons an important instrument for ensuring national security. But the most important new danger seems to be the growing 'nuclearization' of Russian security policy and the manipulation of nuclear weapons with a view towards using them as an instrument for securing Russian interests.

In this light, the threat coming from Russian nuclear weapons is acquiring new dimensions. These armaments are both the only symbol of 'great power' status Russia has left and perhaps the only factor providing Moscow with an ability to influence global international developments. Under conditions of continuing degradation of the Russian army, especially of its conventional forces, nuclear weaponry is regarded by influential groups of the Russian military elites as a relatively cheap potential battlefield weapon. The weakening of the former Soviet early warning systems and the possible imbalance of Russian and American strategic and conventional military capabilities may force the Russian military to adopt de jure or de facto a first-strike strategy. In fact, in the event of acute international crises involving Russia, they may be faced with a real or imagined dilemma 'to strike first or to lose everything'. The evolution of the Russian nuclear attitudes and policy may – and it seems will – have wide repercussions for global politics.

Three Stages of Russian Nuclear Policy after the USSR

Russian nuclear policy can be explained as a result of interrelations between at least two controversial strategic trends in Russia's political thinking and political behaviour. The first is oriented towards a continuing decrease in the role of the nuclear factor in shaping Russian foreign and military policy. It reflects deep conceptual changes in Russia's strategy on the world stage which rejects confrontation, is looking for integration into the world system and gives priority to the economic, social and political improvement of the country.

In contrast, the second strategic orientation is aimed at nuclear deterrence. This policy explicitly or implicitly suggests that Russia's perception of the outer world is still of something hostile. In this orientation, Russia's greatness is made dependent, not so much on social improvements, as on restoring its military might and sphere of influence. This policy represents primarily the interests of powerful groups associated with the military–industrial complex, who are attempting to overcome the industrial crisis through massive investments in military-oriented science and industry. This requires in turn the revival of the old confrontation and consequently of a foreign enemy who threatens Russia's interests.

Since 1992, the influences of these two attitudes on the formulation of Russia's actual nuclear and security policy have been shifting towards the second orientation. During the first stage of this reorientation, which started at the beginning of 1992 and ended somewhere in the middle of 1993, Russian nuclear policy was determined basically by the first type of strategic attitudes. It then had two key objectives. The first was to seek ways to cooperate with the United States, with a view to decreasing nuclear confrontations and reducing nuclear arsenals. In particular, it proceeded from a realistic assessment of Russian military and economic capabilities after the dissolution of the Soviet Union and of budgetary shortfalls regarding defence. Among the main aims of this strategy was the aspiration to use a cooperative policy to close the growing gap with the United States in the number of strategic armaments each country was able to sustain. This policy was implemented first of all through the START-II Treaty signed in January 1993. It allowed Russia to limit the number of strategic warheads of each side to the ceiling of 3500 and thus seriously decrease the potential lag behind the United States.

The other key objective of Russia's nuclear policy in the first year and a half of her independence was to secure her status as the only nuclear power on the territory of the former Soviet Union, and to establish her undivided control over all nuclear weapons left in the newly independent states after the collapse of the Soviet Union. This aim was achieved with the support of the United States, which helped Moscow to resolve a very important issue regarding the Ukrainian strategic assets; without Washington's pressure, the Ukrainian leadership could have delayed the solution of this key problem for years.

However, this cooperative policy faced problems. Already at that time, advocates of Russia's nuclear deterrence policy had a strong lobby in the industrial, military, political and academic communities. For instance, the document 'The Strategy for Russia', which was prepared under the aegis of Sergey Karaganov, a member of the Presidential Council, and published in the middle of 1992, stated:

> Russia's present economic and political weakness, as well as its interests, makes it necessary to preserve its reliance on nuclear weapons and on nuclear deterrence policy. In the near future (10 years) a comparatively powerful nuclear potential will nullify practically any technological breakthrough and superiority of military capabilities. The threat [to Russia] might increase if the role of nuclear weapons continued to decrease.[1]

This orientation towards nuclear deterrence was also expressed in a clear-cut way in the document approved by the leaders of the Commonwealth of Independent States (CIS) in Bishkek in October 1992. It was stated in 'The Concept of the Military Security of the CIS Member States' that 'to prevent a war by nuclear deterrence of the potential enemy' was among the principal tasks of the united armed forces of the CIS. The authors of the 'Concept' have also underlined that 'those powerful groupings of strategic offensive arms ... which are deployed along the outer borders of the Commonwealth during the days of peace ... are unlikely to undergo major reductions and will continue to present the principal military danger to the security of the Commonwealth'.[2] It was almost directly stated that the military threat from the West would continue in the new geostrategic situation. There were hardly any doubts that the aforementioned strategic offensive forces could belong only to a narrow circle of Western states, primarily to the United States, and also to the People's Republic of China.

Until the middle of 1993, Russia's nuclear policy was shaped mainly by the influence of rationally thinking groups striving for cooperative relations with the West in nuclear and security fields, but the balance of power between them and those who advocated nuclear deterrence had been changing in favour of the latter. In November 1993, the new Russian military doctrine was officially approved. Among other key principles, it contained the nuclear deterrence strategy and gave up the principle of no-first-use of nuclear weapons which had been previously adopted. That was the beginning of the next stage in the evolution of Russian nuclear policy.

That second stage ended somewhere in the middle of 1995. In the second half of 1995, more and more indications surfaced that Russian nuclear policy might be reviewed once more. Russia's possible new strategy was outlined in a number of articles, including some published by key figures in the defence and foreign ministries and within the president's administration. Many of them were written by military experts or referred to anonymous sources in military agencies. The most widely known of these articles were written within The Institute of Defence Studies, which was assumed to be a mouthpiece for a militant part of the Russian military establishment.

The proposed concept offered strong confrontational precepts. It can be boiled down to a number of principal points.

1   A number of states, including the leading states of the West, primarily the United States and Germany, are posing a growing threat to Russia.
2   They are attempting to preserve Russia's current geopolitical and military weakness, to isolate her, to penetrate her traditional spheres of influence and even to throw her back from her present positions.
3   The main practical evidence of these malicious intentions is the approaching expansion of NATO eastward, Turkey's efforts to establish strong positions in Transcaucasia and Central Asia (which are considered Russian traditional domains), Japan's claims to the Kuril Islands, and so on.
4   The only possible way to prevent the emerging political and military threats and challenges from the West (along with Japan) in a situation when Russian conventional forces are weak is the nuclear deterrence strategy.
5   It is important not only to preserve the capability to deter the Western threat at the strategic level but also to secure the full use of all capabilities of tactical and sub-strategic nuclear systems to protect Russian interests at the regional level.

A brilliant exposition of this type of thinking was presented early in 1996 by Admiral Edward Baltin, who was then the Commander of the Black Sea Fleet. He has written:

> The expulsion of Russia out of its age-old geopolitical positions is going on. Let us remember, if nothing else, the Ukraine which is more and more drawn into NATO's embrace, Turkey's successful activities in Transcaucasia, to say nothing about the processes in the Baltic zone. The spatial forcing back of our country from Western and Central Europe has expressed itself in the loss of her main ports on the Baltic and Black Seas, as well as in a shortage of communications with Europe.[3]

So far, there have been no direct official statements that Russia's military doctrine should be reviewed. However, it was stated in the president's address, 'On National Security', to the Federal Assembly that was published in June 1996 that 'The Russian Federation is consistently implementing the policy of nuclear deterrence. The key role in this is played by the maintenance of the nuclear potential of the Russian Federation both at the global level (Strategic Nuclear Forces) as well as on the regional tactical scale (operational–tactical and tactical nuclear weapons) as sufficient conditions.'[4]

This particular point is the first official declaration made at the highest possible level about the importance for Russia of not only strategic, but also tactical deterrence. And it is also a serious indication of the nuclearization of Russian security policy. The disturbing signs of some practical implementation of these new attitudes are the long delays in the ratification of the START-II Treaty, the linkage of this ratification with a halt to NATO's expansion; and a growing number of declarations, including some made by high-ranking officials, that Russia's response to NATO's eastward extension will include a deployment of Russian sub-strategic forces aimed at targets within the territory of new NATO members.

Russian Military Doctrine on Nuclear Policy

Since at this moment no revised text of the Russian military doctrine exists, the document approved in November 1993 is still the only official declaration of the principal points of Russian nuclear policy. The first draft of 'The Basic Provisions of the Military Doctrine of the Russian Federation' was prepared in the first half of 1992 and discussed at a special conference in the Academy of the General Staff in May 1992. After some changes, the document was sent to the former Supreme Soviet, without any discussion of it at the formal sessions of the Russian Parliament. There were two reasons for this. There were contentious discussions and disputes within the Russian military and political elites about some basic points of the doctrine, such as the sources of military threats to Russia, the role of nuclear deterrence, the 'first use' issue and so on. At the same time, however, the military leadership and perhaps the president were obviously interested in avoiding a vote on this document in Parliament, because the latter might change it in unpredictable ways.

However, the collapse of the Supreme Soviet in October 1993 opened the way to a rapid and seemingly somewhat superficial examination of the previously prepared text of the 'Basic Provisions' by the Security Council on 6 October and 2 November 1993. It then went on to approval by Presidential Decree N-1833, dated 2 November 1993. This document can be considered to represent Russia's official policy towards major security issues, including nuclear weapons policy.[5]

There is one general issue which is critical for the analysis of Russia's nuclear policy, namely what particular international actor or actors are perceived by the Russian political and military elites as potential adversaries or sources of threats. Without resolving that issue, any rational formulation of a policy aimed at the neutralization of this threat or threats is simply impossible. As was mentioned above, nuclear deterrence of the 'potential adversary' was proclaimed in 'The Concept of the Military Security of the CIS Member States' as one of the main tasks of the joint armed forces of the CIS as well as one of the principal means of ensuring both the common and individual security of the CIS member states. It was strongly stressed, however, that the CIS military structures were dedicated to a defensive posture, and there would be no first use of nuclear weapons.[6]

'The Basic Provisions' seem to be somewhat more careful in formulating descriptions of some politically very sensitive issues. It was announced in them that Russia 'regards no state as its enemy'.[7] This formulation may be interpreted in two ways, however. Some experts, including for instance the first Deputy Minister of Defence Andrei Kokoshin, viewed it as meaning that Russia has no potential enemy.[8] This stance was criticized at times by military specialists who said that the absence of potential adversaries made any military planning senseless and even impossible. However, the exact meaning of what was said in 'The Basic Provisions' was that it was Russia who did not regard any country as its enemy. That does not in fact mean that some other states do not regard Russia as their adversary.

But the main point is that politically very sensitive indications of particular potential adversaries were replaced in 'The Basic Provisions' by a list of sources of external military threats to the Russian Federation. That is in actuality the same as a definition of potential adversaries: a military threat cannot exist 'by itself' without some particular state or other international actor who is able to create that threat by its actions. Among the actual sources of possible external military threats against Russia listed in 'The Basic Provisions' are (1) the possible use (including the unsanctioned use) of nuclear and other types of weapons of mass destruction which a number of states have in service; (2) the possibility that strategic stability might be undermined as a result of the violation of international agreements in the area of arms limitation or reduction, and of the qualitative and quantitative build-up of armaments by other countries; and (3) the expansion of military blocks and alliances to the detriment of the interests of the Russian Federation's military security.[9]

This list is in fact very interesting. It proves that the Russian leadership continues to consider the United States and some other leading Western countries as Russia's potential enemies. No state other than the United States can 'undermine the strategic stability' and no other bloc is likely to be expanded except NATO.

The list of factors which help transform a military danger into an immediate military threat to the Russian Federation is also significant. This list includes such actions as (1) the build-up of troops on the borders of the Russian Federation to the point where they disrupt the prevailing balance of forces and (2) acts by other countries which hinder the functioning of Russian systems that support the strategic nuclear forces and of state and military command and control of (above all) their space component.[10]

These formulations once again confirm that, at the end of 1993, Moscow did not exclude the possibility of hostile actions from the Western and especially the American side. For instance, no country beside the United States has the physical capabilities to hinder the functioning of Russian space-based control and communication systems. It should be mentioned also that some formulations of 'The Basic Provisions' may be interpreted broadly. What, in fact, is the meaning of a disruption of the prevailing balance of forces? What could be the criteria for judging some action to be such a disruption? This kind of ambiguity makes it possible to interpret military developments near Russian borders in a crisis in a way which allows the justification of almost any Russian intentions and moves.

The main content of the nuclear part of the Russian military doctrine can be summarized in three or four particular points. First of all, it was openly declared that nuclear deterrence is one of the basic foundations of Russian military strategy. It was written in the text of 'The Basic Provisions' that 'The aim of the Russian Federation's policy in the field of nuclear weapons is to eliminate the danger of nuclear war by deterring the launching of aggression against the Russian Federation and its allies'.[11] The very focus on deterrence, either nuclear or conventional, means in fact (though in an indirect way) that Russia has some potential adversaries who should be deterred. Otherwise, deterrence is simply meaningless.

Russian official directives with regard to nuclear policy and nuclear weapons have a dual nature. On the one hand, it was stressed that the Russian Federation seeks the reduction of nuclear forces to the minimal level that would guarantee the prevention of large-scale war and the maintenance of strategic stability and – in the future – the complete elimination of nuclear weapons. It was declared that Russia is in favour of the cessation of nuclear testing and would take measures to strengthen the non-proliferation regime.

On the other hand, however, Russia de facto denounced the previous Soviet commitment to no-first-use of nuclear weapons. It was now said that Russia will not employ its nuclear weapons against any state party to the Treaty on the Non-proliferation of Nuclear Weapons ... which does not possess nuclear weapons except in the cases of: (a) an armed attack against the Russian Federation, its territory, armed forces, other troops or its allies by any state which is connected by an alliance agreement with a state that does possess nuclear weapons; (b) joint actions by such a state with a state possessing nuclear weapons in the carrying out or in support of any invasion or armed attack upon the Russian Federation, its territory, armed forces, other troops or its allies.[12]

This means, in particular, that Russia may use its nuclear weapons first against any NPT member state who is a US ally, if this state is in armed conflict with Russia or with its allies. It should be mentioned also that the terms used here, such as 'armed attack' or 'invasion', were not well defined. Strictly speaking, this formulation presumes, for instance, that Russia may use nuclear weapons in any armed clashes between Belarus and Poland if the latter joins NATO and if even a small group of Polish soldiers enters Belarussian territory in a hostile manner.

The other new element of Russian nuclear thinking was giving up the concept of 'strategic parity' with the United States, which had been previously interpreted as the maintenance of equality of 'battle capabilities' of strategic forces. Instead of this, the new concept of 'intended damage' was included in the text of 'The Basic Provisions'. According to this, the numerical and structural characteristics of the Russian strategic forces should be determined by the task of inflicting on the 'potential adversary' some previously defined level of damage, but not by the goal of maintaining numerical equality with it. It was stated that Russian strategic nuclear forces should be maintained 'at a level ensuring guaranteed intended damage to the aggressor in any conditions of the situation'.[13] The key notion here is the 'intended damage' which can be inflicted by any, including a minimal, number of nuclear warheads delivered onto the aggressor's territory either in a retaliatory or in a pre-emptive strike.

Economic crisis and the growing weakness of Russia's conventional forces are among the principal factors inducing these doctrinal changes. The Russian defence industry does not seem to be able to maintain strategic parity with the United States and to produce the whole complex of the most advanced conventional weapons without which Russian troops will not be able to counteract the armed forces of technologically developed countries.

To Use or Not to Use First

The principal points of Russian military doctrine, particularly the first-use question as well as its general orientation, have become a matter of intense political debate. Some of its authors have stressed that this document should give no cause for concern. In commenting on the military doctrine, the Russian first Deputy Minister of Defence Andrei Kokoshin said:

> I would not say there is any departure here from the principles underlying the role of nuclear weapons. ... In fact, the principles which are laid down regarding the role of nuclear weapons are approximately the same as those which currently exist in the USA, Britain and France, which have never stated unequivocally that they would never be the first to use nuclear weapons.[14]

It is true that the current Russian approach to the first-use issue is from a formal logic standpoint almost the same as the American, French or British approaches. Some other experts have pointed out that in fact there was nothing new in the Russian stance on the first use of nuclear weapons, because the former Soviet Union had always envisaged the option of a first strike (which may be quite true).

However, there were some alarming factors. The first was that the probability of a large-scale Russian pre-emptive strategic strike could now be much higher than it had been with the former Soviet Union. Major-General Vladimir Belous wrote that, 'Even the simplest analysis demonstrates that in a course of operations conducted by conventional weapons, Russian Strategic Nuclear Forces may be forced to use nuclear weapons first.'[15] It was pointed out in 'The Basic Provisions' that 'deliberate actions by the aggressor which aim to destroy or disrupt the operations of the strategic nuclear forces, the early warning system, nuclear power and atomic and chemical industry installations may be factors which increase the danger of war using conventional weapons escalating into a nuclear war'.[16] In other words, for instance a conventional US attack on communication centres or reconnaissance satellites or anything else of that kind is now regarded as a reason to use strategic nuclear armaments.

This may mean in fact that the concepts of a retaliatory strike or of a 'launch-on-warning' use of strategic weapons are now gone. There are several reasons for this. First there is the vulnerability of both strategic forces and the command-and-control system. Lieutenant-General Vladimir Larionov pointed out another reason when he wrote that an orientation towards a retaliatory strike 'may be dangerous due to its damping effect on combat readiness' and that some important research and development efforts might cease. He also said that 'it is necessary to have the numerical superiority of the [delivery] means for the realization of the retaliatory strike strategy. Otherwise they simply may not survive the first counterforce strike by the adversary.'[17] This was absolutely correct from the military point of view. However, both naval and land-based Russian strategic forces will be inferior to those of the United States both in numbers and in combat readiness and in invulnerability.

All this means that a pre-emptive strike strategy may be the only 'rational' one for the Russian Federation. It simply cannot risk the 'stronger' side destroying its strategic weapons as well as its command and communication facilities. It is absolutely clear, however, that the 'stronger' side cannot risk being the victim of a first strike and might do its best to prevent this by launching its own pre-emptive strike. So the Russian reorientation towards a first-strike strategy may result in the emergence of a vicious circle which could stimulate the rapid escalation of some international crisis; this could involve Russia in a nuclear war.

The other factor in the growing role of nuclear weapons in Russia's military thinking is, as said before, the deterioration of its conventional forces. The scale of that deterioration is really impressive. One of the reasons for it is the loss of western military districts which were regarded as the deployment bases for the so-called 'second strategic echelon' and as having the most modern hardware, well-developed infrastructure and best-trained manpower. The commander-in-chief of the Russian Air Force, Colonel-General Petr Deinekin, has said that Russia inherited only about one-third of the Soviet MiG-29s and SU-27s, and about one-half of the airfields. Half of its runways over 1800 metres in length are in urgent need of repair, while some basic facilities are lacking, including proper protection.[18]

About 80 per cent of the immobile command centres of the former Soviet Armed Forces stationed in Europe were on the territories of the Ukraine, Belarus and the Baltic states; as was the major part of their modern military equipment and armaments. According to the Ministry of Defence, only 25 per cent of the main battle tanks, 10 per cent of the armoured fighting vehicles (AFV) and about 15 per cent of the personnel armoured carriers remaining the property of the Russian Army after the fall of the Soviet Union are modern types.[19] At the same time, the production of modern types of armaments in Russia has fallen drastically: tanks produced in 1992 were 43 per cent fewer, AFV 70 per cent fewer, artillery pieces 76 per cent fewer and strike helicopters 93 per cent fewer than in 1990.[20] This trend has not changed since 1992, and the prospects of rearmament of the Russian Army with modern weaponry look rather doubtful.

The other cause of the declining fighting capability of Russian conventional forces is the collapse of the conscript system and the resulting undermanning. As Colonel-General Viktor Semenov, the commander-in-chief of the Russian ground forces, has mentioned, they were undermanned by about 50 per cent.[21]

All these and some other crisis phenomena affecting the Russian Army are aggravated by a serious lack of financial resources. The budget requests of the Ministry of Defence have regularly been cut in half by the government and the parliament. Any serious military reform aimed at a transition from armed forces that are too large and poorly trained to armed forces that are much smaller but better equipped and trained, needs a lot of resources which are beyond the current economic capabilities of the Russian government.

In such a situation it is only natural that the Russian military are turning to nuclear weapons as the most effective and cheapest means of compensating for this decline in combat readiness and capability. Major-General Vladimir Dvorkin, the director of the Research Institute for Strategic Rocket Forces, announced that 'Russia was forced to adopt the new policy [of first use] because of the dramatic contraction of its borders following the Soviet Union's collapse and the deterioration of its conventional armed forces'. Mary Fitzgerald, an American expert from the Hudson Institute, agreed with Dvorkin's statement, saying that Russia felt 'that the cheapest, quickest, best way it can react is with what is at hand – limited nuclear strikes'.[22]

However, if this is so, nuclear weapons should be able to fulfil the tasks which previously had been the responsibilities of the conventional forces, including those in large – or even medium-scale – local conflicts. This means in turn that nuclear weapons, basically of tactical and sub-strategic range, should be suitable as a usable battlefield weapon, but not as a 'political' means for the general prevention of armed hostilities between the superpowers. In view of this requirement, the Russian military sometimes speak about the so-called 'systemic' or 'complex' approach to the use of the different types of weapons – conventional, non-strategic and strategic nuclear armaments.

Why Nuclear Deterrence?

There is no direct indication in the text of 'The Basic Provisions,' or in any other official statements, of what might be the possible scenarios of a nuclear confrontation between Russia and the leading Western countries or NATO. However, even in 1993 some experts believed that the particular text of the Russian military doctrine was evidence of the victory of the 'hawks' over the 'moderates' in the Russian military leadership. According to the *Moskovskie Novosti* sources in the general staff, the concept of a pre-emptive strike has become very popular in military circles.[23] The Russian military, as Major-General Gennadii Dmitriev has said, considered nuclear weapons as a tool for applying pressure on neighbouring countries, which itself was mentioned as 'a normal way' of doing international politics: 'Poland, Chechnya, Slovakia, Hungary, as well as the Ukraine, who are dreaming of joining NATO, should know ... that just as they did so they would automatically be included in the list of targets for Russian Strategic Nuclear Forces with all its outcomes.'[24]

This seems, however, only a part of a broader picture. The very spirit of the Russian military doctrine, taken together with the predominant way of thinking of at least a large part of the Russian political elite, may be the basis for the development of the more or less logical strategic concept. The concept lies at the foundation of the military doctrine as well as of the actual Russian policy during the last two years and integrates different aspects of both the doctrine and the policy. It seems that the main task the military have posed for themselves for the coming years, for a decade perhaps, is the establishment of a zone of Russian military dominance in the 'near abroad' as a kind of 'buffer security belt' around Russia: a belt which then might well be a step towards the restoration of a single nation.

This zone might help to manage some serious problems that are challenging Moscow with the collapse of the Soviet Union: to be able once again to use the military infrastructure, including air defence and ABM components lost since 1991, to improve the geostrategic profile of the country and to secure the lines of communications with Europe, most of which have fallen under the control of newly independent states. Two officers of the General Staff wrote in a major article in the *Krasnaya Zvezda*:

> After the disintegration of the USSR, Russia's geopolitical and geostrategic posture deteriorated seriously. A 'buffer zone' of the Socialist Commonwealth used to exist between the USSR and Western Europe, which protected the Soviet Union from sudden attack, decreased NATO's capability to directly affect the Soviet Union, and increased the Soviet ability to affect NATO if it proved to be necessary. Now Russia is separated from Western Europe by a belt of states, including some former Soviet republics, which now forms a 'buffer zone' for Western Europe. Russian access to the open seas has deteriorated. Russia has lost a number of geostrategic advantages which both the Russian Empire and the Soviet Union had.[25]

Having said that, the Russian military does not announce how they would like to improve Russia's strategic posture. But the very attempt to analyse the current role Russia plays in the international system, using the intellectual tools of traditional geopolitical theories and concepts, almost inevitably leads to the conclusion that the only possible way to overcome these disadvantages is to restore the single country to the borders of the former Soviet

Union, or the Russian Empire and – who knows – perhaps even re-establish the former 'buffer zone' in Central and Eastern Europe. There is some concrete evidence that the implementation of this 'grand strategy' has already begun. Russian operations in Tadjikistan are openly endorsed by the need to protect Russian borders from terrorism, drug trafficking and Muslim extremism. Moscow is striving to obtain military bases in the Transcaucasian region and is using 'peace-keeping' operations there as well as in Moldova as a tool of political pressure.

It should be stressed that nuclear deterrence could be used in different ways. First of all, in the most natural scenario nuclear deterrence could be used to prevent foreign aggression or its threat. But there is another scenario as well in which there is a creeping geopolitical expansion behind an outward show of nuclear deterrence. The most simple scenario of this kind could develop as follows. A state that is expanding its sphere of influence might constantly put before the opposing state a choice: either to put up with a comparatively insignificant retreat, or to risk the development of a nuclear confrontation. Russian nuclear deterrence policy could be perceived by the external world as an attempt to disguise attempts to restore the Russian Empire, or to make the 'near abroad' a sphere of influence.

Nuclear weapons may play an important role in the restoration of the new Russian domain, deterring any Western, particularly any American, attempts to prevent such a restoration or to interfere in developments in the former Soviet Union. So the most probable scenario of a nuclear confrontation between Russia and the West could be based on Western attempts to intervene in the regions considered by Moscow as its sphere of influence. One clear piece of evidence of that may be found in the military doctrine:

> The introduction of foreign troops into the territory of neighbouring states of the Russian Federation (if it is not connected with measures to restore or to maintain peace in accordance with a decision of the UN Security Council or a regional body of collective security with the agreement of the Russian Federation) is considered by 'The Basic Provisions' as a factor 'transforming a military danger into an immediate threat to the Russian Federation'.[26]

This means, for instance, that any Western military presence in the Baltic states or in any other part of the former Soviet Union may be regarded by Moscow as a pretext for a sharp military confrontation, which might have a real chance of escalating into war. Possible outcomes and developments of such a confrontation can hardly be predicted. That in its turn poses a serious dilemma for Western leaders and public opinion: to resist restoration of the Russian Empire or to agree to something like a new Yalta agreement leading to a new division of Europe – or Eurasia perhaps – into spheres of influence.

Nuclear Weapons and Russia's Security Policy on NATO's Expansion

In his address to the Federal Assembly in June 1996, President Yeltsin publicly announced that Russian nuclear weapons are regarded not only as a means of deterring military attack on Russia but also as an instrument for securing her national interests. He has declared that strategic stability should be guaranteed by 'the maintenance of Russia's ability to deter nuclear attack as well as actions encroaching upon her vital interests by ensuring her ability to inflict assured planned damage through retaliatory strikes'.[27]

That may mean that in a case where Russian leaders consider someone's move as endangering Russia's vital interests, they could use nuclear weapons as a mean of deterring it or neutralizing it. The important point here is that there is no definition of what particular interests are regarded as vital. Such an approach allows Russia to be rather flexible and, at least theoretically, to use a threat of nuclear blackmail in a wide range of circumstances.

It appears that, since the beginning of 1995, Russian political and military elites are prone to regard an extension of NATO as one of the most serious possible threats to Russian security interests. It seems also that they consider the manipulation of nuclear weapons as an effective tool to prevent such an enlargement. Russian so-called 'independent' experts, as well as some high-ranking officials, are threatening NATO and especially the Central and Eastern European states aspiring to join the North Atlantic Alliance. These threats propose the deployment of new sub-strategic nuclear systems in the Western part of Russia and even in Belarus, as well as aiming nuclear weapons at the military facilities on their territory. Experts from the Russian Defence Research Institute (the so-called INOBIS) wrote quite frankly:

> Under these conditions [for example, NATO's enlargement] the only possible way is nuclear deterrence of NATO not only in the western theatre of military operations (TOO) including the former Soviet–Polish border and the Baltic Sea, but also in the northern TOO, including the Russian–Norwegian border and the Barents Sea, and in the southern TOO including the Black Sea and Russian military bases in the Crimea, Abkhazia, Georgia and Armenia. Tactical nuclear weapons should become the basis of Russia's defence in all three TOOs.[28]

Such offensive attitudes are not only revealed by a marginal group of 'independent' experts recruited from the retired military. The Russian Minister of Atomic Energy, Victor Mikhailov, announced in February 1996 that Russia would destroy the sites in the Czech Republic where nuclear warheads are to be located after that country joins NATO.[29] Academician Evgeniy Primakov, the Russian Foreign Minister who is known as a rather cautious politician, preferred to say that Russia will undertake 'adequate measures' if the Czech Republic, or any other Central European state, enters NATO.[30] The question is what the term 'adequate measures' really means. The head of the Russian Foreign Ministry, being a diplomat, did not explain the term. The Deputy Minister of Defence, Andrei Kokoshin, who at times has appeared to be a democratically oriented politician, was somewhat more definite when he has said in a discussion of the NATO enlargement issue that 'Russia is still a nuclear power and has not exhausted her ability to influence world politics'.[31]

So the first way Russia could use nuclear weapons, although not in a military form, is to prevent NATO's eastward expansion by their deployment near the borders of new NATO members. This way is advocated by a militant part of Russian political, bureaucratic and military elites. A softer version of this approach could be the proposal made by President Yeltsin at the Moscow Summit on Nuclear Safety and Security in April 1996, concerning a nuclear-free zone in Central Europe. That means in fact that Russia could obligate herself not to deploy nuclear systems in Belarus or perhaps in the Kaliningrad zone, in exchange for NATO's refusal to move such weapons into Poland, the Czech Republic or Hungary. An indirect version of this softer approach would be a statement that, if NATO does not firmly reject the possibility of moving nuclear systems into its Central and Eastern European members of the Alliance, Russia will deploy nuclear armaments in Belarus and other regions from where they could threaten new NATO states. The results of such developments would be disastrous for the states of Central and Eastern Europe as well as for Russia and Belarus, especially taking into account what was said above about the first-use strategy as the most probable option for Russian nuclear behaviour in a conflict.

The other measure which is discussed in Moscow as a possible Russian response to an expansion of NATO is the refusal to ratify the START-II Treaty. Some time in the first half of 1993 this idea was presented to the political and military elites in Russia. This option had been posed by militant members of the former Supreme Soviet of Russia when it had discussed the newly signed treaty. The official reply regarding this option, sent to the parliament by the Ministries of Defence and Foreign Affairs, denied that linkage by stating that 'the North Atlantic Alliance confirmed that underlying its policy is the principle of using force only if force is used against any of its members'.[32]

It was also emphasized by these two government agencies that NATO does not regard Russia as an enemy, that it has revised its viewpoint as to the character of possible sources of danger. However, in the first half of 1995 this idea was reborn by the then speaker of the Federation Council, Vladimir Shumeiko, and by the chairman of the State Duma Committee for World Affairs, Vladimir Lukin. The latter has said that 'It will be difficult to explain to the Russian people why we go on disarming when the greatest military machine in the world is approaching our borders'.[33] This approach could be another example of how counterproductive may be the present Russian line in the field of nuclear security. The heart of the matter is that the START-II Treaty allows Russia to minimize the extent to which it lags behind the United States in the number of strategic warheads, and thus allows her to improve her strategic profile.

In fact, out of nine types of ICBM which were deployed by Russia at the time the treaty was signed, only two will still be operable by the year 2003. Hence Russia faced the choice either to dismantle the obsolete weapons, including the most effective 'heavy' SS-18 ICBMs, or to try to prolong their service life by constantly replacing damaged components. But there are certain limits to this option as liquid fuel corrodes the casings of tanks, solid fuel decomposes and cracks can form which may have irreversible consequences. What is more, three types of Russian ICBMs, including the SS-18 and the most modern SS-24 with 10 warheads, were produced in the Ukraine before the break-up of the USSR. Maintaining their fighting capability is possible only with the help and cooperation of the Ukrainian enterprises. But Russian–Ukrainian relations were formerly and are now far from unclouded, and it was recognized as unreasonable to make the development of the Russian strategic potential dependent on Ukrainian affairs.

Ultimately, there remained for Russia only one reasonable course of action: to try by means of the START-II Treaty to make the United States reduce its strategic armaments to limits comparable with those Russia will have at the beginning of the 21st century. Otherwise, Russian strategic nuclear forces will be cut unilaterally down to 3000 – or perhaps even fewer – as a result of losing systems, whereas the United States may maintain from 7000 to 9000 warheads on its strategic delivery systems, without a serious change of its plans.

Conclusions

The principal question is whether Russian nuclear policy may present any danger to the outer world as well as to Russia itself. The Russian positions on nuclear deterrence as well as on the first use of nuclear weapons could by themselves be evidence of deep-rooted feelings of insecurity and of threats coming from global centres of power. It may be also the result of an inferiority complex appearing amongst Russian elites as a result of the collapse of the Soviet Union and the general crisis in the country. If so, then Russia's nuclear policy is arising as a kind of defensive attitude, perhaps a defensive reaction to the international environment. This means in its turn that Russian elites consider their country as something differentiated and alienated from the rest of civilization.

At the same time, and this is in fact more likely, Russia's nuclear thinking could be a part of a new 'great power' strategy aimed at the restoration of a new empire or at least a zone of domination in the 'near abroad'. The most critical problem now appears to be the effect of this policy on European and global stability. Would the eventual restoration of the Russian Empire create greater security or insecurity in Europe? After all, it could quite possibly help to suppress local conflicts and wars in former Soviet territories and to restore political stability. There is no definite answer yet to this question. In any case, the prospect of a new empire rising armed with nuclear weapons provides few reasons for optimism.

Notes

1   'Strategy for Russia: Some Key Points for the Report of the Council for Foreign and Defense Policies', *Nezavisimaya Gazeta*, 19 August 1992.
2   'The Concept of the Military Security of the Member-States of the CIS', *Sodruzhestvo: The Information Bulletin of The Council of the Heads of States and The Council of the Heads of Governments of the CIS*, (7), 1992, pp.36–9.
3   *Nezavisimaya Gazeta: Nezavisimoe Voennoe Obozrenie (The Independent Military Review)*, (3), 18 November 1995.
4   '"On National Security": The Address of the President of the Russian Federation to the Federal Assembly', *Nezavisimaya Gazeta*, 14 June 1996.
5   'The Basic Provisions of the Military Doctrine of the Russian Federation', *Krasnaya Zvezda: Special Appendix*, 19 November 1993.
6   'The Concept', p.37.
7   'The Basic Provisions', p.1.
8   *Nezavisimaya Gazeta*, 3 June 1993.
9   'The Basic Provisions', p.2.
10 Ibid.
11 Ibid.
12 Ibid.
13 Ibid., p.6
14 'Deputy Defence Minister Kokoshin on Military Doctrine', interview given to Ostankino Channel One TV Moscow, 23 November 1993, reported on BBC 'Summary of World Broadcast SU/1855 S1', 25 November 1993.
15 *Obozrevatel*, (10–11), 1994, p.48.
16 'The Basic Provisions', p.5.
17 *Nezavisimaya Gazeta*, 19 December 1992.
18 *Voennaya Misl*, (7), 1993, p.7.
19 *Rossia Segodnia: Realnii Shans (Russia Today: A Real Chance)*, Moscow: RAU-Corporation, 1994, p.425.
20 Ibid., p.462.
21 *Krasnaya Zvezda*, 21 May 1994.
22 *The Arms Control Reporter*, September 1993, p.611, E-2.53.

23   *Moscovskie Novosti,* (47), 21 November 1993, p.B-10.
24   Ibid.
25   *Krasnaya Zvezda*, 30 August 1994.
26   'The Basic Provisions', p.3.
27   *Nezavisimaya Gazeta*, 14 June 1996.
28   Defence Research Institute, 'Key Principles of Countering Major Outer Threats to the National Security of the Russian Federation', *Segodnia*, 20 October 1995.
29   *Segodnia*, 20 February 1996.
30   *Segodnia*, 6 March 1996.
31   *Nezavisimaya Gazeta*, 21 October 1995.
32   Ministerstvo inostrannih del Rossiiskoy Federatzii. Minisrestvo oboroni Rossiiskoy Federatzii (Ministry of Foreign Affairs and Ministry of Defence of the Russian Federation), 'Dogovor SNV-2. Fakti i argumenti. Belaya kniga (START-2 Treaty. Facts & Arguments. The White Book), Moscow: 1993, p.15.
33   *Moscow News*, 7–13 July 1995, p.14.

13 Implications of the Cold War Military Legacy in Northern Europe

Arto Nokkala

Introduction

The European North has been described as a good example of an area of military stability, but like the rest of Europe, with the end of the Cold War it faces many pan-European and global challenges, such as an emphasis on economic performance instead of on security, a revised concept of national security that is much broader than the usual narrow military focus, and increasing regionalization. The northern subregional security problem can be argued to be a very specific Cold War legacy. It is different from what exists elsewhere in Europe and in the former Soviet Union, even though it is linked to wider regional and global security developments. Since Northern Europe is often considered one of the least turbulent regions in the world, many policy makers do not see major problems in this region. However, there are problems and the Cold War history determines many aspects of the current security policies of the Northern European states.[1]

This chapter will first describe the problem and then highlight its possible political implications along three dimensions: the various aspects of security, developments of regionalization, and promotion of disarmament and arms control in foreign and security policies.

Cold War Military Legacy in Northern Europe

The problem created by the Cold War legacy is rooted in the fact that Northern Europe is the region where the former US/NATO–Soviet confrontation expressed itself in extensive military–strategic deployments of a nuclear and maritime nature. These deployments had close connections with conventional military developments in the region. Unlike Central Europe, in Northern Europe the end of the Cold War did not result in a 1000km withdrawal of one of the adversaries, especially not of military installations and of forces with nuclear capabilities. The Cold War legacy most importantly consists of those military structures and activities which continue to make conflict a possibility in the region, conflict that was created during the Cold War period and continues to be connected with it. More generally, the problem is about the military's new role, and its share of responsibility in the post-Cold War world.

Nuclear disarmament

The global nuclear arms race is over, but we still face the risk of nuclear proliferation; we do not yet have a nuclear weapon-free world. The two main northern rivals during the Cold War, the United States and the former Soviet Union, have not accepted a rapid and total dismantling of their nuclear arsenals, in spite of the fact that some argue that this is now feasible. The START-II Treaty is still unratified in Russia, but once it is in force, most of the remaining 3000 to 3500 warheads (up to 1700 to 1750 on each side) will be submarine-launched ballistic missiles (SLBMs). And most of the Russian SLBMs will be stationed in the Kola area of Northern Europe. Today that area holds 28 SLBM nuclear submarines, carrying some 3000 warheads. At the same time, the United States continues to patrol the European Arctic waters with its nuclear attack submarines.

Tactical nuclear disarmament has progressed through unilateral moves. Since 1988, the United States has reduced its tactical nuclear warheads by 90 per cent. Those remaining are air- or submarine-launched nuclear weapons. Even if these are not currently based in Northern Europe, they are well within reach of it. Russia has its tactical nuclear warheads on similar weapons, as well as in artillery rockets, short-range missiles and artillery shells. All of these are no longer deployed, but are still situated in areas adjacent to the Nordic and Baltic countries.

Nuclear disarmament has so far been consistent with a continuing reliance on mutual deterrence, even if the connection between nuclear and conventional deterrence has become even looser than it was in the past. The US Nuclear Posture Review of 1994 still mentioned a need to deter a potentially hostile Russian government, although the role of nuclear weapons is further restricted. On the doctrinal side, NATO continues to consider nuclear weapons to be a last resort, but has not declared a no-first-use policy. The Russian military doctrine of 1993 includes the option of using nuclear weapons against non-nuclear countries. In Northern Europe, nuclear disarmament and the end of the Cold War have not changed the role of the so-called 'submarine bastions' in the strategy of Russia and the United States. Under the START-II Treaty, Russia could deploy all of its allowed submarine-launched ballistic missiles on only her 13 newest submarines, but for strategic reasons a larger number of SLBM submarines seems probable. In any case, a majority of these SLBM submarines would probably be deployed near Northern Finland, since other locations do not have equal access to ports; and construction of new ports and facilities faces many economic and political obstacles.

It is very probable that the relative importance of Russia's strategic submarines will increase. Unless a major effort to continue nuclear disarmament is made soon, the bases and facilities at Kola will remain the focus of military planners in many countries. The Cold War strategic game in Northern Europe and its waters will continue, even though less intensively than in the past. Certainly, Russia lacks alternatives in geography, infrastructure and resources, but even more importantly, the situation displays the security and power-political value that is still attached to nuclear weapons and deterrence, even if that value is easily forgotten in public discussion.

Non-proliferation has become the main political item on the global nuclear agenda. In Northern Europe, non-proliferation has only a contextual meaning, since all the countries there are parties to the Nonproliferation Treaty. The non-proliferation strategies of these countries actually derive a large part of their credibility from their behaviour towards the nuclear states. The non-aligned Nordic countries, Finland and Sweden, have a special political opportunity to point out the lack of military legitimacy of nuclear weapons. Since the European Arctic waters are the most prominent deployment area for weapons of mass destruction, the symbolic importance of acts of states with northern interests has an impact far beyond the North, and structures the relations between Northern and Southern Europe in these matters.

The prospects of getting universal agreement by all the nuclear nations to the Comprehensive Test Ban Treaty (CTBT) are uncertain. The acceptance of the test ban is crucial from the northern regional point of view, since the only remaining Russian nuclear test sites are situated in Novaya Zemlya.

Conventional Disarmament

The strategic nuclear weapons from the Cold War are still coupled to conventional forces, and there are still options for their possible use in some future crises, in which Russia and the United States might not yet be on the same side. But independently, conventional structures in Northern Europe also reflect continuity from the Cold War. This is most visible in the major naval, air and land forces of Russia that surround or are deployable in the Kola area, and in the role played by NATO's forces and reinforcements in controlling Russian military movements.

Russia has kept the tasks, capacities and deployments of her Leningrad Military District largely unchanged on the strategic level, despite major tactical and operational reorganizations, de facto disarmament, low operational readiness due to a lack of conscription, finances and supply, and despite the reduced legitimacy of the armed forces in Russian society. These factors are also visible in the northwestern parts of Russia, where the actual turn-out of conscripts is only about one-quarter of what is required. At the same time, both in Russia and in the West a consensus exists that there is an increased strategic importance attached to the northwest corner of Russia, as compared to that of her other European areas. This does not imply, however, that all of the Cold War strategic framework has retained its former political significance.

The Western perception is that Russia still has considerable offensive capabilities in the North, or at least retains the ability to regain them within a few years if necessary. For instance, the newest version of the *Military Balance in Northern Europe* states, 'It must be assumed that Russia is able to mount a more comprehensive attack against North Norway with the forces which are available in the adjacent area than with the forces which may be transferred to the area immediately before or simultaneously with the attack.'[2] This kind of scenario had been predicted to become less likely after the Cold War. Some have even concluded that the Russian capability for external intervention would be completely lost if the current crisis of the Russian armed forces was not resolved.

But these expectations have not led to a major change in the strategic military pattern in the western part of Northern Europe. Only minor disarmament has taken place during the last three years. The military patterns of NATO and the United States in these areas are unchanged in any major way. The reorganization of NATO's regional control and command system, and of areas of responsibility, may improve the flexibility in NATO's reinforcement capabilities to some extent, but it is clear that the overall pattern of deployments, doctrines and training activities does not show any major change of focus away from an explicitly collective defence against Russia as the major potential adversary in the region.

The military arrangements of Finland and Sweden, especially in their northern areas, exhibit no visible changes in deployment and basic plans of action. Both countries retain their posture of making no military alliances as a way of emphasizing a strong territorial defence. Especially in Finland, a broad general conscription, and a very high societal legitimacy of the military and armed defence if restricted to the European scene, has led to the popularity of traditional defence. It is difficult to talk in terms of disarmament for these countries. Only a little rationalization has happened because of limited financial resources. In Sweden this rationalization is based more on enhanced military technologies than it is in Finland.

Evaluations of Russian actions suggest that NATO and the United States are probably still the external threat on which the Russian military planning is based. This Russian perception is also evident in concerns about NATO's enlargement, since NATO has traditionally been seen as primarily a military challenge. Russia does not seem to hold a strong vision of NATO as an integral part of pan-European stability and cooperative security. If this is its definitive perception of NATO, the analyses that drive military developments in the Northern European parts of Russia are probably more hardline. This would be understandable in a strategic context, since analyses of the future of warfare not only in Russia but also in the West point to a widening difference between political and military conceptions. Such concepts as the non-linear battlefield, cyber or information war, and deep strike, are fast becoming a technological reality among the most advanced states. It would not be surprising if the Russian military were to conclude that NATO has obtained strategic advantages over Russian vulnerabilities and that many of these, such as the position of Kaliningrad, are materializing in Northern Europe.

The obligations imposed by the treaty on Conventional Forces in Europe (CFE) have been modified to allow Russia to keep more of the treaty-limited equipment in her northwestern parts than originally intended. Even if this can be seen as a correction of one Cold War legacy, on the whole it cements the subregional military continuity in Northern European security more than it represents a new stage of disarmament.

Some military developments in Northern Europe do relate more to cooperative international security and change than to continuity from the Cold War. These developments are mainly related to cooperation within the North Atlantic Cooperation Council (NACC) and Partnership for Peace (PfP), or to confidence- and security-building measures within the framework of the Organisation for Security and Cooperation in Europe (OSCE). These changes are more evident in the Baltic area than in the northernmost subregion. Military cooperation between the Nordic countries, and by them with the three small Baltic states, has increased during the last few years. The agenda for change includes almost everything except actual collective defence planning. There are probably still many further, and as yet unexploited, opportunities concerning military contacts, peacekeeping and crisis management, and material and training cooperation. One problem is that bilateral and multilateral cooperation, outside the NACC and PfP framework, does not cross the western border of Russia as readily as it crosses borders between smaller countries. On the one hand, this problem is rooted in the traditions of close Nordic cooperation and, on the other hand, it comes from the new situation created by the regained independence of Estonia, Latvia and Lithuania.

Conclusions

In general, Europe has undergone a rather steady, even sometimes slow, progress in disarmament, confidence building and overall improvements in security. No major setbacks have been experienced, even if Russia has changed its foreign policy course to become a little less pro-Western in its orientation, and even if the United States has also re-evaluated its global policy. Several developments point to a lessening role of the military in the policies of many states and to a much decreased reliance on nuclear weapons. On the whole, the abolition of many former expressions of military rivalry has been a success. These conclusions apply to Northern Europe as well as to other regions.

But North European military structures and patterns of action still reflect a clear Cold War legacy, which in the Arctic is accentuated by the important position held by the military and other security organizations in local society. The present configuration is really most suited to respond to some new potential confrontation between Russia and other states or group of states. Several developments show that concern about such a potential confrontation is still at the core of the active promotion of enhanced stability in Northern Europe, even if some more dynamic acts of cooperation have taken place. The subregion of the European Arctic has continued to be a repository of traditional security instruments. A diminished interest in naval arms control tends to reinforce their residual role.

Why is this Problem Important?

The military legacy of the Cold War has not received much political attention. But various political policy statements do indicate an awareness of its existence. This can be seen particularly in the importance that is assigned, in policies of the Nordic countries, to the framing of security-related political objectives in terms of 'stability'.

Stability is a concept which, like the concept of security, is politically powerful but otherwise rather flexible. The political–military situation in Northern Europe is such that 'stability' carries a large military connotation. This is reinforced by the fact that there are no existing conflicts which can justify the relatively low priority of disarmament efforts. Only secondarily can 'stability' be seen as describing also such objectives as societal cohesion, economic viability, established democracy, rule of law and respect for the quality of life everywhere in the region.

The military sector has several organizational advantages that allow it to claim to be at the heart of the security problématique. Because of its professional norms, the military can claim to occupy a special position in state policies that is different from that occupied by other sectors related to security. These norms include limits the military imposes on the transparency of its actual performance. Because of this special position, the military does much and raises many expectations that do nothing to advance confidence between nations and between different social groups. One of the most important factors affecting this confidence is the need of the military organization to have an adversary, a need that is central for military activities that claim to be an important element of stability. Additionally, in established democracies military organizations are often political forces as well, whose postures allow some political choices and exclude others. This general problem in North European security is special, since here 'stability' for some states means accepting an active military as a solution for a situation that is actually problem free.

The problem posed by this contradiction is important, because disarmament in Europe in general has been slowing down, as the situation of non-military and non-inter-state threats and challenges has become more complex. The rise of conflicts that are not inter-state and of centrifugal forces of integration means that the military forces of states are directed more towards international crisis management and peacekeeping. The difficulties of responding to this variety of non-military threats actually tend to preserve the military as a reliable and predictable instrument of a modern state. At the same time, states are now less and less equipped to deal with the dynamics of continuing qualitative arms races, that are made more difficult by the globalization of economies and the increasing competition between arms-manufacturing industries.

In Northern Europe these factors see to it that there are insufficient major incentives from outside the region to continue disarmament that might reduce the effects of the Cold War legacy on regional security. The political implications of this military situation can be analysed and projected into the future by a review of the three dimensions undertaken below.

Political Implications of the Situation

Scope of Security in Northern Europe

It has become customary to talk about an extended conception of security. Security does concern many aspects of human life other than those of military safety. It is a matter of relative freedom, not only from political and military threats, but also from societal, ecological and economic threats, as far as these have political meaning. Security needs a careful definition about whose and what security is ultimately at stake. The broader conception of security integrates different levels of analysis, as well as different actors and various political objectives, but it does not necessarily claim that security is the most important objective for everyone. Rather than being an issue in itself, security is one dimension of many different issues on the agenda, not only of states, but also of other communal actors. It is more important to clarify linkages between different sectors of society, and between production and relative levels of security, than it is to focus on a single actor and objective.

After the Cold War, both states and international organizations claim that they have policies that aim to achieve security in the broad sense, for example by stressing cooperative security through the OSCE. In its 'Study on Enlargement', NATO defines its security concept very broadly, even if it emphasizes collective defence and transatlantic security more than it stresses non-military and pan-European aspects.

The broad conception of security prescribes that states should have security policies that take into account not only other states but other actors and their security interests as well. States should use the various means available to them to frame a suitable mix of cooperative security strategies to protect national interests and meet international challenges. In the case of Northern Europe, this would imply that the military legacy of the Cold War should receive special treatment. In particular, the counterproductive effects it has on regional non-military security should be pointed out clearly. Among the new opportunities which should be seized are stronger links between military and ecological security, such as possible cooperation in dismantling Russian nuclear submarines and handling nuclear waste. This cooperation would also test the possibility of linkages between closed military establishments and more open ones. But open international and transnational studies are needed to examine different interests that might justify keeping a strong military presence in Northern Europe. Present policies also recognize the residual local value of the military sector, since interests in favour of military continuity are often based on economic and societal–security factors.

Regionalization

Regionalization is a special challenge to centralized state control within the international system, especially when it develops in some new form proposed from below. Europe today faces at least six kinds of regionalization. The North European cross-border and subregional areas include, for example, the region of the Barents European Arctic, North Calotte and the region of the Baltic Sea. Additionally, there are several proposed or emerging regional groupings such as the Baltic–Scandinavian region, the Tallinn–Helsinki–Turku region and an enlarged Barents region including the surrounding sea. Regionalization in the North is very much based on a desire to avoid being marginalized and restricted to the periphery with respect to Europe. But for the stable Nordic countries it is also a way to respond to problems caused by the less stable Baltic states and Russia.

Cross-border regional cooperation in Northern Europe has mainly been economic, social and cultural. The traditional emphasis on political and military security has been left out of this process. This is in spite of the fact that cooperation in the Barents area, for instance, was a Norwegian political initiative connected with its national security interests and that the Nordic cooperation that has been a driving force behind regionalization promoted from above has been related increasingly to security questions.

But the legacy of the Cold War does impose constraints on some forms of regionalization. Some types of security cannot be achieved when political–military security is left out of the process of regionalization at the state level, as in the region of the Barents European Arctic. Building regions by imposition from above, without integrating the different aspects of security, may lead to uneven and divergent regionalization.

Tacit expectations and unilateral demands may interfere with the process of regionalization when no fora exist in which different kinds of security can be considered simultaneously. Some states may experience a specific military threat as a consequence of their efforts at regionalization. For example, this has been the case of the Baltic countries as a consequence of their efforts to obtain traditional security guarantees in the form of NATO membership. Regional cooperation in the Baltic Sea attempts to treat this problem by creating self-confidence in the three Baltic states through non-military security cooperative arrangements. But this problem by its nature is very regional. Unlike a non-military security problem, it involves a special geographic division, that is, the Russian western border. So the solution to this problem would require a broader forum and a wider geographic scope.

Prospects of Disarmament and Arms Control Policies

Overcoming the Cold War legacy in Northern Europe requires taking advantage of new opportunities for regional multilateral disarmament, arms control and confidence- and security-building measures. Problems to be overcome relate to the emerging form of European security architecture, Russia's reform of its armed forces, NATO enlargement, and possible changes in the foreign and security policies of Finland and Sweden away from the current commitments to non-alignment. Present incentives for disarmament include the interest of Nordic countries in reducing public spending, the de facto deterioration of the Russian military force and the restructuring policy of NATO. In many instances there are actually no efforts to disarm, rather there is an interest in maintaining previous military efficiency by exploiting new technological developments.

A common North European arms control effort could include negotiations about a new regional role for the military sector, a role focusing on security broadly defined instead of on the present nationalistic aspirations. Discussions might deal with actual mutual defence needs instead of pretending that inter-state threats have disappeared, a pretence that leaves the military with no apparent purpose. Any military structure and activity is suspect if any country in that region considers it as having roles other than international multilateral peacekeeping, or if it is assigned non-military activities such as search and rescue missions, border control and the cleaning up of the environment. Such suspect structures and activities should be the target of continuing disarmament. The improved confidence about security brought about by the end of the Cold War might permit less attention to be paid to technical details of verification and more to political dialogue, with its ability to encompass many aspects of security.

Conclusions

States in Northern Europe have two reasonable options for adapting the military sector to the emerging international situation. Under the first option, the new military stability produces a basic stable international order, and states have to adjust their actions to it. Under the second option, new political efforts might be carried out to change the role of the military sector. Because they are internally cohesive, Nordic countries could carry out many of these efforts. They have the opportunity to develop a special northern dimension for European institutions and to keep them interested in achieving subregional security in the same way that security is sought elsewhere in Europe. Together the Nordic countries can alleviate Russian fears of the

West, as well as the fears which the Baltic countries have towards Russia. It is important that Nordic countries reconsider their evaluations of threats at all policy levels, but in Northern Europe the general and essential need is for an increased transparency concerning military questions and new initiatives towards disarmament and arms control.

Notes

1 The following publications contain particularly interesting and useful readings on this topic: Robert G. Darst, 'Contemporary Challenges to International Security in the Barents Sea Region', in Jyrki Käkönen (ed.), *Dreaming of the Barents Region*, Tampere: Tampere Peace Research Institute, Research Report No. 73, 1996; Johan Eriksson, 'Security in the Barents Region: Interpretations and Implications of the Norwegian Barents Initiative', *Cooperation and Conflict*, **30**, (3), 1995; Pertti Joenniemi and Carl-Einar Stalvant, 'Baltic Sea Politics: Achievements and Challenges', in Pertti Joenniemi and Carl-Einar Stalvant (eds), *Baltic Sea Politics*, Stockholm: Nordic Council, 1995; Kari Möttölä, 'Political Principles of Security in the Arctic Region, Part I', in Kari Möttölä and Arto Nokkala, *Political and Military Aspects of Security in the Arctic*, background paper prepared for the Second Conference of Parliamentarians of the Arctic Region, 13–14 March 1996, Yellowknife, Northwest Territories, Canada; Iver Neumann, 'A region-building approach to Northern Europe', *Review of International Studies*, **20**, 1994; and Arto Nokkala, 'Security in the Arctic Region: Military Aspects in an Integrative Framework, Part II', in Kari Möttölä and Arto Nokkala, *Political and Military Aspects of Security in the Arctic*, background paper prepared for the Second Conference of Parliamentarians of the Arctic Region, 13–14 March 1996, Yellowknife, Northwest Territories, Canada.

2 The *Military Balance in Northern Europe 1995–1996*, Oslo: The Norwegian Atlantic Committee, 1995.

14 The New World Order and the Tempo of Militant Islam

Hilal Khashan

Introduction

With the end of the Cold War, Islamic fundamentalism has emerged as a global security issue. It poses serious challenges to state authority in the Middle East and produces alarming spillovers in several Western countries. It is a rare historical coincidence to observe that both the southern and northern shores of the Mediterranean seem threatened by a common foe. In the Middle East, Islamic fundamentalism is the product of cultural and intellectual stagnation, Western colonialism and the failure of the secular nationalist model of government. The West, wishing to harass Soviet occupation troops in Afghanistan, tinkered with the ecology of Islamic society and unwittingly gave teeth and muscles to Islamic fundamentalism, which are being exercised in the 1990s. Recent terror incidents attest to the gravity of the fundamentalist threat: these include the bombing of the World Trade Center in New York, the series of suicide missions in Israeli cities, the subway explosions in Paris and the multinational slaughters in Algeria. The destruction of a US military housing complex in Khubar, Saudi Arabia, a country often referred to as an oasis of order and stability in the troubled Middle East, demonstrates the rapidity with which Islamic militancy is spreading.

Islamic fundamentalism in the Arab world grew in a region previously known both for religious tolerance and for the prevalence of traditional religious practices. The emergence of zealous religious groups represents a curious departure from past trends. This chapter seeks to address the question pertaining to the rise of militant Islamic groups by focusing on the modern Arab social and political environment which is believed to have bred religious militancy. The failure of Arab society to come to grips with the requirements of modernity created an institutional vacuum and enabled the radicals to present themselves as serious contenders for political authority. The rise and sustenance of radical Islamic groups would not have been possible without financial and military assistance. In addition to discussing some of the salient factors responsible for the ascendancy of radical Islamic groups, this chapter will also account for the sources of funding and weaponry of these groups. This second component of the study is especially important, since without significant material resources the activities of the radicals would not have expanded to their current breadth and scope, nor would there have been the urgency in the efforts of states to contain them.

There are obviously many misconceptions about the birth and growth of radical Islam. Western media find it convenient to implicate a number of 'pariah' or 'mad' Middle Eastern states – Iran, Syria, the Sudan – in stimulating radical Islam and, more important, in keeping it alive. These charges cannot be completely dismissed; however, the contributions of the West in previous years, and the impact of domestic factors, seem more relevant to explaining the fundamentalist threat than the unsubstantiated theory of pariah states. This assertion will become clearer below as the analysis proceeds.

This chapter looks into the social and political conditions that have led to the emergence of militant Islamic groups in the Arab world, especially since the 1967 Six-Day War. However, it goes beyond the genesis of militant Islam to investigate two aspects of support that help keep the phenomenon alive: their sources of funding and weapons. In turn, these aspects of support are analysed in terms of international, regional and local sources. The discussions support the conclusion that, while the international and regional sources are significant, the local sources of support are decisive for the operations of the militant Islamic groups.

The Origins of Islamic Fundamentalist Movements

The creation of the state of Israel in 1948 put an end to Arab liberalism, a trend that had dominated Arab cultural and political change since the third quarter of the 19th century. It stimulated instead the emergence of radical Arab nationalism. Young and politically inexperienced army officers took charge of the political systems in key Arab countries such as Egypt, Syria and Iraq. The conservative monarchies of Saudi Arabia and Jordan proved impervious to military coups, but they nevertheless adopted the same Draconian security measures as the military juntas in neighbouring countries. The new political elites in the so-called 'revolutionary states' navigated in the turbulence of the Cold War between East and West, and opted to court the former Soviet bloc in exchange for military and economic aid. In fact, both secular and traditional Arab elites convinced their publics that their two most important objectives were to eliminate the state of Israel and to achieve economic prosperity. The masses accepted these declared objectives of the leaders, only to suffer from one frustration after another as neither of them was met.

The Arabs lost every major military confrontation with Israel, which emerged as the region's military superpower – as a result both of Arab leaders' unwillingness to fight and of unconditional American support of Israeli policies. Israel also succeeded in becoming the Middle East's technological powerhouse and leading economy. The Arabs' ineffective handling of the conflict with Israel jolted the masses who had expected that an outright military approach would recover Palestine. Instead of concentrating on Israel, Arab elites focused their attention on other issues that included government efforts to eliminate domestic opposition, violating the basic human rights of their populations, and involvement in inter-Arab disputes. The record of the Arab leaders on the developmental front was equally dismal. Some regimes toyed with socialism and adopted a single-party apparatus to propel modernization. Others, such as the Gulf rentier states, adopted the welfare state approach. In a second, apparently more successful, approach, only a veneer of modernity was imposed on society, while resources were squandered on weapons and grandiose projects of little economic utility. Corruption and nepotism prevailed. Consequently, the concept, never fully understood in the modern Middle East, of the state as a guardian and representative of individual and community interests soon lost its lustre.

Instead of the city acting to transform the village, the city was invaded by the village. Arab cities swelled, to become sprawling living quarters. It is in this atmosphere of ideological and developmental failure that radical Islamic groups sprang up and sought to transform the ailing political systems into systems of their own creation. The ascendancy of radical Islam everywhere in the Middle East and its virtual monopoly of serious political opposition suggest that the present state system in the Middle East is not working very well.

Impact of Global Developments on Islamic Militancy

Apart from local and regional factors, there have also been changes in the international system which spurred the further growth of radical Islam. In December 1979, the Soviet Army invaded Afghanistan at the request of its new communist government. The United States reacted to this invasion in a variety of ways; for this study, the role of the US Central Intelligence Agency (the CIA) in supporting the Islamic resistance movement against the Soviet occupation is particularly relevant. It is widely believed in the Arab world that Afghanistan was 'the melting pot which produced, under CIA leadership, members of terror groups from different Arab countries'.[1] Thousands of Arabs went to fight in Afghanistan with the financial assistance of Usama Bin Ladin, a Saudi Arabian businessman who had strong CIA connections.[2] Following the completion of the Soviet withdrawal from Afghanistan in 1989, many Arab *Mujahidin* (or Arab-Afghans) began heading back to their countries of origin and giving support to militant Islamic groups there. The role of the Arab-Afghans in increasing the pace of Islamic militancy in the Middle East cannot be overestimated. When the United States demanded that the government in Islamabad take more drastic measures to control Arab militants taking refuge in Pakistan, the Pakistani prime minister, Sher Mazari, reacted negatively. He said that 'the Arab militants were originally trained and financed by the Americans. They were the people who began all this, now they pull out and we are left to deal with it. ... It is very unfair.'[3]

The collapse of the Soviet Union contributed to Islamic militancy in at least three ways. First, the radicals saw in the fall of the communist ideology a clear proof of the unworkability of man-made laws and of the limits of authoritarian oppression. If the Soviet Union, one of the two superpowers, could disintegrate without a fight, then the Middle Eastern states, most of which have no real foundations, are ultimately bound to succumb to determined Islamic fundamentalist groups.

Second, the break-up of Yugoslavia, a by-product of the Soviet collapse, triggered an ethno-religious war in Bosnia and Herzegovina which attracted a few thousand Arab-Afghans to fight on the side of Bosnian Muslims. Serb atrocities and ethnic cleansing of the Muslims did not seem to move Western governments to take sufficient actions to deter the increasingly aggressive Serbs; Muslims everywhere watched Serbian excesses in shock and amazement, while the West did very little to stop them. As a consequence, the entrenched notion that the West is irreconcilably hostile towards the Muslim world received a tremendous boost among Arab Muslims. The Bosnian war came in the aftermath of the second Gulf War which resulted in the devastation of Iraq and the subjection of its people to severe sanctions by the United Nations. Most Arabs believe this Gulf conflict was engineered by the United States, who wanted to control Arab oilfields in the Gulf region. The Bosnian and Gulf wars brought anti-Western feelings among Arabs to an unprecedented level. The pervasive feeling among them is that Westerners are constitutionally incapable of being friendly towards Muslims. Hence combating them is not just to be tolerated, but to be strongly supported as well.

Third, the end of East–West ideological rivalry created a vacuum in international relations whose balance had hinged on sustaining a stable confrontation. Quite unexpectedly, the United States found itself without a major enemy. Scholars saw in the end of the Cold War a severe blow to historical progress. For example, Francis Fukuyama considered history to have ended, and lamented the termination of 'the struggle for recognition [and] the willingness to risk one's life for a purely abstract goal'.[4] In this atmosphere, where the fight between 'good' and 'evil' has ceased to inspire American policy makers, playing up the militant Islamic threat seemed a useful way to revive the East–West dichotomy. According to Samuel Huntington, Islam and other purportedly Eastern religions stand in sharp contrast to 'Western ideas of individualism, liberalism, constitutionalism, human rights, equality, liberty, the rule of law [and] democracy'.[5] He asserts that Islam is central to the fault lines that separate the West from the rest of the world and argues, rather emphatically, that the 'centuries-old military interaction between the West and Islam is unlikely to decline. It could become more virulent.'[6] There is merit to Huntington's analysis, for Muslim radicals seem prompted by the idea of historical determinism which considers the ultimate triumph of Islam as prescribed by God.

Terror by Prescription

Organized political terror in the Middle East predates the era of Islamic militancy. The first incident on record goes back to 23 July 1968, when members of the leftist Popular Front for the Liberation of Palestine hijacked an Israeli airliner to the Algiers airport. From that date until June 1982 (when Israel invaded Lebanon with the declared aim of ousting the Palestine Liberation Organization fighters from that country) nationalist and leftist groups – mainly associated with the Arab–Israeli conflict – took responsibility for launching nearly all terrorist activities. In the wake of the Israeli invasion, the *Hizbullah* organization appeared in Lebanon. With this development, the centre of terror actions shifted from the discredited leftists to the rising Islamists. It would be erroneous to explain the use of violence in terms of a pure protest; the radicals, be they leftists or fundamentalists, have a political programme that they seek to accomplish. The fundamentalists start right from the point where the leftists had stopped. Radical Islamic groups believe they launch terror missions for a holy cause. They claim that their aim is to reinstate the Islamic state which Kamal Ataturk, the founder of secular Turkey, had formally abrogated in 1924. According to the fundamentalists, it is completely unacceptable for Muslims to be ruled by any system of government unless it is based on *shari'a* (divine law); Western-inspired secular laws, now applied in most Islamic states, contradict Islamic tenets and ought to be combated until soundly defeated.

The fact that radical Islamic groups are mainly domestic movements operating against state authority within the boundaries drawn by Western colonial powers does not mean that they accept the existing Middle Eastern state order as final. The fundamentalists realize that they need to assemble numerous building blocks before they can achieve the ultimate construction of a universal Islamic state. Even the non-violent Muslim Brethren movement expresses a commitment to the establishment of an Islamic state, although it advocates a moderate approach. The primary aim of the movement is to contribute to Muslim awakening by revitalizing religious values and eliminating Western cultural influences, which they regard as a major threat to the Arab–Islamic culture. Muslim Brethren's eschewal of militant activities emanates from their conviction, based on previous experience, that they cannot possibly win against the state which commands a formidable machinery of coercion. The operating motto of the Muslim Brethren concerns 'moulding an ideal Muslim brother who sets an example to be followed by other co-religionists'.[7]

Other fundamentalist groups do not commit themselves to peaceful tactics. They employ violence as a recipe for change towards the 'right path'. More than that, they claim that fighting the state represents a duty that binds all able Muslims; without it, the concretization of the Muslim state remains wishful thinking. Radical Muslims see in militancy a means to topple their countries' corrupt and illegitimate regimes, which they also conceive of as Western lackeys. The crisis of identity plagues all Arab political systems, and the ruling elites have invariably failed to convince the populations that they embody their cherished goals and aspirations. Arabs do not accept the consequences of the collapse of the Ottoman empire, which had resulted in the formation of arbitrary political units. Iraq, Jordan, Syria and Lebanon provide living examples of this tenuousness of Middle Eastern states. It is worth noting that the Arab–Islamic mind remains essentially unionist, a reality not missed by the radicals who capitalize on it to find young and frustrated recruits.

Islam conferred upon the Muslims a sense of attachment to the *ummah* of believers (the Islamic community). The fall of the Ottoman empire had shifted the focus of affinity from Islam to Arabism.[8] Similarly, community orientation – not comparable to Western definitions in terms of rigour and strength of attachment – drifted from religion towards nationalism, even if it did not do so completely. Arab nationalism reached its peak in the mid-1950s, but received a severe blow as a consequence of the 1967 Six-Day War. The resulting demise of the idea of Arab nationalism led to an instant rise of militant Islam. At this stage, a three-dimensional perspective came to govern the ensuing political environment in the countries gripped by the fundamentalist surge: overthrowing the existing ruling elite, eliminating

Western cultural and political influences and reintroducing *shari'a*-based Islamic rule. The radicals have prescribed unmitigated violence to achieve these stated objectives.

Sources of Funding and Weaponry

Terror activities depend on two major factors: money provides the budget of death; guns and explosives supply the weapons for inflicting death. Judged by the nature of the activities of militant Islamic groups, they do not require large sums of money and sophisticated arms to carry out their operations. Of course, the militants' terror disturbs international peace and exposes the weaknesses of several Middle Eastern regimes. There is a tendency, however, to exaggerate the strength of the radical groups, as well as the resources at their disposal. The United States and beleaguered Middle Eastern states find it expedient to implicate countries such as Iran, Syria and the Sudan in arming militant Islamic groups and providing them with training facilities and funding. There is, indeed, some truth to these charges; but to say that outside support is decisive in the formation and operation of the radical groups misses the entire issue of Islamic militancy. It also points either to a weak understanding of the aspirations of Middle Eastern peoples or to a deliberate avoidance of the complexity of the issue. The beginnings of fundamentalist terror go back to 1975, when a small Egyptian group known as *Jama'at at-Takfir wal-Hijra* (Movement of Repentance and Holy Flight) started a series of limited anti-government activities. There is nothing on record to suggest that this movement received any foreign assistance.

Before this analysis proceeds, a distinction needs to be made between the rise of radical groups and the support they receive from abroad. Radical Islamic groups have emerged for purely indigenous reasons. Outside support only became possible when the rise of radical Islam became a primary source of domestic opposition. Radical Islamic groups receive support from different foreign sources, including countries that are vociferous in their calls for putting an end to terror activities. Foreign supporters have different reasons for dealing with radical Islamic groups. For the sake of simplicity, the main sources of support for radical groups will be divided here into three categories: regional (Middle Eastern), international (Western and Asian) and local.

The architects of the 1979 Islamic revolution in Iran thought that they stood in a unique position to export their version of militancy to other Muslim countries. Their Muslim neighbours proved them wrong. Sunni Muslims viewed with scepticism the generous offers of material aid made by Iran's Shi'i leadership. In view of this, it becomes clear why Iran's only spectacular breakthrough was among Lebanese Shi'is. Iran established itself as the patron of Hizbullah, whose military activities are directed against Israeli occupation forces in Southern Lebanon. Iran's ability to influence radical Islamic groups derived legitimacy in Arab eyes to the extent that it concentrated on promoting anti-Israeli operations. Beyond this, Iran had little influence on militants in the Arab East. The two Palestinian radical Islamic groups, *al-Jihad al-Islami* and *Hamas*, cooperate with Iran to the extent of the willingness of the latter to support their operations against the Hebrew state. Unconfirmed accounts assert that they receive about $10 million a year from Iran.[9] Some conservative and staunchly pro-American Arab states have given material support to Palestinian fundamentalist groups.[10]

Hizbullah does not launch or promote militant activities against the Lebanese government. In fact, this fundamentalist movement won eight seats in the 1992 parliamentary elections and has become fully integrated into Lebanese national politics. Hizbullah leaders do not hide the fact that they receive military and financial aid from Iran, which in good years reach about $100 million; neither does Iran deny giving this aid. This aid is normally channelled through Hizbullah's Resistance Support Authority. Iranian military aid to Hizbullah passes through Syria, itself not known as a supplier of material aid to any radical Islamic group. Nevertheless, Syria provides liaison facilities to radical groups fighting against Israel.

The struggle for position in regional politics, not ideology, explains why Iran gives material aid to the radicals, while Syria provides their leaders with shelter. Tehran aspires to convince the sceptical United States – which seeks to contain Iran – and weary Gulf Cooperation Council states that its regional interests threaten none of theirs. Iranian support of the radicals serves as a retaliatory message to those who attempt to block what Iran regards as its vital regional interests. Similarly, Syria attempts to use the radicals as bargaining chips in peace negotiations with Israel, and to reserve a place for itself in Middle Eastern affairs. Recently, the Jordanian prime minister, Abdul Karim al-Kabariti, whose country is at odds with Syria, said: 'Syria has no right to protect groups and organizations that use violence and terror to erode security and stability in the region.'[11] It is important to observe that al-Kabariti charged Syria with protecting the radicals, not with arming them.

Iran, in collaboration with the Sudan, has extended its support for Islamic militants to North African groups. An undocumented report cited in a Lebanese magazine charges the Iranians with transporting large quantities of high explosives to border areas between Libya and Algeria. The same report claims that 'recent successes by Algerian security forces in preventing the arrival of foreign supplies to the armed groups caused a setback to Iran'.[12] The possible role of the Sudanese government, which is controlled by

Hasan at-Turabi's National Islamic Front, has attracted considerable atten-
tion through its fomenting of radicalism. Rhetorical statements from Khartoum reinforce the charges of the regime's many foreign opponents that the
Sudan has a role in regional terrorism. For example, during the Popular
Arab and Islamic Conference held in Khartoum in March 1996, at-Turabi
called for 'mobilizing all Muslim efforts against the new world order'.[13]
Having failed to fully suppress their own country's intractable *Jama'at
Islamiya*, Egyptian officials together with the state-controlled mass media
direct their wrath against the Sudan's Islamic regime. Thus an Egyptian
magazine implicates the Sudan in allegedly harbouring about 50 Arab fundamentalist and nationalist groups.[14] The shock of the assassination attempt
on 26 June 1995 on Egyptian President Hosni Mubarak in Addis Ababa
seems to have unleashed an unrestrained campaign in Cairo against the
Sudanese leadership. There are claims that the would-be assassins received
their training in Suba, near Khartoum.[15]

Arab scholars tend to belittle the complaints by Egyptian officials about
foreign conspiracies. In this connection, Hasanin Tawfic Ibrahim dismisses
the significance of material and military aid given to Egypt's Islamic militants by some Middle Eastern countries. Ibrahim cites the following com-
pelling example to make his point:

At a time when the head of the [Egyptian] state was insisting that the Sudanese
regime stands behind those [radical] groups, the former Minister of Interior gave
a famous public statement ... insisting that he has no information that implicates
the Sudanese regime in the matter [terror in Egypt]. All that is to the matter is
that some extremists infiltrated into Egypt from Sudan. Shortly afterwards [the
Minister] was dismissed from the Ministry of Interior. He was replaced by
General Hasan al-Alfi in April 1993.[16]

In Egypt, security forces say they have confiscated Israeli weapons ear-
marked for the country's militant Islamic groups.[17] There is no independent
verification of this charge. Nevertheless, it is on record that the Israeli
authorities – in addition to similar efforts by the Saudis and Jordanians –
financed the construction of many mosques in Gaza and the West Bank.
Between 1967 and 1985, the number of mosques in the territories nearly
tripled. These later became a hotbed for the proliferation of militant Islam in
the occupied territories.

No doubt radical Islamic groups receive some logistic support from a few
Middle Eastern countries, but there is a tendency to magnify unduly the
implications of this aid for the rhythm of regional violence. Contributions
from countries outside the Middle East actually seem to have a greater
influence on the march of Islamic radicalism.

Supplies to the militants from Western and Asiatic countries are quite significant. The war in Afghanistan has provided a stepping-stone for escalating violence in the Middle East. This chapter referred earlier to the role of the CIA, and of the Saudi businessman Usama Bin Ladin in recruiting thousands of Arabs to fight alongside the Mujahidin. In Afghanistan, Arab fighters acquired high-level martial skills suitable for the kind of irregular terror activities they currently launch against states in the Middle East. Apart from the Afghan episode, direct Western aid proved vital to escalation of the militants' operations. A Lebanese daily newspaper described the evolving relationship between Islamic fundamentalists and the West as 'yesterday's allies and today's enemies'.[18] Writing in an Arab daily newspaper published in London, Salah ed-Din Hafiz noted the previous Western support of the Islamic militants' involvement in the Afghan war and associated the enmity of Islamic radicals with the end of their utility to Western interests. William Saffire, a Western columnist, does not look at the issue in terms of such an alliance-and-enmity syndrome. Instead, he believes that the Islamic extremists have exploited the 'West's havens and forums'.[19]

The actual motive or reason for providing material aid to Muslim radicals is not so important. The fact remains that the aid came from Western points of origin, and will probably continue to come. A report by an Arab magazine claims that at least 50 radical Islamic leaders sought and obtained political asylum in Europe, 12 in England alone.[20] For Muslim radicals, Europe is not just a refuge from the intelligence and security officers of Arab states, but also an important source of money, training and weapon supplies. In January 1995, German authorities revealed that some Arabs train in mountain camps on German territory. This development occurred after the discovery of the traditional training camps in the Sudan and Afghanistan. Similarly, Algerian security forces in March 1994 intercepted a large shipment of military hardware carried by a cargo ship originating from the Netherlands.[21] Some shipments destined for certain Arab countries were intercepted at the French–German border; Swiss authorities discovered other shipments bound for the Middle East. Arrested Muslim radicals have admitted receiving weapons from the West through several Mafia connections. Observers seem to believe that wealthy Arabs, living in Europe and sympathetic to the objectives of the Islamic militants, contribute generous funds for clandestine arms purchases on the black market. For several years, Bin Ladin provided funds to numerous radical organizations in the Arab world through the Human Concern Agency, which he founded in Afghanistan in 1982.[22] Shadowy philanthropic groups, such as the Sudanese *Muaffaq* organization associated with the National Islamic Front, provide liaison services for the militants. Some claim that this group planned the attempt in Ethiopia on President Mubarak's life.[23]

The most important source of weapon supplies to Islamic militants is probably local. On this matter Nassar says that 'the dependence of these "revolutionaries" on local sources for logistic supplies discredits the Egyptian government's accusation of Sudan and Iran for standing behind terrorism'.[24] Investigations by Egyptian police point to the ability of the Islamic militants to manufacture home-made bombs and Molotov cocktails, and to install explosive devices. Egyptian security forces have recently succeeded in locating arms factories near Cairo, Asyut and Banha owned by the militants and managed by a sympathetic army officer.[25] There is wide speculation that the Egyptian Army itself provides light weapons to the country's militant Islamic groups. It is common knowledge that there are many Islamic fundamentalists in the ranks of the Egyptian Army.[26] One should not forget that it was a fundamentalist army officer who assassinated President Anwar Sadat in 1981. The militants secure some of their weapons from government troops ambushed and killed in armed confrontations.

Abu Amr sheds light on the local sources of support for the Hamas movement in the occupied territories. He observes that 'individuals contribute either directly to the movement or to the zakat committee or other foundations supervised by Hamas or the Muslim Brotherhood. Money from the zakat is used for Hamas's activities in helping the poor, building mosques and schools, and other charitable works.'[27] Although Hamas denies it, Abu Amr insists that it has its own profit-making investment projects.[28] It is very possible that other radical Islamic groups elsewhere in the Arab world receive funds from the proliferating Islamic banks and commercial enterprises.

Three of the military tactics most widely used by the radicals depend exclusively on local resources: suicide missions, stabbings and booby-trapping cars. These tactics, first begun by Hizbullah fighters in Southern Lebanon, have spread among Islamic militants in the Arab world, especially in Algeria. Stabbing of Israelis in the territories is commonplace nowadays. Similar terror activities against policemen, Copts and Western tourists occur in Egypt. The radicals' increasing dependence on suicide operations is alarming, since they tend to inflict heavy human losses and exceed in efficiency all previously used tactics. Yusuf al-Qardawy, an Islamic militant preacher, approves of suicide activities. Bragging about them, he says: 'If the Jews possess the atomic bomb ... we possess the human bomb.'[29] According to state security forces trying to suppress the militants, such operations are difficult to contain since the logic of their execution seems unbounded by human rationality and is therefore uncontrollable.

Conclusion: A Grim Future

The security forces in Egypt and Algeria have scored important successes against the Muslim militants in these countries. Recent Israeli reprisals against suicide bombings in Jerusalem and Tel Aviv, and the Palestinian Authority's Draconian measures, seem to have inflicted serious damage on the infrastructure of the Hamas and al-Jihad movements. In Lebanon, Hizbullah faces a new Israeli government fully determined to stamp out its operations against the Hebrew state, and an unsympathetic Lebanese government bent on stabilizing the country in order to go on with reconstruction. Thus impatient officials and imprudent analysts have predicted the imminent collapse of Islamic militancy in the Middle East. But the successes are not that impressive and the optimistic predictions seem unwarranted by reality.

Levels of religiosity are increasing everywhere throughout the Middle East. The liberalization efforts of the first half of the 20th century in Arab society, as well as the secularization efforts by ruling military elites during the 1950s and 1960s, lost their impetus after the Six-Day War which revealed the extent of Arab political decay. Islamic radicalism built up gradually and sought religious alternatives to secular failures. Continued mismanagement of public assets by the existing elites, eschewal of serious political reform and marginality in the new world order all strengthen the *raison d'être* of Islamic radicalism. As a result, Islamic nationalism is supplanting territorial nationalism and is becoming the main support of the political opposition and its promise for the future. Citing the examples of Iran and the Sudan, Juergensmeyer fears that this process is contagious since 'Islamic nationalism in one country can encourage the growth of Islamic nationalism in other countries'.[30] The long-term objectives of militant Muslims are universal in that they seek to unite the Islamic countries and spread the word of Allah throughout the world.

It would be futile to try to defeat Muslim militants without dealing with the underlying factors that made their appearance possible. Authorities in Cairo say they are aware of 69 radical Islamic groups that have emerged in Egypt during the past few years. This clearly demonstrates that crushing one militant group may lead to the rise of several others. The high religious fervour in the Middle East is likely to facilitate replenishing the ranks of the militant groups. In Egypt alone there are more than 120 000 mosques, 80 per cent of which are under the control of militant Islamic groups.

The only forces of opposition that seem capable of replacing the existing Middle Eastern political orders are Islamic groups. Muslim militants have chosen to challenge the regimes head-on in a number of states in the region. Encouraged by the successful anti-Soviet war in Afghanistan and the

Islamic revolution in Iran, would-be pacifist Islamic groups have turned to militancy. They have found financial supporters and weapon providers in different parts of the world, but the truth is that they depend heavily on the internal political environment in which they operate.

The prospects for containing the threat of militant Islam do not look good. The Middle East policy of the United States seems injudicious as, among several other things, it continues to apply a double standard to its relations with the Arabs and Israelis. Europe appears reluctant to assume an active role in the Middle East and avoids any challenging of the supremacy of the role of the United States in this region. Meanwhile, the performance of most Arab regimes continues to falter, the economies are retreating, government spending is decreasing and the quality of life is worsening. And as if all of the above is not enough, an uncompromising *Likud* government has taken over power in Israel. In Middle East politics the waters are murky and the skies cloudy. In view of the prevailing conditions, the only obviously clear development is the continued spread of militant Islam.

Notes

1 *Al-Arabi*, 3 July 1995.
2 Ibid.
3 *Newsweek*, 31 May 1993.
4 Francis Fukuyama, 'The End of History?', *National Interest*, (16) Summer 1989, p.18.
5 Samuel P. Huntington, 'The Clash of Civilizations?', *Foreign Affairs*, **72**, (3), 1993, p.40.
6 Ibid., p.31.
7 Muhammad Ahmad Khalafallah, 'As-Sahwa al-Islamiya fi Misr', in *Al-Harakat al-Islamiya al-Mu'asira fi al-Watan al-Arabi*, Beirut: Markaz Dirasat al-Wihda al-Arabiya, 1987, p.66.
8 This does not mean that Islam as a belief system was contested. In fact, religion continued to dominate personal matters and social activities throughout the Arab lands. However, the idea of an all-encompassing Islamic state lost its lustre, and was replaced by pan-Arabism.
9 It is on record that Arab states in the Gulf region have given considerable financial support to the Hamas and al-Jihad movements, especially since the end of the second Gulf War. One reason for this was the effort of these governments to appease their own rising fundamentalist groups. For more on this, see Sakr Abu Fakhr, '"Hamas" wal "Jihad" al-Quwatan al-Filistininyyatan al-Mu'ajjalatan', in Hasan A-Sabi' *et al.* (eds), *Al-Harakat al-Islamiya fi Filistin*, Beirut: Al-Markaz al-Arabi lil Ma'lumat, 1996, p.73.
10 It is ironic that Israel, wishing to weaken the Palestine Liberation Organization in the occupied territories, tolerated the rise of the Hamas movement. In view of Israel's exceptional security measures, the movement's acquisition of large quantities of fire-arms evokes surprise.
11 *Al-Hayat*, 21 June 1996.

12   *Al-Watan al-Arabi*, (997), 12 April 1996.
13   *Al-Hayat*, 24 March 1996.
14   *Al-Musawar*, 28 July 1995.
15   *Al-Watan al-Arabi*, (1007), 21 June 1996.
16   Hasanin Tawfic Ibrahim, 'At-Tanzimat al-Islamiya fi Misr', *Shu'un al-Awsat*, (50), March 1996, pp.72–3.
17   Ibid.
18   *Nida' al-Watan*, 10 March 1994.
19   *Herald Tribune*, 19 March 1993.
20   *Al-Arabi,* 3 July 1995.
21   Ibid.
22   *Roz al-Yusuf*, (3549), 17 June 1996.
23   *Al-Hawadith*, (2058), 12 April 1996.
24   *Ali Nassar*, 'At-Tanzimat al-Musallaha fi Misr: Ma'ziq Istratigiyat al-Unf al-Thawri', *Shu'un al-Awsat*, (38), February 1995, p.36.
25   Ibid.
26   *Al-Watan al-Arabi*, (997), 12 April 1996.
27   Ziad Abu Amr, 'Hamas: A Historical and Political Background', *Journal of Palestine Studies*, **22**, (4), 1993, p.16.
28   Ibid., p.17.
29   *Al-Qabas,* 15 March 1996.
30   Mark Juergensmeyer, *The New Cold War? Religious Nationalism Confronts the Secular State*, Berkeley: University of California Press, 1993, p.48.

Index

For Product Safety Concerns and Information please contact our EU
representative GPSR@taylorandfrancis.com Taylor & Francis Verlag GmbH,
Kaufingerstraße 24, 80331 München, Germany

Printed and bound by CPI Group (UK) Ltd, Croydon, CR0 4YY

08/06/2025

01896977-0012